ANGEL SIGNS

ANGEL SIGNS

A CELESTIAL GUIDE TO THE POWERS
OF YOUR OWN GUARDIAN ANGEL

ALBERT HALDANE *and* SIMHA SERAYA
with BARBARA LAGOWSKI

HarperSanFrancisco
A Division of HarperCollins*Publishers*

Author Web site: www.angelsignsonline.com

Designed by Lindgren/Fuller Design

ISBN 0–06–251706–6

To the millions of men and women
who do not converse
with their personal guardian Angel
and don't know that they can;
to the millions who never did
because they don't know how;
to the millions who are called
but don't know to whom to respond.

To all humans around the planet,
who will discover here
the name of their munificent companion,
pronounce it
in the universal language,
and in so doing, unite
forever with their Angels.

—ALBERT HALDANE

To each and every seeker of beauty, truth, and goodness, to all
seekers of excellence, to all lovers of the Divine, which dwells
inside our own heart and outside in the celestial abode.

—SIMHA SERAYA

FOREWORD

One summer afternoon when I was seventeen, my friend Michel and I were driving through the French countryside, daydreaming about our upcoming vacation to Greece. We were leaving the next morning, and we were absorbed in our thoughts, not saying a word. Suddenly, as if out of nowhere, a man materialized in the road in front of us. He was waving a red flag, warning the driver that there was roadwork ahead. But it was already too late. I screamed and slammed on the brakes in an attempt to avoid hitting the man. Then I turned the wheel. Immediately, the car veered off the road and began to somersault through a rocky field.

Inside the car, the metallic noise was horrifying, amplified each time the roof of the car hit the ground. Still fully conscious, I counted each turn as the car spiraled through the air—one, two, three, up and down, up and down. I was aware that the centrifugal force had thrown Michel toward the back and that I no longer occupied the driver's seat. I was also aware that despite the violent pitching of the automobile, no part of my body ever touched the inside of the car. It was as though I was turning again and again inside an invisible, protective sphere and that I was somehow cushioned from all contact. As the car spiraled, I continued to count—four, five turns, then suddenly, silence. The car had come to rest on its wheels.

Michel and I climbed from what we assumed would be horrific wreckage. But when we surveyed the scene, what we found rendered us speechless. The car had sustained no damage. The windows were not broken; the body was not dented. Indeed, it was difficult for us even to find a smudge of dirt on the white paint. Furthermore, we ourselves were totally free of injury. Although the car had flipped violently five times and come to a crashing halt, we had not sustained even a scratch or a bruise. We weren't even dizzy!

Seventeen-year-olds have been known to reach unreasonable conclusions about the important events that mark their lives, particularly when they are overwhelmed by the implications of those events. At the time, I simply assumed that my friend and I had been very lucky. I have since realized that several laws of gravity and physics were miraculously suspended that day and that the metaphysical airbag that protected us during the crash was provided by the only being capable of suspending natural laws, my guardian Angel. Only an Angel can magically transform compassion into action. Only a celestial protector can stay the laws of science or activate other natural laws—some of them still unknown to human science.

My poetic contribution to this book is my ardent thanks to all of God's Angels for the unfailing generosity and illuminating wisdom with which they surround each of us on earth.

—ALBERT

I became vividly aware of the Angelic influence in my life one night in July 1997. I was lying in bed, half asleep, when suddenly I was psychically transported to a conference room, where I found myself seated at a large table with three people I knew well. I was aware that the four of us had been brought together for a business meeting. I also became aware of two questions that occupied my mind: "What is competence?" and "Do I possess competence?"

As soon as the questions formed themselves, a clear, pleasant voice filled the room. It said, "Competence does not exist in and of itself, but it shows up at the crossroads of three realities: first, what you are, what you were born with, the very nature and texture of your being; second, your personal life experience, how you explore the paths of light and darkness, the various actions you undertake that develop the potential of 'who you are'; and third, the way you try to identify and achieve your highest calling in life. You do not have to succeed in that mission, but it is essential that you commit yourself completely to achieving it."

Having received these answers, my friends and I left the room. Outside, the weather was mild, the sky gray and white, dotted with small, light clouds. I recognized that I had been transported to the familiar streets of Paris. While walking, my eyes were drawn to the horizon. Right above it, I could clearly see three Angels, dressed in white linen tunics, each holding an open book. Their eyes sparkled with love and humor, and they seemed to be emitting vibrations of warm compassion and unlimited enthusiasm. Behind them appeared a fourth figure, which seemed to be holding a torch. The three Angels smiled at me. I recall that their lips were moving across their faces at strange angles, resulting in expressions not usually seen on human faces.

The Angels said, "If you want to see us with wings, we can make them come out, but the truth is we don't need them."

I gazed at the figures in rapt wonder, my emotions filled with their presence. Suddenly, a huge transparent dome appeared above us all.

The Angels explained, "Each time a human contacts us, he or she and we are enveloped by a translucent globe called a 'cathedral of light.'"

At that moment, I understood with certainty that I was in contact with Angels and that the fourth character was an Archangel, a uniquely different being with a higher quality of energy. Then each Angel showed me the open book they held in their hands. I could clearly see the fine characters with which the words were written. I could also see that the language of the script was an ancient one. The Angels told me that I should "make an attempt."

I understood. Although I am a scholar in the field of ancient languages, I am always more comfortable researching, probing, and speaking within my field of study than writing. Putting pen to paper would be a professional and emotional leap.

The Angels looked at me intensely, reassuringly. Then they said, "You shall be helped."

A year later, Albert and I suddenly broke the code of Exodus, chapter 14, verses 19, 20, 21, and we saw with awe and wonder the Angels' names, the guardians of the terrestrial humans, reveal themselves, letter by letter, in a luminous and precise chronological design. With that, I began the assiduous study on the meaning and import of the name of each Angel. Using the scientific principles of archaeolinguistic methodology, I endeavored, day and night, to decipher the letter-sounds of each Angel's name, to discern the unique "Angelscope" offered by each celestial guide, and, most of all, to provide everyone everywhere with an opportunity to connect in a personal way with his or her own guardian Angel.

Certainly, as the four celestial beings in my vision had promised, I have been helped! It is a joy for me to acknowledge the guidance of all marvelous Angels, and it is my pleasure to here express my eternal gratitude.

—SIMHA

Now that the work of writing this book is finished, we see how much precious help we have received from the Angels themselves. Many of the ideas, concepts, metaphors, poetic images, and rhythms in this manuscript were inspired by our celestial helpers. We also realize that the Angels have become more active participants in our daily lives. They have sent us an abundance of proof, signs, hints, and even manifestations just to let us know they're near, at every moment. Close companionship with a heavenly protector is what we wish for you, too.

Relationships are two-way propositions, and relationships with Angels are no different. We have to deepen and enlarge our spiritual awareness of the divine spirits among us. Then we can truly hear, see, feel, understand, and act upon the profound messages our guardian Angels are constantly beaming in our direction. It is our hope that, because of this book, more and more people will connect with Angels, listen to them, and speak to them, thus beginning a dynamic dialogue that will never end.

Albert Haldane
Simha Seraya
Manhattan, New York
September 2001

ANGEL SIGNS

INTRODUCTION

There are Angels among us! That's what the ancient texts of every major religion and spiritual tradition tell us. Yet those texts reveal a great deal more than we realize about our celestial guides—about the many ways Angels lift our spirits, enhance our lives, enrich our destinies. Drawn from age-old wisdom, enlightened by modern science, your Angelscope is the key to knowing and communicating with the heavenly guardian who was assigned to you at the moment of your birth.

Our guardian Angels exist to protect us, to reinforce our connection with the spiritual realm, to awaken us to our potential, to support us in times of need and—yes!—to create miracles. Indeed, while researching and writing this book, the authors have been graced with unexpected good fortune (God-sends!), guided by invisible hands, and increasingly enveloped in the warm embrace of the Angels' companionship. Open your awareness to the presence of your celestial guide in your life, and you'll notice them in the strangest places, sometimes in the nick of time.

Our guardian Angels are the messengers of the divine realm, the unbreakable link that connects earth with heaven. Their mission on earth is simple: to deliver our messages, to open a channel through which flows the bounty of the divine spirit, and to be our greatest supporters. We need them to help us live more fully. Without us, they could not fulfill their purpose. Your heavenly protector Angel will always be there for you. All you need do is invite him/her to share your life. Your Angelscope will reveal how you can learn more about yourself, deepen your spirituality, enrich your life, and enhance your talents (talents you never knew you had) by making your guardian Angel a special part of your daily life.

Enlightening Information About Angels

On the day of our birth, each of us receives the gift of life and a wise and constant guide to help us empower that life. Every person on earth is assigned a specific guardian Angel—a unique personality who will inspire and protect us as long as we live. Ancient texts from many traditions tell us that there is a guardian Angel for every five days of the year. Summon your Angel into your life, and this Angel will play an enormous role, awakening your goals, stimulating your abilities, inspiring solutions to your most difficult problems, and guiding you to a brilliant destiny known only to the Angel and the Divine.

How do you begin to make the acquaintance of a personal guardian? The answer lies in your Angelscope.

Each Angelscope includes everything you need to summon your heavenly guardian to your side, including a phonetic pronunciation of your Angel's name, the universal resonance of her/his name, an Angelscope profile, a list of notable people born under each Angel's influence, your best matches with other people born under different Angel signs in many areas of life including romance, a list of the colors associated with your Angel, and a powerful invocation. These elements provide you with a deep knowledge of your guardian's true nature and an unfailing method for summoning your Angel to your side in times of need or for companionship and direction, now and throughout your life.

Say My Name

Just as your radio must be tuned to the right frequency in order to pick up your favorite program, each of us must elevate our communication to a celestial level before we can broadcast our messages to the Angels. Pronouncing each syllable of your guardian's name correctly by using the phonetic key within each Angelscope will ensure that your requests will come through loud and clear.

Religious seekers from the beginning of time understood that sound produces vibration and that the right vibration opens the door to heightened consciousness and profound knowledge. This age-old wisdom inspired mantras, litanies, and chants for many millennia. Although your Angel is literally above all that, pronouncing your guardian's name precisely and correctly will elevate your spirit and transport your message to a higher realm, where it can resonate with divine will.

Universal Resonance

Everything we know about Angels—their names, their duties, their preferences and personalities—has been brought to us, impeccably preserved, through Sumerian, Akkadian, and ancient Hebrew writings. These traditions—and their ancient languages—also hold the key to deep and resonant communication with our heavenly guides. Knowing the universal resonance of your spiritual ally's name will enable you to connect with him or her more intimately, meaningfully, and powerfully.

Universal resonance works like this: in ancient languages, each letter of the alphabet expresses a specific meaning. The letter resonates with this meaning by itself; then, as it is paired with other letters, the meaning both crystallizes and unfolds. When, finally, each letter and combination of letters is compounded into a complete word, the word resonates with all the meanings derived from its combined roots. In your Angelscope, each syllable of your guardian's name is like a stream of energy. When those streams combine to form the Angel's entire name, they create a virtual river of meaning. This moving, flowing current of meaning—or universal resonance—is activated each time you invoke your guardian's name.

This system was born as the result of years of Simha Seraya's and Albert Haldane's work. But you don't have to be an experienced linguist and Angelologist to understand that this method, when applied to each Angel's name, is the key to defining that Angel's nature, understanding her/his power, and marshaling his/her aid. It is a method that allows us to communicate with our guardian spirits in their own language. When you invoke your invisible helper, try to concentrate on the deeper meaning of the Angel's name. You will be communicating with your guardian spirit in that spirit's own language.

Color Harmonization

Just as every sound, every syllable of an Angel's name, is imbued with a specific energy, so, too, does each color carry a distinct vibration. By wearing or concentrating on the colors that resonate with your special guardian, you will multiply the energy of your invocation, provide yourself with a focal point for meditation, and ensure that you are always carrying a tangible reminder of your guardian's constant presence.

To align yourself with your Angel's color harmonization, wear clothing or jewelry in that hue, choose candles or other home accessories in your Angel's color, or even paint in a shade that reflects your guardian's vibration while making your invocation.

Invocation

Each Angelscope features an invocation that has been specially tailored to each guardian's harmony. By repeating this invocation aloud, you produce energy—and a vibration—that carries your message aloft. But that's not the only benefit of making your message audible. Recitation engraves your Angel's name in your memory and on your heart, provides a foundation for those who aren't accustomed to prayer, and gives you a context for making your request. Of course, as you become more attuned to your guardian Angel, you can invoke him/her in other ways: silently, telepathically, or even in a letter. What is important is that you establish a deep and intimate relationship with your celestial guide and make the kind of a request your Angel can answer. Here are some guidelines that will help you do just that.

Consider Your Request

What are you asking for, and why? Your Angel is your spirit-mind-bodyguard; he/she isn't about to supply you with anything that can damage you or others; neither is your Angel likely to be the agent of any result that is not in accord with Providence. Some examples of materially—rather than spiritually— inspired requests might include wealth for wealth's sake, power over someone else, or anything you ask for to satisfy a purely selfish motivation.

It is important to note, however, that there is nothing inherently wrong with asking for money. Wealth in itself is not bad thing, and abundance— that feeling of deep satisfaction that derives from a rich life well lived—is a gift of Providence. However, there is a huge difference between summoning your Angel's aid when you're trying to, say, scrape up medical school tuition and using your guardian as a celestial ATM. A clean request, free from ulterior motives, has the best chance of being answered.

Focus upon Your Intentions

A jazzy, new Jaguar and a beachfront house in Malibu are materialistic desires; a car to transport you to a job that fulfills your goals and a great house that makes the whole family feel happy and secure are desires that further your intentions.

What is an intention? Briefly, an intention is a desire explored. Say you need money. Who doesn't? But why do you feel that you need it? Perhaps you desire love. Who doesn't? But what function will love fulfill in your life? When a desire emerges, it is your privilege and duty to make the mental effort to produce an answer before soliciting your guardian's help. Do you need cash to get through a crisis? Do you need love to boost your morale—or your ego? Questions like these compel you to take a spiritual jump, to move beyond simple answers. They also put you on the path to intentionality, where wishes are born of self-knowledge and petitions are aligned with higher aspirations.

Angels are not good fairies. They don't deal in desires. Make sure you are asking for something that will move you along the road to your full growth and destiny and not just into the fast lane.

Make Sure Your Intention Relates Primarily to You

How generous of you to petition your guardian Angel on behalf of your office manager! She might enjoy the exciting new position you're asking your Angel to provide. But if she happens to be a difficult person to work with and someone you wouldn't mind getting rid of, your "gift" takes on a different cast.

To be sure your intentions are sound, ask for the things *you* need to smooth your own path. If you are inspired to petition on behalf of someone close to you, simply ask your heavenly companion to contact the other person's guardian. He/she can then provide for your friend without outside interference.

Open a Channel Between Earth and the Infinite

Opening a channel between earth and heaven isn't really as esoteric as it sounds. Just do what you do to get in touch with the stillness within yourself. Meditate. Listen to elevating music. Focus upon a piece of jewelry or an object whose color is in tune with your guardian's vibrations. Pray. Just turn your focus inward. Then . . .

Watch and Listen Carefully for an Answer

Angelic responses come to us in the subtlety of a hunch, in the life-changing power of an unexpected experience, or in the adrenaline rush of an accident or close call. They inspire good Samaritans to come to our aid and spirit guides to appear in our dreams. They turn events to our advantage, and if these evidences of their power are not enough, they materialize and touch us with their transformational grace.

Most of All, Express Gratitude!

Your intention may be fulfilled just as you visualized it. It might also be resolved in an unexpected way or go—seemingly—unanswered. Be assured that although your guardian Angel takes a personal interest in you, every request will always be resolved in a way that brings the greatest good to everyone concerned.

Although you may have to look deeply at your Angel's answer to discover the wisdom in it, each connection with the infinite is a miracle! Thank your guardian Angel. He/she has opened a path between you and heaven's bounty. What greater gift could you possibly receive?

Embarking upon the journey to Angelic knowledge is like launching a rowboat. At first glance, it seems your boat is in direct contact with only the water that supports its hull. In reality, your small craft displaces all the water in the lake and all the water in the river that feeds the lake and all the water in the many small streams that merge to form the river.

Make one small step toward your guardian Angel, and you will be transported to the celestial realm where seventy-three loving guides wait to bring together wish and answer, dream and reality. Get to know your guardian Angel. He/she will make you a believer in all the divine nurturers who believe so deeply in you.

Date of Birth	Guardian Angel	page	Date of Birth	Guardian Angel	page
Jan 1–Jan 3	Ye-Ya-La-El	192	Jul 3–7	Ye-Yi-Ya-El	77
Jan 4–8	Ha-Ra-Ha-El	195	Jul 8–12	Mela-Ha-El	80
Jan 9–13	Mitsa-Ra-El	199	Jul 13–17	He-Havi-Yah	83
Jan 14–18	Vama-Ba-El	202	Jul 18–22	Nith-Ha-Yah	86
Jan 19–23	Ye-He-Ha-El	205	Jul 23–27	He-A-A-Yah	89
Jan 24–28	Ânava-El	208	Jul 28–Aug 1	Yeratha-El	92
Jan 29–Feb 2	Me-He-Ya-El	211	Aug 2–6	Se-A-He-Yah	95
Feb 3–7	Damabi-Yah	215	Aug 7–11	Re-Yi-Ya-El	98
Feb 8–12	Mana-Qua-El	218	Aug 12–16	Ova-Ma-El	101
Feb 13–17	A-Ya-Â-El	221	Aug 17–21	Le-Caba-El	104
Feb 18–22	Ha-Bovi-Yah	224	Aug 22–26	Va-Sari-Yah	108
Feb 23–27	Ro-A-Ha-El	227	Aug 27–31	Ye-Hovi-Yah	111
Feb 28–Mar 4	Yaba-Mi-Yah	230	Sep 1–5	Le-Ha-Hi-Yah	114
Mar 5–9	Ha-Ye-Ya-El	234	Sep 6–10	Chava-Qui-Yah	118
Mar 10–14	Mova-Mi-Yah	237	Sep 11–15	Mena-Da-El	121
Mar 15–19	Hova-Vi-Yah	240	Sep 16–20	Ani-Ya-El	125
Mar 20–24	Ve-Hovi-Yah	11	Sep 21–25	Ha-Âmi-Yah	128
Mar 25–29	Yeli-Ya-El	14	Sep 26–30	Re-Ha-Â-El	131
Mar 30–Apr 3	Si-Yata-El	17	Oct 1–5	Ye-Yaza-El	134
Apr 4–8	Âlami-Yah	20	Oct 6–10	He-He-Ha-El	137
Apr 9–13	Ma-Hashi-Yah	24	Oct 11–15	Mi-Yi-Ca-El	141
Apr 14–18	Lela-Ha-El	27	Oct 16–20	Vavali-Yah	144
Apr 19–23	Acha-A-Yah	30	Oct 21–25	Yela-Hi-Yah	147
Apr 24–28	Ca-Hetha-El	34	Oct 26–30	Se-Ali-Yah	150
Apr 29–May 3	Hazi-Ya-El	37	Oct 31–Nov 4	Âri-Ya-El	153
May 4–8	Aladi-Yah	40	Nov 5–9	Â-Sali-Yah	157
May 9–13	Lo-Avi-Yah	43	Nov 10–14	Mi-Ya-Ha-El	160
May 14–18	He-Ha-Â-Yah	46	Nov 15–19	Ve-Hova-El	163
May 19–23	Yezala-El	49	Nov 20–24	Dani-Ya-El	166
May 24–28	Meba-Ha-El	52	Nov 25–29	Ha-Hasi-Yah	169
May 29–Jun 2	Hare-Ya-El	55	Nov 30–Dec 4	Âmami-Yah	172
Jun 3–7	He-Qua-Mi-Yah	58	Dec 5–9	Nana-A-El	175
Jun 8–12	Le-A-Vi-Yah	61	Dec 10–14	Niya-Tha-El	179
Jun 13–17	Cali-Ya-El	64	Dec 15–19	Meba-Hi-Yah	182
Jun 18–22	Levavi-Yah	68	Dec 20–24	Povi-Ya-El	186
Jun 23–27	Pe-Hali-Yah	71	Dec 25–29	Nema-Mi-Yah	189
Jun 28–Jul 2	Nel-Cha-El	74	Dec 30–31	Ye-Ya-La-El	192

Angel VE-HOVI-YAH

Brings fertility and creativity to all areas of life. Stimulates long-term love relationships. Promotes beneficial associations. Overcomes obstacles.

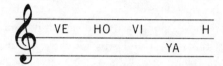

PHONETIC PRONUNCIATION

Ve as in Veracity

Ho as in Holy

Vi as in Victory

Ya as in Yard

H Vocalize the final H as a soft exhalation

UNIVERSAL RESONANCE OF THE ANGEL'S NAME

Ve Vitalizing factor. Fruitfulness and productivity. Catalyst of variety, vitality, verity, will, and vigor.

Ho Spiritual life force. Presence of the universal and all-permeating spirit. Divine call, divine connection.

Vi Vitalizing factor. Fruitfulness and productivity. Catalyst of variety, vitality, verity, will, and vigor.

Yah Final vibration of the Angel's name. Receptivity and reflectivity. The presence of the deity; the abundance of the being.

Guardian Angel Ve-Hovi-Yah

In Akkadian, the name Ve-Hovi-Yah means, literally, "generated by the principle of love" or "the generating life force of the loving God."

Clearly, the ancients knew the Angel Ve-Hovi-Yah to be a powerful, even irrepressible, creative source.

The men and women born under the guidance of Ve-Hovi-Yah are truly can-do people. How could it be otherwise? This guardian

COLOR HARMONIZATION

Gray with iridescent mauve / Violet / Dark blue / Orange

HARMONIC MATCHES FOR VE-HOVI-YAH'S PROTÉGÉS

- *The best matches for success in economic and practical achievements will be among men and women born November 10–14, under the care of Mi-Ya-Ha-El.*

- *The best matches for recognition, fame, personal charisma, and social fulfillment will be among men and women born June 3–7, under the care of He-Qua-Mi-Yah.*

- *The best matches for romance, love, and artistic and intellectual achievements will be among men and women born June 28–July 2, under the care of Nel-Cha-El.*

Angel not only generates the inspirational energies that stimulate creativity and imagination, Ve-Hovi-Yah also enhances the capacity to produce results! If you are in harmony with this Angel, you can bring to life anything your imagination can conceive—and quickly! Those close to Ve-Hovi-Yah can reap the rewards of their innovative efforts often from the inception of a project, sometimes nearly as soon as the original idea emerges. That's because, with the assistance of Ve-Hovi-Yah, every stage of the creative process, from inspiration to perspiration, moves along easily and smoothly. And because this guardian stirs the respect and trust of those around you—your family, your friends, and your professional colleagues—the time and environment will always be right for your inventive brainstorms.

When those under the protection of Angel Ve-Hovi-Yah consider forging a partnership to bring their exciting ideas and boundless talents to fruition, their ability to unite compatibly with others allows them to find just the right counterpart. In fact, in this global marketplace, men and women under the protection of Angel Ve-Hovi-Yah can easily meet their match and network with people around the world. Physical proximity is not necessary for them to maintain stable and intense personal and professional relationships. Happily, Ve-Hovi-Yah's abundance can often lead to satisfying intimate relationships as well as financial success. If you are close to this Angel, you may establish a working relationship that becomes deeply meaningful or even romantic, thus doubling your feelings of satisfaction and prosperity.

If you are a protégé of Ve-Hovi-Yah whose pet projects have yet to take flight, be reassured: a sincere evocation of this Angel will change your luck and allow you to succeed without too much effort in whatever you undertake. In order to benefit fully from the potential of Angel Ve-Hovi-Yah, however, you must keep a few things in mind. Try to think and act from affection and love; avoid striving for personal gain and selfish interests. Angels aren't good fairies; they aren't interested in providing you with a new Porsche or the right ZIP code. If circumstances allow, it is preferable that you stay away from the kind of situations that make people say with a sigh of resignation, "Business is business." Ethics shouldn't be contingent on the bottom line.

Angel Ve-Hovi-Yah encourages projects whose inspiration, intuition, and vision are dominated by generosity and a desire to share and not guided by strict calculation of interest and profit. In all the activities you undertake, if you are under the influence of Angel Ve-Hovi-Yah, you must define your personal ambitions from an altruistic, or at least generous, point of view. Are your desires in alignment with the good of those around you? Will your actions enhance the well-being of those who share your environment? The world? Angel Ve-Hovi-Yah ensures material, intellectual, or spiritual success for those under her/his protection when they faithfully follow the path of thoughtfulness and benevolence.

The dominant qualities reinforced by Angel Ve-Hovi-Yah are creativity and originality. These characteristics urge the mind to act, and always from the loftiest objectives. The harmonic vibrations of Angel Ve-Hovi-Yah will also stimulate those born between March 20 and 24 to embark on a spiritual quest through which they will acquire and refine their knowledge of inner dimensions and invisible worlds.

When in profound harmony with Angel Ve-Hovi-Yah, women and men elevate their thoughts, ideas, and feelings toward the heavens, overcome personal obstacles, including shyness and doubt, make love their lifelong intention, and generously share with others the wonders harvested from the endlessly fertile celestial orchard.

Angel YELI-YA-EL

MARCH 25–29

Encourages enrichment of intellectual thought. Develops the capacity for organization and planning. Encourages the transmission of knowledge. Supports aid and charity work.

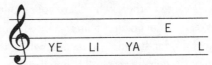

YE · LI · YA · E · L

PHONETIC PRONUNCIATION

Ye as in Yale

Li as in Literature

Ya as in Yard

El as in Elevation

UNIVERSAL RESONANCE OF THE ANGEL'S NAME

Ye Mastery. Dexterity, expertise; human action aligned with divine universal principles.

Li Dynamic learning. The ability to make mental links. Intellectual elevation. An evolving, ascending movement of the mind. Lucidity and enlightenment.

Ya Mastery. Dexterity, expertise; human action aligned with divine universal principles.

El Ending vibration of the Angel's name. Principle of excellence; chosen; elite. Elevating force. Source of perpetual transformation and evolution.

Guardian Angel Yeli-Ya-El

In Akkadian, the name Yeli-Ya-El means, literally, "My intellect is impregnated with the spiritual principle."

Those who can, do. Some of those who do share with the rest of us the profound and transformative lessons they have learned through the fullness of experience. And so it is with the protégés of Angel Yeli-Ya-El, who receive the gift of learning through experience and are encouraged to transmit their knowledge to the world.

NOTABLE PEOPLE BORN UNDER THE INFLUENCE OF YELI-YA-EL

Diana Ross, *singer*

Elle Macpherson, *model and actress*

Elton John, *singer*

Erica Jong, *writer*

Gene Hackman, *actor*

Howard Cosell, *sports broadcaster*

John Major, *former British prime minister*

Lucy Lawless, *actress*

Maksim Gorky, *writer*

Mario Vargas Llosa, *writer*

Morris West, *writer*

Quentin Tarantino, *film director and actor*

Sandra Day O'Connor, *U.S. Supreme Court justice*

Sarah Vaughan, *jazz singer*

Tennessee Williams, *playwright*

COLOR HARMONIZATION

Black / White / Cobalt blue / Orange

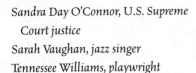

Yeli-Ya-El encourages those under her/his protection to integrate knowledge and action. In this world, where one can find so many examples of action without thought or thought without action, the imaginative, reflective, and productive men and women born between March 25 and 29 are a force to be reckoned with. Every experience they encounter, every challenge they confront, is shaped by knowledge. And each new piece of knowledge they collect leads to a deeper understanding, a fresh perspective, and, ultimately, another new experience. Those women and men who are in harmony with Angel Yeli-Ya-El demonstrate the ability to control their lives, careers, and relationships with thoughtful, well-considered actions. Their natural gifts—curiosity, discernment, creativity, productivity, and an unquenchable desire to discover how things work—often lead them to occupations related to engineering, technological innovation, areas of application requiring planning, or fields of study concerning the complex interrelation of systems or elements, such as ecology, economics, and ergonomics.

But don't get the wrong idea: those under the guidance of Angel Yeli-Ya-El are by no means ivory-tower eggheads. In fact, they are among the world's most gifted teachers, highly adept at transmitting their knowledge and guiding their pupils to new and exciting analyses. Neither do they lecture, harangue, or drone on and on, like lesser teachers we have known. The associates of Yeli-Ya-El can develop powerful and highly original styles of expression, using enlightening analogies and brilliant metaphors, pointing out invisible connections, and opening up countless new and illuminating intellectual pathways. Depending on circumstances, they can be teachers, writers of articles or of scientific works, or creators of fascinating, instructive television programs and of stimulating techniques for teaching and training.

However, the gift of being able to control one's environment is not unconditional. If you are under the protection of Angel Yeli-Ya-El and you hope to reach your fullest potential, you must operate on a high level of harmonic vibration. That means acting with the intent of increasing good and enlightenment in your world. Your own nature as an explorer of the universe's secrets and as an educator will put you center stage. It is important, then, that you avoid mediocrity, suppress any desire for quick gains, and release any rigid

HARMONIC MATCHES FOR YELI-YA-EL'S PROTÉGÉS

- *The best matches for success in economic and practical achievements will be among men and women born November 5–9, under the care of Â-Sali-Yah.*
- *The best matches for recognition, fame, personal charisma, and social fulfillment will be among men and women born May 29–June 2, under the care of Hare-Ya-El.*
- *The best matches for romance, love, and artistic and intellectual achievements will be among men and women born July 3–7, under the care of Ye-Yi-Ya-El.*

points of view that could distort your perception. However and wherever you choose to share your gift, you must build your success from the inspirations and aspirations that gather in the loftiest parts of your mind.

Of course, it isn't always easy to be guided by high intellectual, spiritual, and moral principles in a material world. Ethical choices can lead to difficulties. It is good to know, then, that in times of trouble Angel Yeli-Ya-El helps those under her/his protection to act and think with the flexibility of a snake, the fluidity of water, and the resilience of a reed. You may bend, but you will not break. Best of all, you will add every adversity you confront to your considerable inventory of educational experiences.

If you enjoy a deep connection to Angel Yeli-Ya-El, you will never be bored with your own life—and you will be a constant source of inspiration to others. You will amaze your family and friends with your capacity to understand situations, with the clarity with which you interpret facts, and with the accuracy of your conclusions. Your professional colleagues or students will find in your words, spoken or written, the energy to renew their vision, implement change, and raise their aspirations.

Angel Yeli-Ya-El leads those he/she guides along the path to competence and mental agility. By reinforcing your relationship to Yeli-Ya-El through invocation, you will implement the teachings of your extraordinary celestial instructor and, in your own extraordinary way, generously pass them on.

Angel SI-YATA-EL

MARCH 30–APRIL 3

Stimulates inner life. Encourages knowledge through experience and experimentation. Reinforces the connection between instinct and intuition. Inspires the ability to conceive innovative ideas and to predict the future.

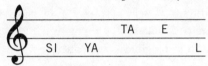

PHONETIC PRONUNCIATION

Si as in See
Ya as in Yard
Ta as in Taboo
El as in Elevation

UNIVERSAL RESONANCE OF THE ANGEL'S NAME

Si Knowledge brought to consciousness. Deep understanding through clarification of creative forces.

Ya Mastery. Dexterity, expertise; human action aligned with divine universal principles.

Ta Perfect instinctual reactions. Knowledge through repetition and recurrence. Understanding of the cycles and rhythms of life on earth.

El Ending vibration of the Angel's name. Principle of excellence; chosen; elite. Elevating force. Source of perpetual transformation and evolution.

Guardian Angel Si-Yata-El

In Akkadian, the name Si-Yata-El means, literally, "From experience and inner knowledge emerges action, whose success dictates its repetition."

Angel Si-Yata-El provides men and women with the ability to draw their knowledge of life directly from their rich inner world. This Angel also gives those in her/his care a kind of innate knowing

COLOR HARMONIZATION

Whiteness / Ocher yellow / Dark green / Speck of red-orange

HARMONIC MATCHES FOR SI-YATA-EL'S PROTÉGÉS

- *The best matches for success in economic and practical achievements will be among men and women born October 31–November 4, under the care of Âri-Ya-El.*

- *The best matches for recognition, fame, personal charisma, and social fulfillment will be among men and women born May 24–28, under the care of Meba-Ha-El.*

- *The best matches for romance, love, and artistic and intellectual achievements will be among men and women born July 8–12, under the care of Mela-Ha-El.*

that flows from a deep well of instinctual information. This profound perception and comprehension encompasses all the stuff of life, including the very essence of the universe. With the help of Si-Yata-El, those under his/her protection have access to the spiritual substance of the cosmos and clearly perceive the fundamental principle of the Creation.

Those who are in harmony with Angel Si-Yata-El are endowed with a strong instinct that provides them with a lot of flair. It also gives them a rather unique perspective on the world around them. For the protégés of Si-Yata-El, the theoretical and abstract dimensions are every bit as tangible as the concrete world. To clarify for those who may not be quite so abstract, the mathematical theorem is just as real as the trajectory it describes, the chemical formula is just as explosive as the combustion it creates. And because, to you, the road map is just as real as the region it represents, you are the best possible person to get lost with—except, of course, that you rarely get lost.

There is, however, one sphere where those under the influence of Angel Si-Yata-El can become bewildered, confused, or turned around: in their ordinary, day-to-day dealings with their fellow creatures, human or animal. While quantum physics poses no challenge for you, you may find people and their changing emotions hard to comprehend. That's because, with the help of Angel Si-Yata-El, knowledge of the laws of the universe emerge spontaneously, as if from a natural spring, from your inner experience. Meanwhile, understanding the people and things around you requires a great effort on your part and constant work.

The men and women in the care of Si-Yata-El can make great strides in theoretical areas, such as mathematics, high-level computer programming, astrological science, primal biology, and philosophy, particularly where it relates to spiritual theories and theology. However, success does not come easily for them in technical or hands-on areas such as medicine, law, and in service, sales, or any field that demands direct and repeated contact with clients. Of course, they *can* succeed in those professions—our guardians will help us succeed at anything we do that contributes to the greater good—but only if they apply all of their perseverance and courage, and only if they accept the risk of failure.

The strengths and qualities engendered by Angel Si-Yata-El create leaders, trailblazers who can move us toward new and futuristic times. Their thoughts and discoveries, especially those within the dynamic realm of science, urge humanity toward wider horizons, where each individual's importance can be seen in context with the vast cosmos. With the help of Si-Yata-El, those under her/his protection develop a deep trust in the unlimited potential of the future and in the constant, uplifting evolution of humanity. This is the reaffirming message they transmit to the rest of us, clearly, simply, and enthusiastically.

By establishing a deep relationship with Angel Si-Yata-El, you can sharpen your intuition, refine your ability to tune into your inner voice, focus your laserlike awareness to get to the heart of any matter, and develop the ability to predict, anticipate, and prophesy. Though you may become something of a curiosity in the workplace or social circle (what do you think the neighbors said about Albert Einstein?), others will seek your guidance, invite your predictions, and accept your enlightened prophecies. Depending on the circumstances of your life, you could become famous by spreading the kind of revolutionary ideas that become models for a better life. You may already be an inspiration to friends and acquaintances who want to progress constructively and harmoniously.

Angel Si-Yata-El bestows on those born between March 30 and April 3 the power of a deep, large, and clear inner vision and the ability to glimpse and grasp the mysteries of the universe. By calling on this Angel, those in his/her care increase their understanding of the invisible laws that make up the world, contribute to scientific progress, and develop a peaceful, truth-based strength that defeats ignorance in every form.

Angel ÂLAMI-YAH

APRIL 4–8

Stimulates a broad, inclusive, and transcendent perception of reality. Opens the door to powerful, important positions. Bestows courage and perseverance. Brings about the realization of desires and dreams.

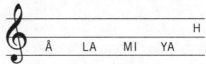

PHONETIC PRONUNCIATION

Â as in Arrow, ending with a soft breath out

La as in Latin

Mi as in Miracle

Ya as in Yard

H Vocalize the final H as a soft exhalation

UNIVERSAL RESONANCE OF THE ANGEL'S NAME

Â The source. The origin of the sensory world; the foundation of human emotions and passions. Enhancement of visual senses and hearing acuity. Supersensitivity.

La Dynamic learning. The ability to make mental links. Intellectual elevation. An evolving, ascending movement of the mind. Lucidity and enlightenment.

Mi The matrix; the model upon which creation is based. Manifestation in the material world. Loving maternal protection.

Yah Final vibration of the Angel's name. Receptivity and reflectivity. The presence of the deity; the abundance of the being.

NOTABLE PEOPLE BORN UNDER THE INFLUENCE OF ÂLAMI-YAH

Bette Davis, actress

Billie Holiday, jazz singer

Colin Powell, U.S. secretary of state

Francis Ford Coppola, film director

Gregory Peck, actor

Horst Stormer, Nobel Prize winner in physics

Jackie Chan, action star

James Dewey Watson, Nobel Prize winner in physiology

Jean H. Fragonard, painter

Maya Angelou, writer

Raphael, painter

Ravi Shankar, musician

Robert Downey Jr., actor

Thomas Hobbes, philosopher

COLOR HARMONIZATION

Lavender / Blue-gray / Old rose / Dark green

Guardian Angel Âlami-Yah

In Akkadian, the name Âlami-Yah means, literally, "Perception and emotion rise together toward the spiritual world. There they come together and are recast in the dynamic shape of the Creator."

Those who keep close to Angel Âlami-Yah thrive at high altitudes. This is to say that those born between April 4 and 8 seem destined to reach lofty material or intellectual positions. Indeed, like the great climbers of the world's mountains, these men and women scale the most challenging personal and professional peaks. Once they reach the summit, they are rewarded with a breathtaking view: a transformative vision of their own future and a perception of the world that is wide, deep, and boundless.

Ancient writings suggest that the Angels reside in a particular band of space that cloaks our planet, a kind of celestial stratosphere that wraps around the earth. Perhaps this elevated perspective is what endows Angel Âlami-Yah—and those in her/his protection—with such an uncanny sense of the big picture. Whether they are considering a career move or a personal transition, the protégés of Âlami-Yah simply aren't satisfied to make purely subjective or snap decisions. Given their druthers, they act only after they've stepped back, broadened their points of view, and considered all the options. While others may make their move more quickly, these men and women proceed only once they have arrived at a complete understanding of the situation and the way it affects the cosmos. With this knowledge, they can predict with great accuracy the way their plans will manifest themselves in the world. No wonder the friends of Âlami-Yah are able to distinguish themselves as experts within their chosen fields, successfully implement vast projects (without a hint of fear!), and completely revolutionize businesses, areas of study, and the lives of those around them.

If you are in harmony with Angel Âlami-Yah, you can use your unique brand of wide-angle vision to determine the scope of even the most complex business and personal situation, bring to light factors that have been invisible, and push beyond the limits of current understanding. Whether you turn your considerable attention

HARMONIC MATCHES FOR ÂLAMI-YAH'S PROTÉGÉS

- *The best matches for success in economic and practical achievements will be among men and women born October 26–30, under the care of Se-Ali-Yah.*
- *The best matches for recognition, fame, personal charisma, and social fulfillment will be among men and women born May 19–23, under the care of Yezala-El.*
- *The best matches for romance, love, and artistic and intellectual achievements will be among men and women born July 13–17, under the care of He-Havi-Yah.*

to a professional, family, or social matter, whether you are delving into a natural phenomenon or a police investigation, you will always shatter the bounds of common knowledge by pointing out yet another view or revealing the secret factors less thorough observers might have left in shadow.

Of course, we humans do not live in an enlightened band somewhere above the fray. Ability alone—even a keen awareness that borders on prescience, like yours—does not ensure prominence in this world. Not to worry! Because your mission is to enlighten those around you, you and all those favored by Âlami-Yah like to shine in public. Your message may be a little shocking, your discoveries a bit provocative, but your innate understanding of how to attract people in large numbers will ensure that your message—and *you*—will certainly attract notice. To put it in spiritual terms, you are a carrier of light. It is impossible to hide the kind of wattage you generate. Âlami-Yah and your own nature would never permit it.

Those born under the influence of Angel Âlami-Yah often take paradoxical emotional and intellectual points of view. This tendency to move against the current of popular thought, accepted belief, and even political correctness provides everyone within earshot with an intense intellectual workout. Your curiosity is fearless. It travels wherever it must in order to uncover the errors that mask the truth, chase away habits that dull the senses, and dispel the ignorance that keeps the mind a prisoner. That doesn't make you reckless or inconsiderate, however. Those under the protection of Âlami-Yah meld their ideas with ethics and temper their ambitions with ideals. In fact, with the help of this Angel, a dynamic, motivated person born between April 4 and 8 can actually create something of a utopia, or at least the modern-day equivalent of one. They are dynamic enough to bring about the kind of changes that bring their complex, forward-looking dreams to life. Although these changes may not reap the immediate approval of others, they will certainly raise the level of any debate, point the way to new paths, and, ultimately, pay off in notoriety and success.

For those who call on her/him with sincerity, Angel Âlami-Yah sends, from the depth of the heavens, gigantic beams of penetrating lights to illuminate their path to the truth. With the help of Âlami-Yah, these men and women can undertake the ultimate journey: the ascension into shadowless, enlightened worlds, to the far depths that lead to the highest summits, to the heart of the gigantic circles of universal knowledge, "of which the center is everywhere, and the circumference nowhere."

Angel MA-HASHI-YAH

APRIL 9–13

Encourages the creation of material wealth. Inspires the design of fashion and the creation of trends. Enriches romantic, emotional, and spiritual life.

	HA		H
MA		YA	
	SHI		

PHONETIC PRONUNCIATION

Ma as in Matter
Ha as in Habit
Shi as in Ship
Ya as in Yard
H Vocalize the final H as a soft exhalation

UNIVERSAL RESONANCE OF THE ANGEL'S NAME

Ma The matrix; the model upon which creation is based. Manifestation in the material world. Loving maternal protection.

Ha Spiritual life force. Love that underlies all things. Presence of the universal and all-encompassing spirit. Divine call, divine connection.

Shi Diffusion, radiation. The ability to comprehend and use the forces enclosed in the nucleus. Birth of science, sentience, and sapience. Radiating knowledge. Cosmic fire; archetype of every sun in the universe.

Yah Final vibration of the Angel's name. Receptivity and reflectivity. The presence of the deity; the abundance of the being.

NOTABLE PEOPLE BORN UNDER THE INFLUENCE OF MA-HASHI-YAH

Charles Baudelaire, *poet*

Claire Danes, *actress*

David Letterman, *talk-show host*

Dennis Quaid, *actor*

Eudora Welty, *writer*

Gary Kasparov, *chess champion*

Joseph Pulitzer, *writer*

Montserrat Caballé, *opera singer*

Omar Sharif, *actor*

Robert B. Woodward, *scientist*

Samuel Beckett, *writer*

Thomas Jefferson, *U.S. president*

Tom Clancy, *writer*

Vince Gill, *singer*

COLOR HARMONIZATION

French blue / White / Ocher / Apple green

Guardian Angel Ma-Hashi-Yah

In Akkadian, the name Ma-Hashi-Yah means, literally, "The matrix generated by the spiritual life force and liberated knowledge."

The Angel Ma-Hashi-Yah provides a call to action for those visionary, energetic women and men capable of starting and managing large companies, manufacturing concerns, or a number of other activities within the areas of economics, finance, commerce, or art. At a time when so many businesses produce nothing but paperwork, those who call upon this Angel will stand out as true entrepreneurs, building new and innovative businesses from the ground up, discovering more efficient methods of production, implementing changes that improve tools and machinery, and trailblazing new routes for mass distribution.

Depending on the circumstances of their lives, those under the protection of Angel Ma-Hashi-Yah can succeed as fashion designers, hairstylists, decorators, architects, or furniture designers, or they can flourish in some other artistic, creative field. They might also apply their skills in the areas of public transportation, sports, and leisure. Whatever path they choose, Ma-Hashi-Yah will see to it that their innovative ideas come to be widely known. In fact, the cutting-edge designs (including those philosophical, political, or esoteric constructs we might call "designs for living") produced by those born between April 9 and 13 have been known to transform long-held cultural traditions. Many of the progressive-minded friends of Ma-Hashi-Yah, like Thomas Jefferson, are remembered for creating new ways of living, reenergizing the culture, and profoundly transforming the lifestyles of their contemporaries. In fact, these people and their ideas can be so attractive and original, people flock to the causes they support and businesses they create nearly as soon as these concerns establish themselves in the world.

Some innovations, of course, are consumed—often mercifully—after their fifteen minutes of fame, while others endure. The brainchildren of the men and women under the protection of Angel Ma-Hashi-Yah have the power to revolutionize the way things look in everyday life, to alter forever the way people move, rest, communicate, seduce, imagine, and think. They are not the purveyors of pet rocks or passing trends; they are an evolutionary force.

HARMONIC MATCHES FOR MA-HASHI-YAH'S PROTÉGÉS

- The best matches for success in economic and practical achievements will be among men and women born October 21–25, under the care of Yela-Hi-Yah.
- The best matches for recognition, fame, personal charisma, and social fulfillment will be among men and women born June 23–27, under the care of Pe-Hali-Yah.
- The best matches for romance, love, and artistic and intellectual achievements will be among men and women born June 8–12, under the care of Le-A-Vi-Yah.

If you are in harmony with Ma-Hashi-Yah, you are an outgoing person who does not hesitate to make the first move, turn a stranger into a friend, and seek contact with others. It really doesn't matter to you whether these associations are short-lived or long-term; what's important to you is that you engender feelings of goodwill. You and all those under the protection of Angel Ma-Hashi-Yah love people. You also love to be loved. You immerse yourself in your social circle with delight and find within it many opportunities to make an emotional connection. Because you are often surrounded by a coterie of admirers and followers, you may confuse flattery with genuine praise. You also run the risk of letting your ego overrun your more altruistic goals. Although sweet-talking admirers may turn your head, you must always remember that your ideas and talents are the characteristics that make you so irresistibly attractive to others. Lose sight of them, and you may also see the last of those breathless devotees.

By establishing a close relationship with Angel Ma-Hashi-Yah, you can hone your intuitive perception and set your imagination free. You will also maximize your opportunities for creating products, forms, colors, and sounds that stimulate others to reach for their billfolds. Depending upon the circumstances that surround you, you could produce the next must-have item and reap a windfall that includes commercial success, artistic recognition, social prestige, and fame.

Whether you are a writer, composer, political reformer, or actor, if you are in deep harmony with Angel Ma-Hashi-Yah you respond to the unifying call that elevates the mind toward principles of truth, goodness, and generosity. Consequently, you do not consider public service a sacrifice but a gift. You have a deep understanding that time and energy, invested in noble humanitarian causes, can pay huge dividends, from material success and fame to social progress and spiritual enlightenment.

Calling upon Angel Ma-Hashi-Yah opens the doors to prosperity, encourages men and women to share the tangible and intangible gifts they have received, and enables them to spread the sunny warmth of celestial love. Invoke Ma-Hashi-Yah, and you will dissolve the limits of ordinary perception, understand the difference between earthly desires and universal aspirations, and turn your world into a magnificent model of divine creation.

Angel LELA-HA-EL

APRIL 14–18

Encourages knowledge through intuition. Aids in the formation of significant relationships and connections. Develops flexibility and adaptability. Stimulates creativity and imagination. Bestows a profound sense of beauty and a sophisticated aesthetic.

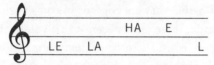

PHONETIC PRONUNCIATION

Le as in Letter
La as in Ladder
Ha as in Habit
El as in Elevation

UNIVERSAL RESONANCE OF THE ANGEL'S NAME

Le Dynamic learning. The ability to make mental links. Intellectual elevation. An evolving, ascending movement of the mind. Lucidity and enlightenment.

La Dynamic learning. The ability to make mental links. Intellectual elevation. An evolving, ascending movement of the mind. Lucidity and enlightenment.

Ha Spiritual life force. Love that underlies all things. Presence of the universal and all-encompassing spirit. Divine call, divine connection.

El Ending vibration of the Angel's name. Principle of excellence; chosen; elite. Elevating force. Source of perpetual transformation and evolution.

Guardian Angel Lela-Ha-El

In Akkadian, the name Lela-Ha-El means, literally, "The spin of the mind bringing one into constant contact with the source of universal love."

COLOR HARMONIZATION

Yellow / Lavender / Green of foliage / Red-rust

HARMONIC MATCHES FOR LELA-HA-EL'S PROTÉGÉS

- *The best matches for success in economic and practical achievements will be among men and women born October 16–20, under the care of Vavali-Yah.*

- *The best matches for recognition, fame, personal charisma, and social fulfillment will be among men and women born June 18–22, under the care of Levavi-Yah.*

- *The best matches for romance, love, and artistic and intellectual achievements will be among men and women born June 13–17, under the care of Cali-Ya-El.*

Whoever suggested that bookworms were quiet, shy, unadventurous, and dull? Surely those stereotypes don't apply to those curious, open-minded, and adventurous men and women born under the influence of Angel Lela-Ha-El. This Angel not only stimulates their intellectual capacities, he/she directs their thoughts toward the discovery of unexpected. As a result, the protégés of this Angel are always up for a search for those invisible connections that link beings and things. And those who are in particularly close concert with Lela-Ha-El can put on an especially dazzling display of brainpower! Whether they are engaged in conversation or groundbreaking research, their minds seem to rise and spiral, breaking through what we consider to be ordinary dimensions of perception. While others plod from point to point, these make fascinating intuitive jumps from one subject to another, linking unlikely ideas and images to bring to light a new and innovative understanding of a phenomenon or an event. Known for their flexible minds and unique viewpoints, they are quirky, penetrating thinkers who constantly redefine the world.

Because those under the guidance of Lela-Ha-El feel the need to run all the data available through their computerlike brains, they tend to be attracted to literary works or works of fiction based on profound scientific research that respect facts. But they are hardly introverted, factoid collectors. Those in harmony with Angel Lela-Ha-El follow their irrepressible sense of curiosity to its limits, balancing the reading they love with a yen for travel, experience, and learning through interaction with direct witnesses to events or discoveries that interest them.

If you enjoy the patronage of Angel Lela-Ha-El, you may feel that you live, through your imagination, in two worlds at once—the world of simple, day-to-day pleasures and the vast and profound universe of knowledge. Consequently, you are just as moved by the miraculous opening of a wildflower in spring as you are by an earthshaking discovery; as mesmerized by the brightening hues of autumn as you are by the arcane brilliance of the world's mystics.

If you are in deep harmony with Angel Lela-Ha-El, you enrich your visions and interpretations of the world with a deep sense of commitment to the world and its people. It is important to you that you use your gifts to bring diverse people closer together, to foster a real sense of communion. Consequently, you and everyone under the protection of Angel Lela-Ha-El are unlikely to speak in confusing technical jargon or take on an exclusionary, holier-than-thou attitude. Instead, you frame your ideas with simple and clear reasoning and present the many truths you have gathered in language that is easily understood by most people.

Angel Lela-Ha-El reinforces the desire to aim high and achieve, even in her/his youngest protégés. Indeed, this powerful spiritual ally endows men and women, young boys and girls alike, not only with the desire to excel, but with the power to learn *how* to learn. As any teacher will attest, this is a life-changing ability. With such a power, the entire universe becomes a schoolroom, a constant and generous source for learning. The friends of Lela-Ha-El browse the world the way they might peruse the stacks of a limitless library, scanning the sources that capture their interest, filing away everything they learn in their fascinating minds. In this way, they maximize their capacity to comprehend, learn with pride but never arrogance, and attain a complete mastery of the understanding of the world.

If you are under the protection of Angel Lela-Ha-El, you may have a unique gift for teaching, whether in a classroom, a boardroom, or your own living room. And if circumstances bring you into contact with pupils who actively and sincerely seek out the truth, so much the better. An unimaginative audience made up of dullards who can't appreciate your audacious, daring, sometimes scandalous conclusions is not worthy of your talent. But be forewarned: those born between April 14 and 18 are rarely accepted by traditional or conformist people and institutions. You may have to seek out your students among those who do not fear dangerous liaisons, like the powerful melding of the unfettered intellect and universal love.

When in deep harmony with Angel Lela-Ha-El, men and women run with enthusiasm toward the ultimate truth, unite with the universal beauty, and let the goodness of divine love enlighten them. Their spirit then vibrates like a celestial harp, sounding the purest notes, filling the world with the harmony of boundless knowledge.

Angel ACHA-A-YAH

APRIL 19–23

Bestows vibrant psychological and physical vitality. Activates the stamina to see creative ideas through from conception to implementation. Brings material wealth.

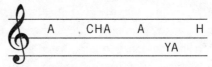

PHONETIC PRONUNCIATION

A as in Apricot

Cha as in Javier (Spanish) or Ach (German)

A as in Apricot

Ya as in Yard

H Vocalize the final H as a soft exhalation

UNIVERSAL RESONANCE OF THE ANGEL'S NAME

A The original ultimate energy, before form, universal, infinite, unifying.

Cha Cohesive substance that unifies the universe. Capability; analysis; breaking down, then reassembling components to a new coherence.

A The original ultimate energy, before form, universal, infinite, unifying.

Yah Final vibration of the Angel's name. Receptivity and reflectivity. The presence of the deity; the abundance of the being.

Guardian Angel Acha-A-Yah

In Akkadian, the name Acha-A-Yah means, literally, "Different energies that come together and unify within the realm of the Creator."

"I feel a need to reconnect with the source, to get back to basics." Increasingly, this is the lament of the world-weary, the mantra of the harried, haggard, and put-upon. It needn't be so for those born

NOTABLE PEOPLE BORN UNDER THE INFLUENCE OF ACHA-A-YAH

Anthony Quinn, *actor*

Ashley Judd, *actress*

Eliot Ness, *organized-crime fighter*

Harold Stanley Marcus, *businessman*

Immanuel Kant, *philosopher*

J. M. W. Turner, *painter*

Jack Nicholson, *actor*

Joan Miró, *painter*

John Paul Stevens, *U.S. Supreme Court justice*

Max Planck, *physicist*

Paloma Picasso, *fashion designer*

Richard Wagner, *composer*

Robert Oppenheimer, *physicist*

Shirley Temple Black, *actress and diplomat*

Vladimir Nabokov, *writer*

William Shakespeare, *poet and writer*

Yehudi Menuhin, *violinist*

COLOR HARMONIZATION

Fuchsia red / Rusty brown / Apple green and dark green

under the care of Angel Acha-A-Yah. This powerful Angel opens for those in her/his protection direct access to the creative source and inspires a profound and personal knowledge of the universal life force. He/she also bestows the deep sense of inner peace that informs those fortunate people, who ride to their destinies on subtle energy currents that turn the world.

While others give in to the rigors of modern life or give up on their dreams entirely, the friends of Angel Acha-A-Yah never tire in completion of their many projects. In fact, they don't even need to tank up on coffee! The unstoppable men and women born between April 19 and 23 draw their prodigious physical and psychological energy directly from the source that fuels the universe. And because this is an endless resource, constantly available and self-renewing, they rarely even experience any fatigue or weariness, no matter how difficult the challenge or bumpy the path.

If you are in accord with Acha-A-Yah, your friends and colleagues may consider you one of the Don Quixotes of the world, always pitting your wit and skill against life's obstacles. Indeed, you give those around you reason for speculation; it can appear that you take on difficulties willingly, as though you never even considered the possibility of avoiding them. That's because while others sink under the burden of life's travails, you surf the waves that come your way; and while others lose their direction in life's storm, you catch the blustery winds and use them to move you ever closer to your objectives. And as for the possibility that all that Sturm und Drang might overwhelm you or fill you with fear, don't even give it a thought. Angel Acha-A-Yah introduces those under her/his protection to the elemental and even somewhat scary forces that formed the universe. Because Acha-A-Yah has seen to it that you understand the necessity of an occasional big bang, you are able to face chaos and disorder without anxiety and fear. To you, change and conflict don't bring pandemonium; they create opportunity! So what if limits shatter? You're equipped to recombine the fragments and use them to make something new, dynamic, and personally fulfilling.

Those in harmony with Angel Acha-A-Yah, like Jack Nicholson, artist Joan Miró, and other independent souls, are guided more often by their own free will than they are by social conventions or values. Some particularly strong-willed men and women are totally

HARMONIC MATCHES FOR ACHA-A-YAH'S PROTÉGÉS

- *The best matches for success in economic and practical achievements will be among men and women born October 11–15, under the care of Mi-Yi-Ca-El.*
- *The best matches for recognition, fame, personal charisma, and social fulfillment will be among men and women born June 13–17, under the care of Cali-Ya-El.*
- *The best matches for romance, love, and artistic and intellectual achievements will be among men and women born June 18–22, under the care of Levavi-Yah.*

free of any constraints imposed from the outside. This exuberant spirit comes with the blessing of Acha-A-Yah, whose protégés often develop ebullient, free-wheeling personalities. While these people, refusing to censor themselves, rarely go with the flow and tend to make spectacles of themselves, their exciting individuality makes them lively companions, unpredictable lovers, and wildly attractive personalities. It also makes them subject to the deep and vengeful jealousy of the less enchanting people around them, who resent their easy manner and personal liberation. By sincerely calling on Acha-A-Yah, this Angel's friends will easily deflect these hostile and demeaning attacks. They will also continue to spread their unique brand of joie de vivre, widening their understanding of the universe—and their circle of friends—at the same time.

Those under the protection of Angel Acha-A-Yah know how to stabilize what is in movement and move what is stable. This means that, like philosopher Immanuel Kant and scientist Max Planck, they can bring shape to what is shapeless and loosen what is rigid. With their sharp powers of perception, they produce penetrating analysis, which become the source of worthy projects and productions. Those under the protection of Angel Acha-A-Yah, for example, might start a company based on their personal talents or a school based upon startling, new educational methods; they might introduce an unheard-of theoretical or scientific system or turn some homely raw material into a jewel, artistic medium, or decorative object.

With the help of Angel Acha-A-Yah, women and men develop the ability to create, achieve, and produce great things seemingly from nothing. In fact, everything they create flows from their own prodigious creativity and unbridled independence. It is common for these men and women to found companies based on little more than their own imaginations. Although they are able to engage in warm and intimate relationships with others and share the joy and benefits provided by their achievements, they are, at their hearts, self-directed entrepreneurs. They are most likely to attract financial benefits when they put their brilliant analytical abilities and their unique perspectives to work for them as counselors, independent consultants, or in some other field of endeavor that minimizes the need for teamwork and allows them to act alone.

Establish a close relationship with Angel Acha-A-Yah, and you will be richly rewarded. Acha-A-Yah bestows an agile intellect, a mind that travels easily from one dimension to another. He/she also imparts the ability to accurately anticipate events still to come. If you are born to Acha-A-Yah's care, your family, friends, and professional contacts may call upon you often to report your sense of things, your feeling about an individual, or your impression of how events might proceed. Your psychic gifts won't disappoint them.

Thanks to Angel Acha-A-Yah, men and women are aware of the celestial origin of their freedom and the rousing power of the life force within them. With this Angel's aid, they will follow their higher impulses, stay enthusiastically involved with life on Earth, and pursue, not the hope for fleeting glory or social prestige, but their true destiny. This is the path that will reap them riches—and the boundless spiritual wealth that flows from the immense and generous source of the divine Creator.

Angel CA-HETHA-EL

APRIL 24—28

Encourages practical intelligence. Inspires action at the most appropriate moment. Bestows a gift for exact calculation and precise analysis. Promotes deep emotional harmony.

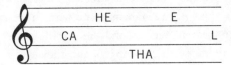

PHONETIC PRONUNCIATION

Ca as in Caress

He as in Hebrew

Tha as in Tarot

El as in Elevation

UNIVERSAL RESONANCE OF THE ANGEL'S NAME

Ca The practical, physical, and material manifestation of ideas and thoughts. A solidifying, coalescing force within the fluid substances of the universe. Energies of cohesion and collusion, connivance, collaboration, cooperation. A force of strength and power.

He Spiritual life force. Love that underlies all things. Presence of the universal and all-encompassing spirit. Divine call, divine connection.

Tha Experience of time. Evolving temporal cycles eternally recurring. Mutation coupling mortality with immortality.

El Ending vibration of the Angel's name. Principle of excellence; chosen; elite. Elevating force. Source of perpetual transformation and evolution.

NOTABLE PEOPLE BORN UNDER THE INFLUENCE OF CA-HETHA-EL

Al Pacino, *actor*

Barbra Streisand, *singer, actress, and director*

Bobby Rydell, *singer*

Carol Burnett, *comedian*

Coretta Scott King, *civil rights activist*

Ella Fitzgerald, *singer*

Jay Leno, *talk-show host*

John James Audubon, *painter and naturalist*

Morris West, *writer*

Renée Zellweger, *actress*

Shirley MacLaine, *actress and writer*

Talia Shire, *actress*

COLOR HARMONIZATION

Ocher / Dark brown / Rust / Forest green / Red-burgundy

Guardian Angel Ca-Hetha-El

In Akkadian, the name Ca-Hetha-El means, literally, "The cohesive force of the real world touched by the infinite life force of divine love, which eternally crosses cycles."

Should I or shouldn't I? Now or never? You'll never have to worry about it if you're under the guardianship of Angel Ca-Hetha-El. This Angel bestows the gift of practical intelligence and an unfailing intuition for the appropriate time to act.

Men and women in harmony with Angel Ca-Hetha-El can analyze and evaluate, quantify and qualify, categorize and organize the visible world with great precision and act with a clear and profound understanding of ideas, feelings, things, and beings that surround them. They also have an uncanny intuition for the rhythms of time and of the phases and cycles that control the natural, material, intellectual, and emotional events of life. Consequently, those under Ca-Hetha-El's influence develop a remarkable sense about the amount of time necessary for an idea, talent, or project to mature. They are masters at predicting how long to let a venture lie and when to act to bring it to its final resolution.

Jay Leno, who has built a career on his razor-sharp insights, and other April 24–28 babies can excel in occupations or professions that necessitate acute observation, an appreciation for the personal quirks that make people unique, and quick and precise analysis. Hardly the indecisive Hamlets of the world, these are men and women who can jump into the right place at the right time and land with panache. Circumstances permitting, they can successfully apply their practical intelligence to complex fields of endeavor, including ecology (John James Audubon), societal change (Coretta Scott King), and satire-based entertainment (Carol Burnett).

If you are in harmony with Angel Ca-Hetha-El, you temper your intellectual observations with a refined sense of emotional sensitivity. In fact, your facility for understanding and discerning your emotions is nearly as quick as your talent for calculation. You can describe the various qualities of feelings—yours and others'—with the same precision you rely on to evaluate distances, shapes, structures, and masses. Your innate understanding of subtle feelings and your profound comprehension of the importance of emotions in all

HARMONIC MATCHES FOR CA-HETHA-EL'S PROTÉGÉS

- *The best matches for success in economic and practical achievements will be among men and women born October 6–10, under the care of He-He-Ha-El.*
- *The best matches for recognition, fame, personal charisma, and social fulfillment will be among men and women born June 8–12, under the care of Le-A-Vi-Yah.*
- *The best matches for romance, love, and artistic and intellectual achievements will be among men and women born June 23–27, under the care of Pe-Hali-Yah.*

human transactions make you a respectful, deeply loyal friend, a loving and faithful mate, and a caring, responsible businessperson. At work and at play, you are careful to give everyone what they are owed, emotionally or monetarily, and you take great pains that everyone around you is compensated in proportion to their contribution. Though your gifts are many, you are known for your fairness, sense of justice, and ability to resolve conflicts without prejudice. Depending on the circumstances of your life, you and others under the protection of Angel Ca-Hetha-El can excel as psychologists, therapists, doctors, company consultants, decorators, religious leaders, directors of human resources, legal mediators, popularizers of science, school directors, and in any other field relying on intelligence, timing, and sound mediation skills.

Ca-Hetha-El enkindles great love in the personalities of those under her/his care, and men and women who stay close to this Angel always act from love. They make their decisions, establish their goals, and form their beliefs from the heart and the head. Faced with a dilemma, you act with the wisdom of Solomon, not for your own gain but for the best interest of all involved. In whatever you do, it is important to you to preserve relationships. You will never suggest a solution that appears fair on the surface if it is divisive at its heart.

By calling on Angel Ca-Hetha-El, you can enhance your intimate knowledge of cycles, seasons, and rhythms of the earth, ultimately coming to understand that many levels of time unfold eternally in the cosmos. Your heart will then beat in unison with the rhythm of universal love. Your love will be one with the basis of all love, your intellect a part of the celestial wisdom. Then your spirit will move toward the universal light of the Creator of all creations.

Angel HAZI-YA-EL

APRIL 29–MAY 3

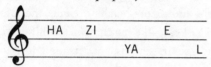

Opens the door to love. Stimulates a satisfying emotional life.
Brings a flow of happy opportunities, unexpected gifts,
pleasant surprises. Bestows a faculty for clairvoyance
and prophecy.

PHONETIC PRONUNCIATION

Ha as in Habit
Zi as in Zebra
Ya as in Yard
El as in Elevation

UNIVERSAL RESONANCE OF THE ANGEL'S NAME

Ha Spiritual life force. Love that underlies all things. Presence of the universal and all-encompassing spirit. Divine call, divine connection.

Zi The seed of life; the energy that bestows vitality and nourishment. Light of life. Sexual energy. High velocity. Power of simultaneity and instantaneity. Zen powers.

Ya Mastery. Dexterity, expertise; human action aligned with divine universal principles.

El Ending vibration of the Angel's name. Principle of excellence; chosen; elite. Elevating force. Source of perpetual transformation and evolution.

NOTABLE PEOPLE BORN UNDER THE INFLUENCE OF HAZI-YA-EL

Bing Crosby, singer
Calamity Jane, legendary gunslinger
Catherine the Great, empress of Russia
Daniel Day-Lewis, actor
Duke Ellington, composer and bandleader
Golda Meir, former Israeli prime minister
James Brown, singer
Jerry Seinfeld, comedian
Joseph Heller, writer
Judy Collins, folk musician
Michelle Pfeiffer, actress
Niccolò Machiavelli, Italian statesman, writer, and political theorist
Pete Seeger, folk musician
Theodor Herzl, writer and founder of Zionism
William Randolph Hearst, media mogul
Willie Nelson, country singer

COLOR HARMONIZATION

Warm brown / Speckles of black /
Ocher / Cameo brown to beige /
Strikes of red rust with sparks of gold

Guardian Angel Hazi-Ya-El

In Akkadian language, the name Hazi-Ya-El means, literally, "The love of God produces universal creation, instantaneously and forever."

Angel Hazi-Ya-El activates intellectual curiosity, stimulates emotions, and encourages men and women to act on their decisions without self-doubt, without regret, and, most of all, without delay.

Irrepressible and unpredictable, comic and provocative, the friends of Hazi-Ya-El are like mischievous children. They zero in on any adults engaged in serious conversation just to make them laugh. Always young at heart, the men and women under the protection of Angel Hazi-Ya-El are always up for a new idea. They love to stir up intellectual excitement, and they work constantly to bring about change, move minds, and enflame romantic passions.

To sum up: these personalities are impossible to overlook. Where others are content to go with the flow, the associates of Hazi-Ya-El fight the current. Their quest is to break up paralyzing inertia, contravene any and all uselessly constraining habits, and propose anything and everything that might stimulate vitality and open new horizons. If their circumstances allow them the freedom to express their innermost passions, those under the protection of Angel Hazi-Ya-El are sure to be noticed for the originality of their hypotheses, their fresh—even unexpected—approach to relationships, the force of their intellects, and the high-mindedness of their aspirations.

If you have established a relationship with Angel Hazi-Ya-El, you live in the now. And unlike most people, you wring all of the experience, emotion, and potential from every moment available to you. You think, act, and relate to others in the present. You neither clutter your path with the burdens of the past nor trip yourself up with the uncertainty of the future. If you have found accord with Hazi-Ya-El, the present extends before you without limits. It is like a fertile field that cradles the precious seeds sown in the past and trusts they will be nurtured by the rejuvenating rains of the future but grows its harvest moment by moment, in each and every now.

Angel Hazi-Ya-El provides those in her/his care with a dynamic mix of intellectual agility and physical dexterity that, added to their innate efficiency, increases their originality and output. In fact, the

HARMONIC MATCHES FOR HAZI-YA-EL'S PROTÉGÉS

- *The best matches for success in economic and practical achievements will be among men and women born October 1–5, under the care of Ye-Yaza-El.*

- *The best matches for recognition, fame, personal charisma, and social fulfillment will be among men and women born July 13–17, under the care of He-Havi-Yah.*

- *The best matches for romance, love, and artistic and intellectual achievements will be among men and women born May 19–23, under the care of Yezala-El.*

rapidity with which those favored by Hazi-Ya-El accomplish complex tasks often leads those around them to misjudge them. They are often written off as superficial, careless, or haphazard. Slower co-workers suspect that they are too fast to be accurate or too verbose to be deep. Indeed, Hazi-Ya-El's dynamos often appear to act impulsively, without preparation or plan. They can even appear somewhat frantic, as though they are following up an endless series of impulsive decisions with a succession of arbitrary actions. Yet, Angel Hazi-Ya-El invites men and women to enlighten their minds at the original source of truth, and when they come back from such celestial trips, they use their energy to spread their burning message of hope and truth to the whole world.

Judy Collins, Golda Meir, and Niccolò Machiavelli are just a few of the protégés of Hazi-Ya-El who have transformed their time by reminding those around them to cast off complacency and live with passion. In exchange for delivering their much-needed messages, those under the protection of Angel Hazi-Ya-El are paid back generously with unexpected presents, beneficial encounters, revelations of precious secrets, offered opportunities, and open doors.

If your birthday falls between April 29 and May 3, it is important that you refine your knowledge of the people and things around you by tuning in to your own brilliant intuitions and clairvoyant dreams. And always, always fearlessly follow the path of your prophetic visions. By doing so, you will become an authentic messenger of light and a beacon for your human brothers and sisters.

If you are in harmony with Angel Hazi-Ya-El, you will calibrate the rhythm of your passions by the powerful beat of divine love and match your personal goals to the will of the universe. When you do, you will become one with the Infinite, an inhabitor of boundless space, where even the most rousing passions come together in the stillness of celestial peace.

Angel ALADI-YAH

MAY 4–8

Provides the courage to undertake and the energy to conquer. Helps to overcome obstacles by implementing creative and original solutions. Encourages access to spiritual dimensions.

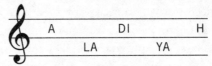

PHONETIC PRONUNCIATION

A as in Aloft
La as in Lagoon
Di as in Direct
Ya as is Yard
H Vocalize the final H as a soft exhalation

UNIVERSAL RESONANCE OF THE ANGEL'S NAME

A The original and ultimate energy; before form, universal, infinite, unifying.

La Dynamic learning. The ability to make mental links. Intellectual elevation. An evolving, ascending movement of the mind. Lucidity and enlightenment.

Di Discovery. Unveiling the unknown. Drama of all changes. Transference, translocation, translation. Mobility and transfer from one world to another. Appreciative perception of contrasts, differences, and variances.

Yah Final vibration of the Angel's name. Receptivity and reflectivity. The presence of the deity; the abundance of the being.

Guardian Angel Aladi-Yah

The literal meaning of the name Aladi-Yah in Akkadian is "The swirling knowledge that soars toward the discovery of divine universes."

NOTABLE PEOPLE BORN UNDER THE INFLUENCE OF ALADI-YAH

Audrey Hepburn, actress

Eva Perón, Argentinian political figure

Gary Cooper, actor

George Clooney, actor

Harry S. Truman, U.S. president

Johannes Brahms, composer

Orson Welles, writer, producer, and director

Peter I. Tchaikovsky, composer

Rabindranath Tagore, poet and philosopher

Robert Browning, poet

Robert Peary, explorer

Roberto Rossellini, film director

Rudolph Valentino, silent-film actor and matinee idol

Sigmund Freud, founder of psychoanalysis

Willie Mays, baseball hall of famer and philanthropist

COLOR HARMONIZATION

Dark gray / Beige / Dark green / Lemon yellow

What would a photograph of the men and women under the protection of Angel Aladi-Yah look like? A blur! That's because those born under the influence of this energizing Angel develop supercharged temperaments, an abhorrence for rigidity and stagnation, and attractive, extroverted personalities. To get to the point—and these people love to get to the point!—these are women and men who are always in the forefront and on the move.

Those of us with less stamina can't help but wonder where the protégés of Aladi-Yah get their exuberant energy. With the help of their guardian, they draw their amazing stamina directly from the original energy source, the force that conceived and created the universe. Connected to such a powerful lineage, these people seem wired for personal growth, supercharged in the exploration of their world, and socially and professionally electrifying.

It would be selling these miracles of motion short, however, to describe them as merely vibrant. In fact, they are virtually unstoppable! Angel Aladi-Yah encourages men and women not only to knock on doors but also to open those doors; not only to identify obstacles but also to unilaterally build passages over them. No doubt this indomitable spirit empowered Willie Mays, explorer Robert Peary, U.S. president Harry Truman, and the unforgettable Eva Perón to overcome their limitations, create opportunities for success, and discover even more opportunities to connect with their auspicious destinies.

If your birthday falls between May 4 and 8, you tend to view the world through rose-colored glasses, focusing only on the good of a given situation or relationship. Where others see conflict, you find mutual interest. You have the power to defuse anger in even the worst of situations and are able to dispel hostility with a few compassionate words or a warming smile. To sum up, you are living proof that happiness is, indeed, contagious. It could not be otherwise. The Angel Aladi-Yah's harmonic vibrations are powerful neutralizers. They not only disperse the gravity of space and time, they also dissolve the doubts and fears that weigh heavily on the mind and spirit. Consequently, men and women in this Angel's care move freely, lightly, and with ease. Because, in their presence, difficulties disappear and obstacles drop, they become the leaders who guide others through points of resistance, urging them on toward

HARMONIC MATCHES FOR ALADI-YAH'S PROTÉGÉS

- *The best matches for success in economic and practical achievements will be among men and women born September 26–30, under the care of Re-Ha-Â-El.*
- *The best matches for recognition, fame, personal charisma, and social fulfillment will be among men and women born July 8–12, under the care of Mela-Ha-El.*
- *The best matches for romance, love, and artistic and intellectual achievements will be among men and women born May 24–28, under the care of Meba-Ha-El.*

their fulfillment with unflagging joie de vivre, courage, energy, and laughter. It is no wonder that those under the protection of Angel Aladi-Yah find themselves surrounded by loyal friends and lifelong admirers.

If you seek the aid of Angel Aladi-Yah, you will find your adventurous intellect leading you to new and unexpected points of view, expressing transformational ideas that break routines for others, and conceiving of startling new ways to overthrow old habits. You will also acquire the capacity to envision every problem you encounter from a uniquely creative angle and to devise solutions that are simple to implement yet truly one of a kind.

If it is your wish, you can climb the social ladder all the way to the top. Or if professional achievement is more your style, you can work your way into positions others might have thought beyond your reach. The joy you bring to your surroundings and your innovative contributions reinforce confidence and hope in others. You are an invigorating addition to any social group or professional environment.

Angel Aladi-Yah provides men and women with the power to fully understand that what is above can be a model for what is below. In other words, from inspiration comes tangible action. This understanding bestows upon those who invoke this Angel a great deal of wisdom and power. If you are in deep harmony with Aladi-Yah, you too can acquire the superior powers of the wise, provided that you are open to it. This profound knowledge will enable you to perceive the spirituality of all things, from animals to atoms, and forge a deep connection between your day-to-day reality and the celestial worlds and beings. When in complete accord with Angel Aladi-Yah, your mind will be enveloped within the great spinning life force of the universe. There it will gather strength, cross all thresholds of space and time, and travel to the source of light, where it will be immersed in eternity. Then, having reached your ultimate goals, you and all of those under the protection of Angel Aladi-Yah can continue your journey on earth with renewed enthusiasm, arousing hope in everyone around you, pointing the way to a refreshing spring from which all spiritual energy flows.

Angel LO-AVI-YAH

MAY 9–13

Increases love for life. Encourages a deep communion with nature. Provides the capacity to generate and share happiness. Helps harmonize day-to-day experience with that of the celestial world.

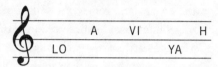

PHONETIC PRONUNCIATION

Lo as in Love
A as in Arrow
Vi as in Victory
Ya as in Yard
H Vocalize the final H as a soft exhalation

UNIVERSAL RESONANCE OF THE ANGEL'S NAME

Lo Dynamic learning. The ability to make mental links. Intellectual elevation. An evolving, ascending movement of the mind. Lucidity and enlightenment.

A The original and ultimate energy; before form, universal, infinite, unifying.

Vi Vitalizing factor. Fruitfulness and productivity. Catalyst of variety, vitality, verity, will, and vigor.

Yah Final vibration of the Angel's name. Receptivity and reflectivity. The presence of the deity; the abundance of the being.

Guardian Angel Lo-Avi-Yah

The literal meaning of the name Lo-Avi-Yah in Akkadian is "The desire for knowledge rises up to the ultimate source of energy to experience the spiritual oneness that creates life."

The harmonic vibrations of Angel Lo-Avi-Yah help men and women draw their thoughts, actions, and experiences from the

HARMONIC MATCHES FOR LO-AVI-YAH'S PROTÉGÉS

- *The best matches for success in economic and practical achievements will be among men and women born September 21–25, under the care of Ha-Âmi-Yah.*
- *The best matches for recognition, fame, personal charisma, and social fulfillment will be among men and women born July 3–7, under the care of Ye-Yi-Ya-El.*
- *The best matches for romance, love, and artistic and intellectual achievements will be among men and women born May 29–June 2, under the care of Hare-Ya-El.*

earth's regenerative source. Consequently, those in sync with Lo-Avi-Yah enjoy sports and activities that bring them into the great outdoors. Those who make their homes in the city are sure to use the parks or spend their weekends in some bucolic area where they can commune with nature. And we do mean *commune*. These outdoorsy spirits have an acute and loving awareness of the natural drives that live in them, as in all things. The hills, grasses, animals, brooks, rocks, caves, winds, lakes, flowers, bees and their honey—all of them nourish the energy and renew the senses of Lo-Avi-Yah's protégés. In fact, only when they are immersed in natural splendor, filled with wonder at the earth's artistic creations, do those under the protection of Angel Lo-Avi-Yah awaken to the fullness of their intellectual quest and open themselves to the primal knowledge that constantly renews the world.

By the grace of Lo-Avi-Yah, those in this Angel's kinship can come to know the profound truths that form the very catalyst of creation. They can also learn to use these truths with skill and power. Depending on their familial and personal circumstances, those under the protection of Angel Lo-Avi-Yah can be exceptionally intuitive and proficient herbalists, naturalists, biochemists, aromatherapists, therapists, healers, doctors, magi, priests, or shamans. In fact, they would succeed in any occupation that demands a knowledge of the powers of plants and scents, a recognition of the power of winds, a feeling of oneness with forests and wild animals, and an understanding of what it means to live and act in empathy with the forces of nature, no matter what their form.

If you are close with Angel Lo-Avi-Yah, you are led by love in all of its carnal, emotional, intellectual, or spiritual manifestations. Love, after all, is a powerful, primal natural force. Once the friends of Lo-Avi-Yah give themselves over to this transformational affection, it begins to work within them, inspiring and encouraging the shape and transitions of their lives. Love for all the creatures who share the earth may inspire them to embark on humanitarian or medical ventures or to undertake scientific, anthropological, ethnological, or botanical research. It may inspire them to follow religious callings, experience mystical encounters, or produce artistic and educational works. Those who become deeply influenced by the harmonic vibrations of Angel Lo-Avi-Yah live on love, at least in the spiritual sense.

Love given and received becomes their nourishment, and they are blessed with the insatiable desire to create and share it—not in hope that it will be reciprocated, but for its own sake.

If you are under the guidance of Angel Lo-Avi-Yah, you receive, as if tied together in a bouquet, the gifts of love, prestige, intellectual brilliance, and renown. Your social relationships are strong and alive, as are those you enjoy with your celestial benefactors.

Your shining charm fascinates your contemporaries—and so do your deep humanitarian beliefs. Don't be surprised, then, when a crowd of fascinated friends and suitors beats a path to your door. They want to accompany you on your journey to enlightenment or at least gather whatever fruit they can from your bounty.

If you do achieve prominence, be aware: others might be impressed by your achievements, but you won't. Money doesn't motivate you, so success and prestige seem merely coincidental. The real happiness for you lies in being nourished by the eternal source so you can bring what you have learned back to terra firma, where you can do your fellow creatures some good. If you had your druthers, you and all the men and women who enjoy the kinship of Lo-Avi-Yah would gravitate toward occupations and activities that are guided by selfless love. You might even choose a mystical, spiritual, or religious path. The friends of Lo-Avi-Yah are so high-minded, admirable, and passionate they can attain not only glory but beatification and sanctification. Whatever lifestyle you choose, you are sure to lead a self-directed and unconventional life. And if you discover your passion, you will become a fascinating and timeless example of altruism at work, of a life dedicated to service.

By the grace of Angel Lo-Avi-Yah, your mind and heart draw their energy directly from the celestial source of the most powerful generative and creative forces of the universe. You will obtain tangible rewards through spiritual thoughts and selfless action.

INVOCATION

O Angel Lo-Avi-Yah,
When my heart becomes parched
And hope wanes, help me!
When my thoughts lose their flame,
Guide me!
I invoke you,
Angel Lo-Avi-Yah,
So dense is my night! Awaken me!
Revive my hopes,
Illuminate my memories of heavens.
O Lo-Avi-Yah, help me rise,
Reveal to me the absolute love
That, in eternal life,
Unites humans with Angels.

Angel HE-HA-Â-YAH

MAY 14–18

COLOR HARMONIZATION

White / Pale yellow / Indigo /
Apple green / Orange

Promotes happy and long-lasting love relationships. Allows for the development of radiant and charismatic personalities. Opens the way to the heart. Makes one receptive to synchronicities and providential messages.

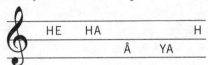

PHONETIC PRONUNCIATION

He as in Help

Ha as in Habit

Â as in Arrow, ending with a soft breath out

Ya as in Yard

H Vocalize the final H as a soft exhalation

UNIVERSAL RESONANCE OF THE ANGEL'S NAME

He Spiritual life force. Love that underlies all things. Presence of the universal and all-encompassing spirit. Divine call, divine connection.

Ha Spiritual life force. Love that underlies all things. Presence of the universal and all-encompassing spirit. Divine call, divine connection.

Â The origin of the sensory world; the foundation of human emotions and passions. Enhancement of the visual senses and hearing acuity. Supersensitivity.

Yah Final vibration of the Angel's name. Receptivity and reflectivity. The presence of the deity; the abundance of the being.

Guardian Angel He-Ha-Â-Yah

In Akkadian language the name He-Ha-Â-Yah means, literally, "Love that draws its source from the Supreme Being and changes all experiences into love."

Angel He-Ha-Â-Yah bestows upon the men and women in his/her care the power to weave their deep feelings into a radiant and sensual aura that surrounds and protects them—and enhances their charisma and personal magnetism. When in harmony with Angel He-Ha-Â-Yah, women and men attract an endless supply of loving and friendly energy. This energy is the source from which they draw to bring new life to their emotional relationships.

Love is a game of give and take; to be successful in love one must be, in turns, the giver and the taker, the seducer and the seduced. This knowledge, which some people don't learn in a lifetime, is second nature to the men and women born under the care of He-Ha-Â-Yah. They initiate or wait to be approached; they call or answer, always adjusting their desires in order to further the relationship. And their relationships prosper. How could they fail? These are lovers who can read the subtle, unspoken signals that precede grand passions. They are true romantics who can inspire and receive great whirlwinds of emotion.

If you have an affinity for Angel He-Ha-Â-Yah, love is blissful but definitely not blind. In spite of your strong inclination for affection, although you can be governed by intense love, you keep your mind and heart open. The protégés of He-Ha-Â-Yah do not give in to the blindness and imprisonment that result from envy, a need to control, or other forms of lovesickness. Love is love only when it is given and received freely. Although you may be dazzled by the object of your affection, you remain clear-eyed enough to look objectively at your relationship and its limitations.

Perceptive and sensitive, open and empathetic, you can be as pleasant to break up with as you are to romance! Those under the protection of Angel He-Ha-Â-Yah possess an acute sense of what to say, how to say it, and when to deliver their message. With talents like these, they can make even bad news seem good! They can also use their skills to build a lucrative future. Those under the protection of Angel He-Ha-Â-Yah are loyal, trustworthy, and tight-lipped. With a gift for listening in silence without interfering, with a deep belief in keeping the secrets entrusted to them, they win the confidence of everyone they encounter. Consequently, the friends of He-Ha-Â-Yah make wonderful family and marital counselors and can provide precious advice to people who wish to establish or improve

HARMONIC MATCHES FOR HE-HA-Â-YAH'S PROTÉGÉS

- *The best matches for success in economic and practical achievements will be among men and women born September 16–20, under the care of Ani-Ya-El.*
- *The best matches for recognition, fame, personal charisma, and social fulfillment will be among men and women born June 28–July 2, under the care of Nel-Cha-El.*
- *The best matches for romance, love, and artistic and intellectual achievements will be among men and women born June 3–7, under the care of He-Qua-Mi-Yah.*

emotional relationships. They can also succeed in occupations that require them to predict trends or perceive and fulfill the unspoken desires of the public. As a result, they make adept literary agents and editors or art gallery owners.

During the course of their lives, those under the protection of Angel He-Ha-Â-Yah tend to indulge in introspection and meditation. To others, this tendency to daydream can make them seem inactive, dull, or even inert. But those who know you best understand that within you abide powerful forces that result in profound inner visions. When you retreat into a state of deep silence with little or no external stimulation, you aren't isolating yourself; you are connecting with the powerful sources that enlighten your feelings and direct your thoughts. Through this process, Angel He-Ha-Â-Yah offers the special men and women in her/his kinship to see and hear to the very heart of beings and things.

Angel He-Ha-Â-Yah predisposes you to reject or avoid hostile relationships or situations, and because you like to balance your busy life with long periods of rest, calm, and daydreaming, you will feel the need to turn away, every time it is possible, from any upsetting relationship or situation. But that doesn't mean you should excuse yourself from life's hustle and bustle altogether. You need your periods of contemplation; they elevate your thoughts. But if you find that you are contemplating your navel, it's time to ask for help. By invoking Angel He-Ha-Â-Yah, you will ensure that you do not fall into a state of total physical passivity or intellectual laziness, and you can focus your thoughts ever on the stimulating celestial sources that open to you.

With the aid of Angel He-Ha-Â-Yah, spiritual awakening instead of apathy, a deep passion for life instead of futile agitation, loving relationships instead of rivalries are the joys that men and women spread generously throughout the world. Those born between May 14 and 18 are a joy to know.

Angel YEZALA-EL

MAY 19–23

Bestows a gift for manual and technical work. Confers an intuition for swift and successful action and reaction. Develops intuition and inspiration. Fosters personal evolution, growth, and development.

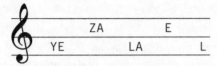

PHONETIC PRONUNCIATION

Ye as in Yes
Za as in Zachary
La as in Larry
El as in Elevation

UNIVERSAL RESONANCE OF THE ANGEL'S NAME

Ye Mastery. Dexterity, expertise; human action aligned with divine universal principles.

Za The seed of life; the energy that bestows vitality and nourishment. Light of life. Sexual energy. High velocity. Power of simultaneity and instantaneity. Zen powers.

La Dynamic learning. The ability to make mental links. Intellectual elevation. An evolving, ascending movement of the mind. Lucidity and enlightenment.

El Ending vibration of the Angel's name. Principle of excellence; chosen; elite. Elevating force. Source of perpetual transformation and evolution.

Guardian Angel Yezala-El

In Akkadian language the name Yezala-El means, literally, "The right action travels at great speed through the universe, from which it draws evolving knowledge."

COLOR HARMONIZATION

Blue / Orange / Beige-brown / Turquoise blue

HARMONIC MATCHES FOR YEZALA-EL'S PROTÉGÉS

- *The best matches for success in economic and practical achievements will be among men and women born January 9–13, under the care of Mitsa-Ra-El.*
- *The best matches for recognition, fame, personal charisma, and social fulfillment will be among men and women born April 4–8, under the care of Âlami-Yah.*
- *The best matches for romance, love, and artistic and intellectual achievements will be among men and women born April 29–May 3, under the care of Hazi-Ya-El.*

Angel Yezala-El fosters practical minds, the ability to control reality, and quickly obtain any necessary results and solutions. Known for their efficiency and reliability, the women and men stimulated by the vibrating harmonics of Angel Yezala-El develop active personalities and the desire to become deeply involved in the world. Their achievements are based on know-how, dexterity, and a gift for producing a job well done, particularly if the job has manual and technical applications.

If you have established a deep connection with Angel Yezala-El, you are quick-witted and able to think on your feet. You are also known for the sparks of understanding and flashes of insight (gifts from Yezala-El) that enliven your conversation and increase your capacity for achievement. Whether you are applying your astute mind in private or the professional sphere, you display an uncanny knack for pinpointing the best possible solution, even if you can't completely explain the reason your remedy will work. But work it invariably does, and before long your flashes of brilliance become part of your glowing reputation—and you have become everyone's alternative to 911.

As much as you'd like to, you may not always be available to help. While those under the protection of Yezala-El display an aptitude for technical tasks, they are unlikely to become bogged down in dull, repetitive chores. Those under this dynamic Angel's care learn to apply their practical, down-to-earth knowledge to wider intellectual questions. This mental muscle and their far-ranging curiosity make them great natural teachers. And that's not all. Those blessed by Angel Yezala-El are given the courage as well as the smarts to undertake and implement any projects that spring to their fertile minds. They know how to create opportunities for change, widen their horizons, and communicate to others how they, too, can become more active and dynamic.

In whatever field or art they choose, those under the protection of Angel Yezala-El can easily acquire the status of master. For example, a dancer born between May 19 and 23 can become a choreographer; a musician can become a conductor; a technician, a producer. In fact, if they so desire, any man and woman in Yezala-El's kinship can take a position of leadership in their social or professional lives. They are living proof of the biblical adage "By their acts, you shall know them." Everything these people do reflects their competence and capacity for achievement.

If you are in harmony with Angel Yezala-El, the key to your success is your ability to make decisions and act quickly. You probably don't need to be reminded, however, that this strategy is not without pitfall. To avoid disappointments or quick and catastrophic errors, it is imperative that you constantly refine your will, clarify your mind, and ensure that your intentions are in alignment with the highest and purest of moral stands. More specifically, it is crucial that you avoid duplicity of all sorts and never, *ever*, wander into the shadows of what could be considered a double life. These aren't secrets; they are lies, and lying is too tawdry an occupation for a mind as fine as yours.

Men and women in deep harmony with Angel Yezala-El are endowed with a natural and physical dynamism, a powerful intellectual swiftness, and a lifetime supply of spiritual and cosmic power. By activating these celestial gifts, they ensure that they will pass through life with enthusiasm, producing valuable ideas that reinforce freedom in the world and contribute to the general well-being.

Angel MEBA-HA-EL

MAY 24–28

Nurtures a feeling of wonder. Reinforces a sense of communion with the immensity of the cosmos. Bestows artistic talent. Encourages authenticity, truth, and justice.

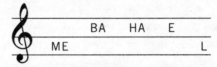

PHONETIC PRONUNCIATION

Me as in Merit
Ba as in Balance
Ha as in Habit
El as in Elevation

UNIVERSAL RESONANCE OF THE ANGEL'S NAME

Me Matrix, matter, model. Maternal loving protection. The force that brings life into the material world. Mustering of energies. Generation and regeneration.

Ba The universal paternal force; that which contains the code of all codes. The formative energy generating all data and shapes. The energy that begins all lives, all manifestations, all experiences.

Ha Spiritual life force. Love that underlies all things. Presence of the universal and all-encompassing spirit. Divine call, divine connection.

El Ending vibration of the Angel's name. Principle of excellence; chosen; elite. Elevating force. Source of perpetual transformation and evolution.

Guardian Angel Meba-Ha-El

In Akkadian language the name Meba-Ha-El means, literally, "Out of the original shape and code of the creation comes the truth wrapped in love, light, and purity."

NOTABLE PEOPLE BORN UNDER THE INFLUENCE OF MEBA-HA-EL

Al Jolson, *singer and actor*

Bob Dylan, *folk singer*

Henry Kissinger, *Nobel Peace Prize winner*

Ian Fleming, *writer and journalist*

Isadora Duncan, *dancer*

Jerry West, *basketball player*

Jim Thorpe, *Olympic athlete*

John Wayne, *actor*

Mike Myers, *actor and comedian*

Miles Davis, *jazz musician*

Queen Victoria of England

Ralph Waldo Emerson, *writer*

Robert Ludlum, *writer*

Rudolph Giuliani, *former mayor of New York City*

Sally Ride, *astronaut and first American woman in space*

Thomas Moore, *writer*

COLOR HARMONIZATION

Forest green / Reds / Spots of yellow / Dark browns / Spots of dark violet (heather tones)

The harmonic vibrations of Angel Meba-Ha-El refine the sensual capacities of humans: sight, touch, smell, and hearing are all rich sensory experiences from which they draw a perpetually renewed sense of wonder. Under the influence of Angel Meba-Ha-El, men and women use the sensory part of their experiences to unite with and integrate themselves into the invisible dimensions of the cosmos.

Angel Meba-Ha-El helps women and men transform their everyday joys into love, union, and harmony with celestial worlds. Touched by the harmonic vibrations of Angel Meba-Ha-El, they can, if they so desire, recast their life experiences through celestial inspiration. They can then channel their observations through a number of creative outlets, including songwriting (like Bob Dylan), dance (like Isadora Duncan), fiction writing (like Ian Fleming), or other art forms, including poetry, painting, sculpture, and pottery. Men and women who are in harmony with Angel Meba-Ha-El look at and perceive the world with a childlike clarity and innocence. They question long-held beliefs and customs with pure and unprejudicial intentions. Their open minds and far-reaching curiosity make it possible for them to unveil truths that have been carefully hidden by defensive people or concealed by self-protective institutions or that have been distorted by time and history.

If you are born to the care of Meba-Ha-El, you have a strong sense of justice and moral righteousness and are most comfortable when your deeply felt ethics form the basis of your personal, familial, and professional relationships. Straightforward, honest, and scrupulous, you are most fulfilled in circumstances that require your laser-sharp authenticity and accuracy. Needless to say, you would make a fair and honest detective, judge, interviewer, reporter, counselor, or historian and would fare well in any pursuit in which you could exercise your ability to extract elements of truth from ambiguities and lies.

As canny as you are, however, you wander beyond your depth when you become involved with shady characters, people who disseminate "spin," relationships built upon secret compromises, and institutions that promulgate half-truths and hidden lies. In other words, politics, public relations, and mysterious strangers are not for you. If the circumstances of your life force you to function in

HARMONIC MATCHES FOR MEBA-HA-EL'S PROTÉGÉS

- The best matches for success in economic and practical achievements will be among men and women born January 4–8, under the care of Ha-Ra-Ha-El.
- The best matches for recognition, fame, personal charisma, and social fulfillment will be among men and women born March 30–April 3, under the care of Si-Yata-El.
- The best matches for romance, love, and artistic and intellectual achievements will be among men and women born May 4–8, under the care of Aladi-Yah.

these environments, Angel Meba-Ha-El can help you preserve your vital link with the truth, authenticity, justice, and purity of purpose. Bear in mind, though: your straight-up manner and strong desire to avoid any complicity with the forces of misrepresentation, dissimulation, and oppression will make your stay in the shadows a temporary one, at best.

Angel Meba-Ha-El transmits and reveals to humans the light and luminous transparency of the original creation. Those who call upon and receive her/his protection, therefore, appreciate purity in all its manifestations. Those born between May 24 and May 28 can thus succeed in all careers whose objectives are clear and pure, such as hygienic and prophylactic medicine; professions that ensure the purity of food; trades that require working with glass, crystal, or diamonds; ecology and related fields that work to clean up nature; biological research and applications; health food; social work; and any pursuits involving the law and justice. It is interesting to note that Rudolph Giuliani, the crime-fighting mayor of New York, and John Wayne, whose movie roles led him to rid the West of bad guys, are both protégés of Meba-Ha-El.

Life can be difficult for the friends of Meba-Ha-El. Constantly stumbling onto hidden truths and rattling the bones of carefully hidden family skeletons don't do much for a person's popularity. Although you act only on the highest of motivations, you may be subject to the slander and vengeance of those who don't live by a similar code of honesty and openness. Therefore, before you begin to clarify and purify a murky situation, it is recommended that you always invoke Meba-Ha-El. Your guardian will bring light to your true goals and make it more likely that your discoveries will be accepted in the loving, accepting manner they are offered.

When you establish a deep closeness with Angel Meba-Ha-El, you will be immersed in the pure and unifying harmonies that underlie the universe. During your time on earth, you will become a participant in the eternal innocence and purity of all creatures engendered by the original Creator. By the grace of Angel Meba-Ha-El, your inner vision will be activated. You will see though people's external appearances and penetrate to the invisible center of all beings. There you will discover the eternal, immaculate, and radiant light that stirs life and reveals the truth.

Angel HARE-YA-EL

MAY 29–JUNE 2

Bestows rich, fruitful love relationships and friendships.
Deepens intuition and creative vision. Stimulates growth of
inner life. Promotes access to prestigious social status.

HA / RE / YA / E / L

PHONETIC PRONUNCIATION

Ha as in Habit
Re as in Ray
Ya as in Yard
El as in Elevation

UNIVERSAL RESONANCE OF THE ANGEL'S NAME

Ha Spiritual life force. Love that underlies all things.
Presence of the universal and all-encompassing
spirit. Divine call, divine connection.

Re Rotation, return, renewal; the natural cycles of
existence. Radiance. Charisma. Inner vision and
foresight on a universal scale. Princely leadership.

Ya Mastery. Dexterity, expertise; human action aligned
with divine universal principles.

El Ending vibration of the Angel's name. Principle of
excellence; chosen; elite. Elevating force. Source of
perpetual transformation and evolution.

Guardian Angel Hare-Ya-El

In Akkadian language the name Hare-Ya-El means, literally, "The
loving radiance of the Supreme Being, which propagates the
Creator-Word eternally."

Angel Hare-Ya-El opens the way to the boundless supply of
divine love and fills the minds of her/his protégés with a powerful

NOTABLE PEOPLE BORN UNDER THE INFLUENCE OF HARE-YA-EL

Benny Goodman, *jazz musician*
Bob Hope, *actor and comedian*
Brigham Young, *Mormon leader*
Brooke Shields, *actress*
Clint Eastwood, *actor*
Edward B. Williams, *lawyer*
Fred Allen, *comedian*
Gale Sayers, *football player*
John F. Kennedy, *U.S. president*
Johnny Weissmuller, *Olympian and actor*
Lea Thompson, *actress*
Marilyn Monroe, *actress*
Melissa Etheridge, *rock singer*
Morgan Freeman, *actor*
Nelson Riddle, *conductor*
Walt Whitman, *poet and writer*

COLOR HARMONIZATION

Lavender / Transparent whiteness /
Pastel light yellow / Pastel green /
Light gray-rose

yearning to reunite with the creative forces from which all life was formed.

By forging a direct inner dialogue with the divine force, those under the protection of Angel Hare-Ya-El become the chosen recipients of invisible celestial signs and, in the course of their lives, can come to speak like visionaries and prophets.

Does that mean those born between May 29 and June 2 are pale-faced, pie-in-the-sky oracles, fresh from a lengthy hermitage in some cave? Not quite! Those in the care of Angel Hare-Ya-El benefit from a nonstop supply of radiant energy, which constantly renews their physical, mental, and spiritual vitality. They are bursting with enthusiasm—and with the desire to share their invigorating ideas, robust health, and personal warmth with others.

If you are a friend of Hare-Ya-El, you need not worry about hitting the glass ceiling. Men and women under this powerful Angel's care are given the key to the loftiest social positions and positions of professional prominence at birth. From these aeries, they apply the highest principles, and always to the benefit of great and noble causes. You, like former president John F. Kennedy, the Mormon leader Brigham Young, and actors Morgan Freeman and Bob Hope, are enlightened by the universal radiance of Angel Hare-Ya-El. You can in turn distribute the spiritual gifts you have been given, convert your energy to acts of knowledge and faith, and enlighten the world.

When in deep affinity with the harmonic vibrations of Angel Hare-Ya-El, you can reach a level of visionary perception that creates social, philosophical, or religious change. A carrier of the idealistic seeds of the future, you and others under the protection of Angel Hare-Ya-El are endowed with the power to shake up the earth and make those seeds grow! No namby-pamby, you apply yourself to a cause with force, persistence, and love. Not only are you certain to see the fruit of your efforts in your lifetime, but also you will live secure in the knowledge that the changes you have made will stand the test of time and continue to enlighten the world long after you have gone.

In your day-to-day family, social, and professional lives, you and your brothers and sisters in the care of Hare-Ya-El attract good energy, goodwill, good ideas, and good people. Then, having mustered

HARMONIC MATCHES FOR HARE-YA-EL'S PROTÉGÉS

- *The best matches for success in economic and practical achievements will be among men and women born December 30–January 3, under the care of Ye-Ya-La-El.*
- *The best matches for recognition, fame, personal charisma, and social fulfillment will be among men and women born March 25–29, under the care of Yeli-Ya-El.*
- *The best matches for romance, love, and artistic and intellectual achievements will be among men and women born May 9–13, under the care of Lo-Avi-Yah.*

such beneficent forces, you spread them through the world. The public relations mavens of the spiritual realm, you are endowed with a powerful and magnetic charisma that socially prestigious personalities simply cannot resist. Before they know it, these high-profile men and women are enlisted in *your* cause, increasing your impact in the world. In return, you will never disappoint those who trust you. Even in times of crisis, conflict, battle, or violent hostility, you and all those close to Angel Hare-Ya-El always remain faithful to the highest humanitarian ideals. With your balanced viewpoint and sincere concern, you are a gracious envoy whose visionary proposals do the greatest good for the greatest number of people—and are a powerful source for healing.

When in complete harmony with Angel Hare-Ya-El, women and men elevate their hearts and their minds to the universal source of love and goodness and, on earth, lend their hands to the perfect application of celestial ideals and divine objectives.

Angel HE-QUA-MI-YAH

JUNE 3–7

Develops a sense of proportion, ratio, and balance. Provides the gift of fair and wise judgment. Helps build economic security. Improves social status.

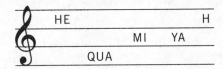

NOTABLE PEOPLE BORN UNDER THE INFLUENCE OF HE-QUA-MI-YAH

Adam Smith, *economist and philosopher*

Alexander Pushkin, *poet*

Allen Ginsberg, *poet*

Björn Borg, *tennis player*

Dalai Lama, *Tibetan religious leader*

Diego Velázquez, *painter*

F. García Lorca, *writer*

Isaiah Berlin, *philosopher and historian*

Izabella Scorupco, *actress*

John Maynard Keynes, *economist*

Josephine Baker, *singer*

Larry McMurtry, *writer*

Liam Neeson, *actor*

Paul Gauguin, *painter*

Prince, *singer*

Ruth Westheimer, *sex therapist*

Thomas Mann, *writer*

Toni Braxton, *singer*

COLOR HARMONIZATION

Red / Orange / Saffron yellow / Khaki green

PHONETIC PRONUNCIATION

He as in Hero

Qua as in Kabala

Mi as in Mirror

Ya as in Yard

H Vocalize the final H as a soft exhalation

UNIVERSAL RESONANCE OF THE ANGEL'S NAME

He Spiritual life force. Love that underlies all things. Presence of the universal and all-encompassing spirit. Divine call, divine connection.

Qua Intelligence; knowledge of the principles of calculation, evaluation, quantification. Equilibrium and balance. Multiplication of natural riches and material abundance. Cosmic consciousness.

Mi Matrix, matter, model. Maternal loving protection. The force that brings life into the material world. Mustering of energies. Generation and regeneration.

Yah Final vibration of the Angel's name. Receptivity and reflectivity. The presence of the deity; the abundance of the being.

Guardian Angel He-Qua-Mi-Yah

In Akkadian language the name He-Qua-Mi-Yah means, literally, "One who is wise in judgment, using human intelligence and accurate knowledge of the laws of nature."

The harmonic vibrations of Angel He-Qua-Mi-Yah provide men and women with the capacity to measure, estimate, evaluate, and weigh the disparate elements that make up their environment. Angel He-Qua-Mi-Yah helps them calculate in a fair and equitable manner, divide portions, and factor ratios with accuracy. This ability allows those born between June 3 and 7 to excel as regulators, moderators, and logisticians in economics or judicial arbitration.

Angel He-Qua-Mi-Yah encourages a deep knowledge of the rules and laws that govern the balance of each dimension of reality. Thanks to this ability to evaluate and weigh, balance and harmonize, those who live in resonance with this Angel can attain great wisdom—and the ability to think, search, reach a conclusion, then make a judgment on any subject with intelligence and compassion.

Some great thinkers are out of touch. They apply themselves to the abstract; their theories, though fascinating, can be difficult to comprehend. Not so with those under the guardianship of He-Qua-Mi-Yah. Down-to-earth, practical, and sage, their wisdom is like that of Solomon. Their pragmatic solutions are reasonable, enlightening, and easily accepted by others. Whether they are shedding light on a technical problem at work or mediating an awkward social situation, their suggestions are so succinct and to the point, their friends can't help but wonder, "Hey, why didn't I think of that?"

The fact is, it is quite unusual for someone to think like the savvy friends of He-Qua-Mi-Yah. These people don't just assimilate the evidence and draw a conclusion; they are among the chosen few who pluck their answers from the universal storehouse of abundance, intelligence, and wisdom. Their answers aren't just correct; they are catalysts for action, the fertile nuggets from which intellectual, scientific, technological, or artistic breakthroughs grow. For proof of that, one need look no further than the revolutionary poetry of Alan Ginsberg, the irresistible shock of Prince's musical genius, or the profound yet simple message carried by the Dalai Lama.

HARMONIC MATCHES FOR HE-QUA-MI-YAH'S PROTÉGÉS

- The best matches for success in economic and practical achievements will be among men and women born December 25–29, under the care of Nema-Mi-Yah.
- The best matches for recognition, fame, personal charisma, and social fulfillment will be among men and women born March 20–24, under the care of Ve-Hovi-Yah.
- The best matches for romance, love, and artistic and intellectual achievements will be among men and women born May 14–18, under the care of He-Ha-Â-Yah.

If the Angel He-Qua-Mi-Yah is your celestial guardian, you may be perceived as an unusual and unique personality—someone who stands head and shoulders above the crowd. Needless to say, you will almost certainly reap the recognition from others and distinguish yourself, possibly in the fields of sports, justice, education, or the human sciences.

Angel He-Qua-Mi-Yah encourages women and men to reject, avoid, or stay away at all costs from the systems and rules that suppress freedom and lead to oppression. (That urge—to discover an environment where an artist could be free—led Josephine Baker to Paris and eventually to her destiny.) When you and other associates of this emancipating Angel are confronted with stifling or limiting situations, it is important that you invoke your powerful friend. Angel He-Qua-Mi-Yah can help you to implement solutions that are so simple and balanced, you will encounter very little resistance.

When in harmony with Angel He-Qua-Mi-Yah, you can easily succeed in all areas that call on your talents as a moderating, harmonizing force. Wherever tyranny or injustice appears, you act quickly to bring about judgments, rules, and laws that compensate for the imbalances. This skill will win you praise, whether you apply it as a Supreme Court justice or a sublimely fair and judicious parent of several children. In the economic arena, you may excel at creating methods of mass distribution or other approaches that serve the needs of the people. You may also build upon the strength of your idealism and discover new sources of wealth that ensure durable growth while promoting social progress.

To sum up, those who attain kinship with Angel He-Qua-Mi-Yah achieve the highest degree of wisdom and reach the home of the celestial spirit, immersing themselves in the universal ocean, where all quantities transform themselves into qualities and where all the numbers prompt the regeneration of life. Then, enlightened by the precise beauty of the cosmos, those under the protection of Angel He-Qua-Mi-Yah reproduce in real life the models of evolution, progress, and harmony they perceive in the heavens.

Angel LE-A-VI-YAH

JUNE 8–12

Stimulates the capacity to generate abundance and fertility. Provides success in research and investigations. Encourages generosity and gift giving. Develops psychic powers.

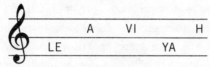

	A	VI		H
LE			YA	

PHONETIC PRONUNCIATION

Le as in Legend
A as in Application
Vi as in Vision
Ya as in Yard
H Vocalize the final H as a soft exhalation

UNIVERSAL RESONANCE OF THE ANGEL'S NAME

Le Dynamic learning. The ability to make mental links. Intellectual elevation. An evolving, ascending movement of the mind. Lucidity and enlightenment.

A The original and ultimate energy; before form, universal, infinite, unifying.

Vi Vitalizing factor. Fruitfulness and productivity. Catalyst of variety, vitality, verity, will, and vigor.

Yah Final vibration of the Angel's name. Receptivity and reflectivity. The presence of the deity; the abundance of the being.

Guardian Angel Le-A-Vi-Yah

In Akkadian language the name Le-A-Vi-Yah literally means, "The journey into the universe of energies that instill life."

The harmonic vibrations of Angel Le-A-Vi-Yah change abstract and intangible thoughts into a continuous flow of conscious energies that fertilize ideas and stimulate action. Consequently, those under the protection of Angel Le-A-Vi-Yah are known for their

---

COLOR HARMONIZATION

Contrasting combinations:
White and black / Red and black / Dark green and yellow / Dark brown and yellow

HARMONIC MATCHES FOR LE-A-VI-YAH'S PROTÉGÉS

- The best matches for success in economic and practical achievements will be among men and women born December 20–24, under the care of Povi-Ya-El.

- The best matches for recognition, fame, personal charisma, and social fulfillment will be among men and women born April 24–28, under the care of Ca-Hetha-El.

- The best matches for romance, love, and artistic and intellectual achievements will be among men and women born April 9–13, under the care of Ma-Hashi-Yah.

ability to breathe creative life into projects, revitalize human groups, build territories, energize epochs, and rejuvenate any temporarily sterile and dry situation.

Upbeat and resourceful, the men and women who live in harmony with Angel Le-A-Vi-Yah are true wonder workers who know how to spread the vitalizing seeds they receive from their celestial guardian. Under their care, projects long believed dead come to fruition; bygone relationships revive. Not only that, those relationships and projects then produce seeds themselves, thus generating and regenerating the vital energy that flows from Le-A-Vi-Yah.

If you are born to this Angel's care, your vitalizing power can ensure success in a number of fields. If, for example, you are involved in science, you can become a successful experimenter known for your magical touch. Your innovative methods will be used by your peers for a long time to come. If you apply yourself to business and finance, you will almost certainly create new products or services, but you may also make your mark as a turnaround specialist who focuses upon revitalizing failing or struggling companies. If you choose to make a career in an intellectual or educational profession, Le-A-Vi-Yah will see to it that you develop a gift for communication. You will introduce new concepts clearly, disseminate new knowledge with ease, and perhaps even discover an exciting new method for acquiring knowledge. Whatever career path you choose, you will not make your selection without forethought. Those who know Le-A-Vi-Yah always explore their options carefully. They examine their motivations, their feelings, and their expectations before making a move. This is, at least in part, the key to their success.

By invoking Angel Le-A-Vi-Yah, you will be encouraged in your ongoing effort to prepare, develop, organize, and implement the ideas that spring from your fertile mind. Depending on your circumstances and individual potential, you could evolve in one of two seemingly different directions: a deeply intellectual one, focused upon the abstract dimensions such as mathematics, astronomy, or nuclear physics, or a more sensuous route in which your intellect melds with your refined musical, artistic, or poetic aesthetic. Although we humans tend to believe there is a world of difference between a math nerd and an artist, really, the two are much alike.

In the celestial universes, creativity is creativity, no matter how it is applied. In fact, your link with Angel Le-A-Vi-Yah may also enhance your ability to perceive the subtle waves that cross the psychic dimension. You may have a profound psychic gift. If so, it is important that you memorize your dreams and learn to analyze them. The messages they contain could transform your life.

With the guidance of Angel Le-A-Vi-Yah, human beings always choose fecundity over profit. They freely distribute their ideas, abilities, and the fruit of their fertile minds with little thought of personal benefit or payback. In fact, they rarely receive the gratitude or recognition they deserve from those who benefit from their generosity. Nevertheless, the harmonic vibrations of Angel Le-A-Vi-Yah protect her/his friends from worldly greed and ensure that they will receive their reward, not from the human realm, but from the very source of the powerful forces of life. By constantly renewing their vital energy, those under the protection of Angel Le-A-Vi-Yah set their sights and intentions on a higher plane—and make their desires one with the celestial origin of love.

Angel CALI-YA-EL

JUNE 13–17

Provides the gift for precise calculation and measure.
Stimulates earnings and savings. Develops capacities for
learning, knowing, and teaching.

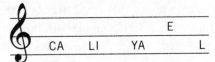

PHONETIC PRONUNCIATION

Ca as in Calla lily
Li as in Liberty
Ya as in Yard
El as in Elevation

UNIVERSAL RESONANCE OF THE ANGEL'S NAME

Ca The practical, physical, and material manifestation of ideas and thoughts. A solidifying, coalescing force within the fluid substances of the universe. Energies of cohesion and collusion, connivance, collaboration, cooperation. A force of strength and power.

Li Dynamic learning. The ability to make mental links. Intellectual elevation. An evolving, ascending movement of the mind. Lucidity and enlightenment.

Ya Mastery. Dexterity, expertise; human action aligned with divine universal principles.

El Ending vibration of the Angel's name. Principle of excellence; chosen; elite. Elevating force. Source of perpetual transformation and evolution.

NOTABLE PEOPLE BORN UNDER THE INFLUENCE OF CALI-YA-EL

Barbara McClintock, Nobel Prize
  winner in genetics
Christo, artist
Courteney Cox, actress
Donald Trump, entrepreneur
Harriet Beecher Stowe, writer
Helen Hunt, actress
Igor Stravinsky, composer
Joyce Carol Oates, writer
Sir James Black, Nobel Prize winner in
  medicine
Steffi Graf, tennis champion
W. B. Yeats, poet
William Crookes, chemist and physicist

COLOR HARMONIZATION

Swirls of purple-red / Saffron yellow /
Ocher-sienna / Warm maroon /
Specks of dark purple-violet

Guardian Angel Cali-Ya-El

In Akkadian language, the name Cali-Ya-El means, literally, "The cohesive life force and the unifying spiritual intelligence propelled into the universe by the Divine Verb."

If your idea of heaven on earth is the boardroom of a powerful corporation, tune in to the harmonic vibrations of Angel Cali-Ya-El! More than any other guardian, Cali-Ya-El bestows upon the men and women in her/his care powerful capacities for uncovering the cohesive forces that are present in all areas of the human experience, whether they are of emotional, intellectual, or spiritual origin. Such capacities allow those under the protection of Cali-Ya-El to develop true expertise in all areas of employment requiring coherent thought, such as scientific reasoning, technical definitions, business presentations, or any venture that hinges on a political, educational, or religious consensus.

The Angels inspire us to understand the world around us in so many ways: artistically, perhaps as a sculpture-in-progress, musically, politically, or architecturally, as a foundation upon which we might build our dreams. The harmonic vibrations of Angel Cali-Ya-El allow men and women to see how numbers control and define the nature of the structures and beings around them. Thanks to this Angel, those in his/her care develop a deep understanding of the way numbers modify or transform the nature of a reality. Like an architect calculating the aesthetic effect of the golden mean in the dimensions of a building, like a science teacher observing the numeric precision in the spiral of a sea shell or a galaxy, like an artist marveling at the distinctly mathematical arrangement of petals in a rose or seeds in a sunflower, these men and women see the beautifully exact patterns in everything around them. They also come to know how to uncover the energy of intelligence in everything that is being, becoming, dying, being reborn, and being transformed.

How does one use such esoteric knowledge in the real world? The way entrepreneur and Cali-Ya-El protégé Donald Trump does—precisely, calculatedly, and successfully! In their private or professional occupations, those under the protection of Angel Cali-Ya-El are known to be meticulous quantifiers with a gift for measuring and evaluation, accurate calculation, and prediction. When in harmony with Angel Cali-Ya-El, these astute men and women learn how to identify and evaluate the forces that motivate others and move obstacles. When they put such dynamic and transformational

HARMONIC MATCHES FOR CALI-YA-EL'S PROTÉGÉS

- *The best matches for success in economic and practical achievements will be among men and women born December 15–19, under the care of Meba-Hi-Yah.*
- *The best matches for recognition, fame, personal charisma, and social fulfillment will be among men and women born April 19–23, under the care of Acha-A-Yah.*
- *The best matches for romance, love, and artistic and intellectual achievements will be among men and women born April 14–18, under the care of Lela-Ha-El.*

energy to use, they can dramatically change the shape of their environment, the culture, or the world.

The world? Absolutely! And beyond! Thanks to Angel Cali-Ya-El, those in her/his care acquire a strong confidence in their capacity to influence material realities. This belief, added to their clear understanding of the laws of coherence and cohesion, adds up to an unbeatable combination. When the protégés of Cali-Ya-El make up their minds, no obstacle can thwart them. These are people who can really move mountains.

If your birthday falls between June 13 and 17, you amuse yourself intellectually by putting together, taking apart, and recombining the various bits of your world as if they were a child's building blocks. To you, "What if?" isn't just a game, it's a workout for your mental muscle! What if you shook up that physics course you teach by bringing in some ten-year-olds to demonstrate difficult theories using Silly Putty? What if you put a different spin on your stuffy client's PR by bringing in a hip-hop DJ? At work and at play, you are constantly deconstructing, reconstructing, analyzing, and recombining. That capacity, as well as your natural talent for learning and teaching, makes you a natural success in several fields, including science, technology, industry, manual arts, communications, and social and political organizing.

Of course, all experimentation and no artistry could make the protégés of Cali-Ya-El predictable—even in their unpredictability. There is no danger of that. If you are born to the kinship of this Angel, you are blessed with a unique and agile voice, which you use to attract a cooperative, appreciative, and unified audience. Whether you are an actor, singer, speaker, teacher, salesperson, politician, consultant, or counselor, with the help of Angel Cali-Ya-El you can use your voice to convince the doubtful, sway the opposition, and eventually preach to the converted. You'll have no trouble influencing others to reward you generously for sharing your talents. Your earning power will almost certainly match your abilities.

Nevertheless, wealth will never spoil you. Cali-Ya-El ensures that his/her friends make money to live—and never live to make money. Philanthropy comes naturally to you, and you will almost certainly redistribute, selectively and carefully, a generous portion of your income. If you have been particularly fortunate, you may even start a foundation or offer a financial prize to those who achieve in a field that benefits mankind. Philanthropy is good medicine for your soul.

If you are in deep harmony with Angel Cali-Ya-El, you will orient your will toward higher and higher pursuits and refine your intentions to transform the world. Then, you and all those under the protection of Angel Cali-Ya-El will become a force for the universal good, uniting all men and women so that the whole of humanity can move, without apprehension or fear, toward its bright, celestial future.

Angel LEVAVI-YAH

JUNE 18–22

Opens the heart. Stimulates love and the love of life. Paves the way for affectionate and generous emotional relationships. Encourages altruistic and charitable behavior.

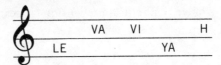

PHONETIC PRONUNCIATION

Le as in Leonard
Va as in Varsity
Vi as in Vigorous
Ya as in Yard
H Vocalize the final H as a soft exhalation

UNIVERSAL RESONANCE OF THE ANGEL'S NAME

Le Dynamic learning. The ability to make mental links. Intellectual elevation. An evolving, ascending movement of the mind. Lucidity and enlightenment.

Va Vitalizing factor. Fruitfulness and productivity. Catalyst of variety, vitality, verity, will, and vigor.

Vi Vitalizing factor. Fruitfulness and productivity. Catalyst of variety, vitality, verity, will, and vigor.

Yah Final vibration of the Angel's name. Receptivity and reflectivity. The presence of the deity; the abundance of the being.

NOTABLE PEOPLE BORN UNDER THE INFLUENCE OF LEVAVI-YAH

Audie Murphy, soldier and actor

Blaise Pascal, mathematician and writer

Cyndi Lauper, singer

Errol Flynn, actor

Isabella Rosselini, actress and model

Jeanette MacDonald, singer and actress

Jean-Paul Sartre, philosopher

Lou Gehrig, baseball hall of famer

Meryl Streep, actress

Nicole Kidman, actress

Paul McCartney, musician

Phylicia Rashad, actress

Terence Stamp, actor

COLOR HARMONIZATION

Soft pastels / Blues / Peach-rose / White / Pale yellow-green / Specks of violet / Royal blue

Guardian Angel Levavi-Yah

In Akkadian language the name Levavi-Yah literally means, "The spiral of Intellect, which surges and unites with the seed of the Divine Verb, engendering love."

Do nice people finish last? Not when Angel Levavi-Yah elevates their minds, warms their hearts, and leads them to the riches of universal love.

Born under the care of an Angel who calls upon beings to unite in a deep and sacred way, the men and women in kinship with Angel Levavi-Yah are truly blessed. Through their harmonic affinity with their guardian, they are granted a deep understanding of everything that forms, weaves, and connects in a meaningful way. This understanding encourages them to meet and choose compatible partners, people with whom they can form profound romantic liaisons and enduring friendships and provide them with the opportunity to express their generosity and altruism.

The sensitive, compassionate men and women in kinship with Levavi-Yah have many talents and skills, but what they are most appreciated for is their ability to bring people together. Whether in a personal, social, or professional setting, these kindly souls always follow their hearts. Consequently, they become natural conduits for celestial love and benevolent earthly leaders who invariably suggest methods and arrangements that bring about the most fruitful and equitable solutions for everyone involved.

There are those cynics who say that no good deed goes unpunished. All we can say is, they must not know the contented men and women guided by Levavi-Yah. Through the grace of this generous Angel, the people in her/his care enjoy a comfortable way of life, rich in shared affection and simple, everyday joys. Nor are their rewards always intangible. Though Levavi-Yah encourages simplicity, sincerity, and the quest for inner happiness, he/she also provides material wealth in proportion with the wealth of emotions that emanate from these kind and charitable people. They are richly rewarded, within and without.

If you are in harmony with Angel Levavi-Yah, you will find your way to success and economic independence by following your heart. Depending on circumstances, you will excel in activities involved with caring and helping, such as medical and paramedical professions, careers in social work, or any profession involved with psychological support of individuals and groups. In the right position, you will be a cheerful and motivational worker, immune to job burnout. That's because Levavi-Yah enables you to quickly overcome any feelings of disappointment and sadness that come upon you. By invoking your guardian, you will be relieved of the stress, delivered from pressure, and uplifted when life circumstances bring you

HARMONIC MATCHES FOR LEVAVI-YAH'S PROTÉGÉS

- *The best matches for success in economic and practical achievements will be among men and women born December 10–14, under the care of Niya-Tha-El.*
- *The best matches for recognition, fame, personal charisma, and social fulfillment will be among men and women born April 14–18, under the care of Lela-Ha-El.*
- *The best matches for romance, love, and artistic and intellectual achievements will be among men and women born April 19–23, under the care of Acha-A-Yah.*

face-to-face with difficult projects, highly charged situations, and self-centered people. In fact, many protégés of Levavi-Yah find that everyday actions motivated by kindness, friendship, and love work as well as invocations do to attract the protection of this powerful Angel. In other words, when friends and co-workers misbehave, disarm them with kindness. Your goodness will be a blessing to you.

Angel Levavi-Yah encourages those near to his/her heart to extend their experience of love and togetherness to all forms of life around them: animals, plants and flowers, landscapes, waterfalls, lakes, mountains—all of nature. By establishing a rich relationship with other species and life forms, such people open a link to invisible celestial forces that created the world. Those under the protection of Angel Levavi-Yah often find happiness in a natural environment, live in communion with its rhythms and cycles, are filled with wonder when things bloom and are born, and immerse themselves daily in the richness and beauty of nature and of the beings that inhabit it. If you feel you need to renew your connection to nature, consider volunteering for some organization that works to benefit plants and animals, bolster the environment, or preserve the delicate systems that ensure the continued fertility of the planet.

By invoking Angel Levavi-Yah, you can pass through difficult experiences in your life with patience and wisdom and neutralize your feelings of frustration and hostility. You will think so positively and creatively that your problems will seem to dissolve by themselves. These abilities, inspired by the grace of Levavi-Yah, allow you to avoid useless conflicts and to preserve the richness and innocence of your energies.

If you achieve alignment with this harmonizing Angel, you will activate your capacity for intellectual improvement and awaken your most loving impulses. Thus you will live a life that is rich and balanced, in which love underlies everything you think and do. It is then that you and all those under the protection of Angel Levavi-Yah can reach the fulfillment of harmony and happiness. Your heart will pulse with the rhythm of life; your mind will draw enlightenment from the living source of the celestial light.

Angel PE-HALI-YAH

JUNE 23–27

Inspires the ability to compose inspired and inspiring words. Stimulates intellectual and spiritual growth. Promotes talent for artistic expression and for educational communication.

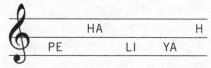

PHONETIC PRONUNCIATION

Pe as in Perfect
Ha as in Habit
Li as in Liberty
Ya as in Yard
H Vocalize the final H as a soft exhalation

UNIVERSAL RESONANCE OF THE ANGEL'S NAME

Pe Inspiration-expiration. A facility for speech, prose, poetry, expression, and proclamation. Power, possibility, passion. Pronunciation, vocalization of the universal language.

Ha Spiritual life force. Love that underlies all things. Presence of the universal and all-encompassing spirit. Divine call, divine connection.

Li Dynamic learning. The ability to make mental links. Intellectual elevation. An evolving, ascending movement of the mind. Lucidity and enlightenment.

Yah Final vibration of the Angel's name. Receptivity and reflectivity. The presence of the deity; the abundance of the being.

Guardian Angel Pe-Hali-Yah

In Akkadian language, the name Pe-Hali-Yah literally means, "Human speech, magnetized by universal love, changes into spiritual words and merges with the energy of the Divine Verb."

COLOR HARMONIZATION

Red / Orange / Bright green / Yellow

HARMONIC MATCHES FOR PE-HALI-YAH'S PROTÉGÉS

- *The best matches for success in economic and practical achievements will be among men and women born December 5–9, under the care of Nana-A-El.*
- *The best matches for recognition, fame, personal charisma, and social fulfillment will be among men and women born April 9–13, under the care of Ma-Hashi-Yah.*
- *The best matches for romance, love, and artistic and intellectual achievements will be among men and women born April 24–28, under the care of Ca-Hetha-El.*

The harmonic vibrations of Angel Pe-Hali-Yah guide men and women toward the profound "I Am," a deeply transformative self-expression that marks the emergence of the self into the world. Those under the protection of this compelling Angel of Expression are blessed with the capacity to climb the ladder that reaches from human speech to celestial language to the activating force of the universe known as the Divine Verb. This knowledge enables them to hold and follow, without interruption, the golden thread of love, which links all forms of human communication.

Thanks to Angel Pe-Hali-Yah, the encourager and inspirer of intellectual and spiritual elevation, those born between June 23 and 27 are able to charm with their passionate words and educate with the powerful content of their message. Although the gifts and abilities attached to this Angel's harmonies allow for material, economic, and social success in all fields of endeavor based upon human speech, Angel Pe-Hali-Yah does not encourage in men and women lukewarm forms of expression that are empty of meaning. The creation of doggerel, maudlin sentiment, or puff pieces, simply will not sustain the men and women who have been touched by Pe-Hali-Yah's creative spark.

The rigorous inspiration of Angel Pe-Hali-Yah is a gift and, like most gifts, comes with responsibilities. When the talented communicators in this Angel's care turn their backs on the values of authenticity and truth that link their prose and poems to the utterances of the Angels, their gift may erode. If they use their gifts to seduce, depriving their expression of the fire, sincerity, and authenticity inspired by Pe-Hali-Yah, they may experience a loss of coherence and perhaps even the breakdown of their inner life. If that happens, they will continue to shine, externally, with the fire of stars, while inwardly they are consumed with sadness and regret.

If you are in deep harmony with Angel Pe-Hali-Yah, you know how to successfully defend causes and projects you believe in. You are an efficient spokesperson for individuals or groups that need to have their rights or visions recognized. You are also a protective ally, unafraid to assert yourself as the defender of your friends and valorous enough to clear the path that will lead them to progressive growth. Sometimes your role in your friends' lives may seem parental. Angel Pe-Hali-Yah encourages men and women to take on a nurturing or parental role on behalf of a dear acquaintance, project, social cause, technological innovation, or even a national revolution. In fact, this guardian provides the light and the faith by which great ideas are conceived. This Angel also blesses those in her/his care with reassuring words to share with those who have anxious hearts or who need protection against adversity.

If you are close to Pe-Hali-Yah, you will be able to succeed in all activities and occupations that require reliable, convincing, credible words that are filled with emotional warmth, including prose and poetry writing, drawing, singing, and musical composition. Angel Pe-Hali-Yah sometimes guides men and women toward social, religious, or spiritual vocations, through which they generously give to the world the words of truth that help, console, and heal. Your innate flair with words could also make you a standout in the field of religion, education, communication, or the arts or perhaps aid you in business, economics, politics, or diplomacy. In contrast, the areas of finance and science do not come naturally to you, unless you hold a communication-based position—spokesperson, public relations specialist, or interpreter—within those fields.

With the help of Pe-Hali-Yah, you can develop a magnetic and charismatic personality and could reach a position of fame as a preacher, teacher, speaker, singer, stage actor, or any other occupation that allows your unique light to shine. Angel Pe-Hali-Yah improves the chances of social and professional success when their protégés "keep it real" and base their communication on knowledge and truth. By invoking Pe-Hali-Yah often, you will ensure that you are firmly rooted in integrity and that everything you express reinforces your—and your celestial guardian's—loftiest goals.

When you call upon Angel Pe-Hali-Yah often, your gift for speaking passionate words that educate and convince will grow, just as you grow in faith. Ultimately, this ability will allow you to receive and know the spiritual light that will eventually guide you to your true country: the world of the ultimate, cosmic, and eternal truth.

INVOCATION

O Angel Pe-Hali-Yah,
Your words join the hymns
Cascading in the heavens
And you bestow their harmonies
Near the edge of eternity.
O Angel Pe-Hali-Yah,
Help me,
Guide my soul,
Which spirals in darkness.
O Pe-Hali-Yah
Your voice resounds, the vowels crackle,
My memory opens up
Under the flame of your chant of love.
And I join the immense dream
Where humans meet the Angels.

Angel NEL-CHA-EL

JUNE 28–JULY 2

Inspires the attainment of deep knowledge. Encourages the completion of projects. Develops conceptual imagination. Stimulates fruitful discoveries. Reinforces moral rectitude.

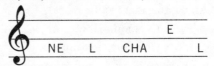

PHONETIC PRONUNCIATION

Nel as in Nelson

Cha as in Javier (Spanish) or Ach (German)

El as in Elevation

UNIVERSAL RESONANCE OF THE ANGEL'S NAME

Ne Nucleus, center, essential; identity, individuality. Penetration to the center of every reality. Negation and rejection of superficial and perverse realities.

L Dynamic learning. The ability to make mental links. Intellectual elevation. An evolving, ascending movement of the mind. Lucidity and enlightenment.

Cha Cohesive substance that unifies the universe. Capability; analysis; breaking down, then reassembling components to a new coherence.

El Ending vibration of the Angel's name. Principle of excellence; chosen; elite. Elevating force. Source of perpetual transformation and evolution.

Guardian Angel Nel-Cha-El

In the Akkadian language the name Nel-Cha-El means, literally, "From the nodal center of the Universe rises and spins the flame of the intellect, which enlightens and nurtures the conscious minds."

The harmonic vibrations of Angel Nel-Cha-El provide men and women with the capacity to penetrate and deepen essential information that defines reality, situations, and events in the world.

NOTABLE PEOPLE BORN UNDER THE INFLUENCE OF NEL-CHA-EL

Alfred G. Gilman, *Nobel Prize winner in medicine*

Antoine de Saint-Exupéry, *writer*

Carl Lewis, *Olympic runner*

Dan Aykroyd, *comedian and actor*

Estée Lauder, *cosmetics entrepreneur*

George Sand, *writer*

Jean J. Rousseau, *political philosopher*

John Gray, *relationship counselor and writer*

Kathy Bates, *actress*

Mike Tyson, *boxer*

Pamela Anderson Lee, *actress*

Paul Berg, *Nobel Prize winner in chemistry*

Peter Paul Rubens, *painter*

Princess Diana

COLOR HARMONIZATION

Black / Burgundy red / Bronze / Silvery Gray / Forest green

Such a gift often allows those born under Nel-Cha-El's guidance to quickly and precisely detect the central point, the underlying structure, the essence, and the principle that define beings and things. Those influenced by Nel-Cha-El feel comfortable in the study of current and historical events and use both the discipline of logical reasoning and the freedom of the imagination to understand them. Depending on the specific circumstances that have shaped the details of their lives, such persons may apply their gifts in the areas of mathematics, physics, biology, theology, architecture, poetry, computer programming, and bioelectronics. In their private lives, they go straight to the point, without meandering and getting lost in false illusions and superficialities.

With the help of Angel Nel-Cha-El, men and women aspire to become researchers and teachers, philosophers, theoreticians, or engineers of artificial intelligence. They can apply their considerable mental and intellectual gifts to deepening a specific field of knowledge, looking for logical differences between systems, or to detecting and pointing out particular aspects of each individual structure. Those under the protection of Angel Nel-Cha-El often acquire historical fame based on their powerful capacity to find the profound simplicity of seemingly complex ideas, categorize what appear to be disparate elements, formulate relationships between them, and identify by name (sometimes their own!) the results of their discoveries. There is one caveat, however: the harmonic vibrations of Angel Nel-Cha-El that allow for intellectual discoveries do not provide the necessary gift for their direct applications. That means that although you may find that you have been given a stocked refrigerator, so to speak, you may not be in possession of a functioning stove. You may have to use some of that natural inventiveness to find an outlet for your considerable gifts before your life can really start to cook. If your job is boring or repetitive or does not allow you to exercise your mental muscle, you should compensate for the monotony by getting involved in hobbies or studies that stimulate your intellect, energize your imagination, and elevate your aspirations.

If you're beginning to get the idea that men and women born under the protection of the Angel Nel-Cha-El are something akin to flesh-and-blood perpetual motion machines driven by their own

HARMONIC MATCHES FOR NEL-CHA-EL'S PROTÉGÉS

- *The best matches for success in economic and practical achievements will be among men and women born November 30–December 4, under the care of Âmami-Yah.*
- *The best matches for recognition, fame, personal charisma, and social fulfillment will be among men and women born May 14–18, under the care of He-Ha-Â-Yah.*
- *The best matches for romance, love, and artistic and intellectual achievements will be among men and women born March 20–24, under the care Ve-Hovi-Yah.*

boundless energy and curiosity, you're thinking right. These people are truly independent personalities that put individualism and uniqueness ahead of all else. But just because they're impressive doesn't mean they care to impress. Nel-Cha-El's charges couldn't care less about public opinion. In their view, each person on earth is the ultimate engine of free will in search of truth. Only finding the solutions to the mysteries that intrigue them will satisfy them. Acclaim will not.

Of course, an ongoing quest to the bottom of the matter can lead a person to hide inside himself or herself, to become isolated in an ivory tower (or a library or the Internet), to the detriment of deep personal and social relationships. Carried to an extreme, such behavior can be perceived by others as social rejection and emotional negativity and can also weaken the very creative and imaginative abilities that characterize those under the protection of Angel Nel-Cha-El. With the help of Angel Nel-Cha-El you can blossom in activities where you can combine your search for the truth with your respect of honest and morally righteous principles and put them both into the service of the community. Depending on their personal circumstances, those under the protection of Angel Nel-Cha-El can make excellent judges, counselors, referees, or government officials and are trusted friends who can be counted upon for deeply considered, well-balanced advice.

To sum up: if you are in harmony with Angel Nel-Cha-El, you are a lifelong learner who can come to know intimately the underlying structure of all reality, from the cellular microcosm to galactic macrocosm, from the simplest human feelings to the wonders of the universal consciousness. All you need to do is ask Nel-Cha-El to point the way to your limitless horizon.

Angel YE-YI-YA-EL

JULY 3–7

Encourages the renewal of social relationships. Paves the way
for the resolution of crises and conflicts. Enhances the ability
to organize and coordinate. Bestows a gift for recognizing—
and taking advantage of—good opportunities.

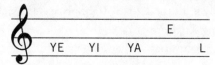

PHONETIC PRONUNCIATION

Ye as in Yes

Yi as in Ying

Ya as in Yard

El as in Elevation

UNIVERSAL RESONANCE OF THE ANGEL'S NAME

Ye Mastery. Dexterity, expertise; human action aligned
with divine universal principles.

Yi Mastery. Dexterity, expertise; human action aligned
with divine universal principles.

Ya Mastery. Dexterity, expertise; human action aligned
with divine universal principles.

El Ending vibration of the Angel's name. Principle of
excellence; chosen; elite. Elevating force. Source of
perpetual transformation and evolution.

Guardian Angel Ye-Yi-Ya-El

In Akkadian language, the name Ye-Yi-Ya-El means, literally, "The
Force that masters action in all forms: vision, conception, accomplishment."

The harmonic vibrations of Angel Ye-Yi-Ya-El provide men and
women with the capacity to set goals, devise the means of reaching
their aspirations, then carry out the plan of action necessary to
accomplish them. When these people share a deep empathy with

COLOR HARMONIZATION

Burgundy / Rust / Coral / Bright peach

HARMONIC MATCHES FOR YE-YI-YA-EL'S PROTÉGÉS

- *The best matches for success in economic and practical achievements will be among men and women born November 25–29, under the care of Ha-Hasi-Yah.*

- *The best matches for recognition, fame, personal charisma, and social fulfillment will be among men and women born May 9–13, under the care of Lo-Avi-Yah.*

- *The best matches for romance, love, and artistic and intellectual achievements will be among men and women born March 25–29, under the care of Yeli-Ya-El.*

Ye-Yi-Ya-El, this Angel of creation—and *self*-creation—leads those close to him/her to find themselves as initiators of events, founders of organizations, reformers of societies. Nor are the resolute and ready friends of Ye-Yi-Ya-El bogged down by obstacles, glitches, or problems with the plan. When difficulties or conflicts block the path to achievement, these indomitable women and men know just what detour to take to arrive at their destination in style. No matter where they have come from and where they are going, their route invariably leads them to the right place at the right time.

By invoking Angel Ye-Yi-Ya-El, those in her/his care can make the most of opportunities as they come and fulfill them at just the right time, that is, when they are at the optimal stage of their maturity to capitalize on the break their guardian has thrown their way. Aware of the unique, transformational power in every action, those under the protection of Angel Ye-Yi-Ya-El understand the urgency of the following celestial message: "Thinking is acting. Do what you think, and think what you do." Guided by this wisdom, and enlightened by the prescience of Ye-Yi-Ya-El, these people create spiritually rich, powerful, and lasting works. Depending on the circumstances that characterize their personal lives, they may use their impressive talents to expand and improve vast organizations, to renew social or national structures, or to build culture or understanding or nations.

If you are close to the vibrating force of Angel Ye-Yi-Ya-El, you may feel put upon by local organizations or even your co-workers. You may suspect that you are being called upon more than your colleagues, for a new idea, a new plan, an innovative strategy that will bring results. Your suspicions are probably correct. Angel Ye-Yi-Ya-El channels the creative force of the ultimate Creator through those under his/her protection. Your friends and co-workers can't help but notice your superior know-how. Unless you devalue your abilities with self-serving pursuits, like a single-minded quest for material gain, you will be the one others turn to for novel ways of thinking and groundbreaking ways of getting things done.

Do these qualities make you the designated workhorse within an organization? Absolutely not! If you are protected by Angel Ye-Yi-Ya-El, you are given a keen sense of discrimination about the men and women around you. When you have decided upon a project, you know how to select the most worthy and beneficial partners for the advancement of that project. Whether you are an architect, a CEO, the organizer of an expedition, or a military leader, for example, Ye-Yi-Ya-El will lead you to the most efficient help, the most cunning lieutenants, and the most clever project managers.

Because you thrive on action in all its forms, and the courage to take dynamic action has become so rare in the modern workplace, you will almost certainly be praised, stroked, applauded, and generally celebrated from the watercooler to the corner office. But beware: too much acclaim can turn even your usually level head. You may find yourself dabbling in militancy, opportunism, and materialism. You may even forget the high principles that have guided you to success and begin to see yourself as the sole architect of the pedestal you've put yourself on. When this occurs, you may lose contact with the true founder of the feast: your invisible guide. In order to reconnect with your celestial source of strength and renew your creative freshness, it is important to redirect your conscience and invoke Ye-Yi-Ya-El. This Angel is a forgiving friend who will restore your connection to the celestial Creator, the only true Origin of all occurrences in the world.

When under the influence of Angel Ye-Yi-Ya-El, men and women can integrate themselves within the flow of creative energies that constantly build and rebuild the universe. By channeling these invisible forces for the betterment of life on earth, those close to Ye-Yi-Ya-El then become a vibrating and beaming source of transforming fire.

The brightness of that fire attracts the help and recognition of other men and women who, guided by the shining presence of Angel Ye-Yi-Ya-El, become new and powerful radiating centers of imagination, achievement, and love.

Angel MELA-HA-EL

JULY 8–12

Encourages a desire to harmonize and mediate situations. Inspires the discernment of simple and practical human truths. Enhances love for life. Encourages strong and loyal relationships.

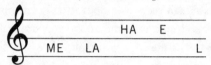

PHONETIC PRONUNCIATION

Me as in Metal
La as in Labrador
Ha as in Habit
El as in Elevation

UNIVERSAL RESONANCE OF THE ANGEL'S NAME

Me Matrix, matter, model. Maternal loving protection. The force that brings life into the material world. Mustering of energies. Generation and regeneration.

La Dynamic learning. The ability to make mental links. Intellectual elevation. An evolving, ascending movement of the mind. Lucidity and enlightenment.

Ha Spiritual life force. Love that underlies all things. Presence of the universal and all-encompassing spirit. Divine call, divine connection.

El Ending vibration of the Angel's name. Principle of excellence; chosen; elite. Elevating force. Source of perpetual transformation and evolution.

Guardian Angel Mela-Ha-El

In Akkadian language, the name Mela-Ha-El means, literally, "The generative matrix of intellectual and emotional connections gathers, in the oneness of the universe, the bits of eternal Truth that cross the dimensions of the future."

NOTABLE PEOPLE BORN UNDER THE INFLUENCE OF MELA-HA-EL

Barbara Cartland, writer

Bill Cosby, comedian and actor

Buckminster Fuller, architect and inventor

Carl Orff, composer

David Brinkley, television journalist

Giorgio Armani, fashion designer

John D. Rockefeller, industrialist and entrepreneur

John Quincy Adams, former U.S. president

Julius Caesar, Roman emperor

Kevin Bacon, actor

Marcel Proust, writer

Nelson Rockefeller, politician and businessman

Paul Braun, football coach

Saul Bellow, writer

Steve Forbes, politician and businessman

Suzanne Vega, singer

Tom Hanks, actor

Yul Brynner, actor

COLOR HARMONIZATION

Apple green / Warm maroon / Very dark green / Navy blue / Sparks of yellow and cream / Blue-green

The vibrating harmonies of Angel Mela-Ha-El provide the men and women in his/her care with an intimate knowledge of the patterns and laws that organize and transform people's lives, careers, relationships, and greater realities. Those under the protection of this perceptive Angel clearly understand how subtle shifts in opinion and evolving trends affect the world.

Judicious, thoughtful, and deliberate, the men and women born between July 8 and 12 tend to live their lives on what they perceive to be the up-and-up. They respect the sovereignty of the law and are happy to build their lives on a traditional, moral foundation. Their goal is to bring people together in harmony. They are not interested in rocking the boat.

If you are born in affinity with Mela-Ha-El, you enjoy acting as the peacemaker, whether in your personal, professional, or social sphere. A natural matchmaker, you have the ability to bring people together in fruitful unions of all sorts, including successful marriages, happy alliances, and solid contractual, professional, or political relationships. This subtle skill, and your natural inclination toward peace, harmony, and negotiation, may cause those who don't understand you to label you a people pleaser. But Angel Mela-Ha-El, who encourages your desire for harmony, has also blessed you with clear intentions and a logical, flexible mind. You are not a pushover or even a peacenik: you are a seeker of justice for all, an earthly conduit for the most equitable solution the Angels can conceive. By keeping close to your celestial guardian and your values, you will earn the admiration and trust of your friends, partners, and colleagues and bring a unique purity of intention to your surroundings. Tom Hanks did this when he focused his considerable talent on larger issues including AIDS awareness and veterans' rights.

You may also develop a powerful gift for healing. Angel Mela-Ha-El provides men and women with access to traditional and ancestral wisdom and plants in each of her/his protégés a memory of the laws and principles that underlie the existence of all beings and things. As a result, if you seek knowledge you will find it possible to reconnect with the formulas and methods applied by scholars of ancient civilizations, such as the priests of Chaldea and Egypt, alchemists, and shamans. That divine connection, and the help of Angel Mela-Ha-El, will enable you to succeed in any pursuit

HARMONIC MATCHES FOR MELA-HA-EL'S PROTÉGÉS

- The best matches for success in economic and practical achievements will be among men and women born November 20–24, under the care of Dani-Ya-El.

- The best matches for recognition, fame, personal charisma, and social fulfillment will be among men and women born May 4–8, under the care of Aladi-Yah.

- The best matches for romance, love, and artistic and intellectual achievements will be among men and women born March 30–April 3, under the care of Si-Yata-El.

whose goal is to balance and regenerate life, such as nutrition, the creation of flavors and scents, homeopathy, aroma and breathing therapy, and alternative medicine. You will also be comfortable in occupations that put you in daily contact with earth and water, mountains, fields, forests, rocks, and nature. Many men and women under the protection of Angel Mela-Ha-El have been able to find in such occupations a source of material wealth and professional renown.

When under the influence of Angel Mela-Ha-El, women and men are deeply drawn to calm, harmony, and peacefulness. Circumstances that put them into the unknown or lead them to adventurous and risky situations can disturb them and diminish the feeling of safety that is so necessary to their well-being. By consciously and lovingly invoking Mela-Ha-El, by asking to be enveloped in the strength of his/her love, this Angel's friends activate a powerful, heaven-sent protective shield. They can then pass safely through life's dark phases without disturbing the spiritual balance so necessary to their happiness.

When those under the protection of Mela-Ha-El want to elevate their daily activities to the level of an exciting mission, the notions of harmony and concord are their best guides. When they meditate on these principles, when they attune their objectives to the laws that guide nature and move the universe, the ecology of the planet opens up to them. Then, with the assistance of Angel Mela-Ha-El, they can become active partners in the beautiful dance that is life on Earth.

Angel HE-HAVI-YAH

JULY 13–17

Reinforces loving attractions and lasting friendships.
Stimulates emotions and passions. Purifies and enlightens
intentions. Encourages feelings of generosity and compassion.
Enhances the love for life and deep feeling for
all living things.

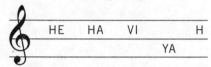

HE	HA	VI		H
			YA	

PHONETIC PRONUNCIATION

He as in Helix

Ha as in Habit

Vi as in Victory

Ya as in Yard

H Vocalize the final H as a soft exhalation

UNIVERSAL RESONANCE OF THE ANGEL'S NAME

He Spiritual life force. Love that underlies all things. Presence of the universal and all-encompassing spirit. Divine call, divine connection.

Ha Spiritual life force. Love that underlies all things. Presence of the universal and all-encompassing spirit. Divine call, divine connection.

Vi Vitalizing factor. Fruitfulness and productivity. Catalyst of variety, vitality, verity, will, and vigor.

Yah Final vibration of the Angel's name. Receptivity and reflectivity. The presence of the deity; the abundance of the being.

Guardian Angel He-Havi-Yah

In Akkadian language the name He-Havi-Yah literally means, "The universal life force of the Loving Being is attracted to itself and, through the ultimate union of One to Oneself, conceives,

Clement Clark Moore, *poet and writer*

Donald Sutherland, *actor*

Gerald Ford, *former U.S. president*

Ginger Rogers, *dancer and actress*

Harrison Ford, *actor*

Ingmar Bergman, *film director*

Isaac Bashevis Singer, *writer*

James Cagney, *actor*

Mary Baker Eddy, *founder of Christian Science*

Phoebe Cates, *actress*

Rembrandt, *painter*

Roald Amundsen, *explorer*

Woody Guthrie, *folk musician*

COLOR HARMONIZATION

Translucent white speckled with
pastel blue / Straw yellow /
Diaphanous green / Gray-lavender

HARMONIC MATCHES FOR HE-HAVI-YAH'S PROTÉGÉS

- *The best matches for success in economic and practical achievements will be among men and women born November 15–19, under the care of Ve-Hova-El.*
- *The best matches for recognition, fame, personal charisma, and social fulfillment will be among men and women born April 29–May 3, under the care of Hazi-Ya-El.*
- *The best matches for romance, love, and artistic and intellectual achievements will be among men and women born April 4–8, under the care of Âlami-Yah.*

engenders, and creates." Also, "Awareness that the unity is the creative energy of multiplicity."

The harmonic tonalities of Angel He-Havi-Yah expose men and women to the life force of the divine love in its totality. The lives of those touched by this Angel find their basis and expression in the attractions, impulses, and emotions of love.

The world loves a lover, and that saying goes double for the compelling men and women born between July 13 and 17. Guided by their positive emotions and deep passions, such people can become magnetic centers that draw admirers near. With the help of their guardian, these generous men and women draw their emotional depth directly from the divine source, then share these feelings unconditionally with others.

Love is blind, or so it is said, but these sensitive souls are definitely not blinded by their emotions. On the contrary, the feelings that enhance the nuances, colors, and richness of their relationships and experiences lend clarity to their lives. These are the powerful energies they use to evaluate, learn, and act in the world. If they can find the courage to follow their passions, they will discover their fulfillment. In fact, most of the difficult times suffered by those close to He-Havi-Yah are caused by their own apprehension and the fear-based decision to deny their dominant preferences and attractions.

If you are under the protectorship of this brilliant Angel, your heart is true; it will always lead you to the most positive path. Whatever occupation you pursue, you will succeed *if you do what you love.* The influence of Angel He-Havi-Yah is strongest when emotions, feelings, and passion prevail. If you choose your life's work for financial reasons or convenience—do you think explorer Roald Amundsen found it easy to follow his true calling?—you expose yourself to disappointment and failure.

Many men and women who are in kinship with He-Havi-Yah find that occupations and pastimes that connect them with things being born, growing, and flourishing increase their happiness and potential for success. For those who keep close to their Angel, just the sight of creatures that live and thrive—animals, flowers, vegetables, small children—is a source of wonder and happiness. They appreciate these pleasures the way a gardener would, finding the reward, not in payment for labors, but in the bliss of a perfect rose. Because such simple yet profound things bring them joy, these men and women tend to seek out a simple life, one that is removed from social turbulence, superficial relationships, and sources of agitation.

Should the friends of He-Havi-Yah become enmeshed in human dramas that cause them to stray from the preferred path or lose sight of their true passions, they may become temporarily disoriented. They may even disappoint those who trust them most implicitly. Still, they need only invoke their guardian to reawaken the soft light of innocence in their souls. Angel He-Havi-Yah helps his/her friends to keep their goals pure. Consequently, those in alignment with this Angel will almost certainly see the error of their ways and receive forgiveness from heaven. Against all logic, they will also receive the compassion and forgiveness from those they have wronged as well. That's because the honest souls born between July 13 and 17 are immersed in the enlightened truth. Although they may veer from the right path, they will always find their emotions, attractions, impulses, and passions lead back to the original substance of intuitive knowledge.

If you are faithful to He-Havi-Yah, and circumstances confront you with hostile situations or social and political upheaval (the office is a great setting for upheaval!), you will survive only by moving to a place where your generous love—for what you do, for what you are, and for everyone you know—encounters no restrictions. By purifying your emotions in the fire created by the high harmonic vibrations of Angel He-Havi-Yah, you will orient your life toward helping others, with simplicity, humility, and a full and selfless heart.

INVOCATION

O Angel He-Havi-Yah,
Your eternal light,
Rekindles the sparks
Scattered in heaven.
O He-Havi-Yah,
Near the fire of galaxies,
Under your sublime guidance,
My soul joins in with other souls
And together, humans and Angels
Are singing the harmony of God.
O Angel He-Havi-Yah,
When I am comforted by your fire,
Fears vanish,
My heart calls for other hearts,
And, uniting courage and dreams,
We spiral
In eternity.

Angel NITH-HA-YAH

JULY 18–22

Leads to knowledge of essential matters. Increases intellectual depth. Provides a gift for anticipating and predicting. Stimulates the search for and love of truth.

		HA	H
	NI		YA
	TH		

PHONETIC PRONUNCIATION

Ni as in Nirvana

Th as in the final T in Knit

Ha as in Habit

Ya as in Yard

H Vocalize the final H as a soft exhalation

UNIVERSAL RESONANCE OF THE ANGEL'S NAME

Ni Nucleus, center, essential; identity, individuality. Penetration to the center of every reality. Negation and rejection of superficial and perverse realities.

Th Experience of time. Evolving temporal cycles eternally recurring. Mutation coupling mortality with immortality.

Ha Spiritual life force. Love that underlies all things. Presence of the universal and all-encompassing spirit. Divine call, divine connection.

Yah Final vibration of the Angel's name. Receptivity and reflectivity. The presence of the deity; the abundance of the being.

NOTABLE PEOPLE BORN UNDER THE INFLUENCE OF NITH-HA-YAH

A. J. Cronin, writer

Chester Himes, writer

Danny Glover, actor

Edgar Degas, painter

Ernest Hemingway, writer

Gregor Mendel, pioneering geneticist

H. A. Lorentz, physicist

John Glenn, astronaut

Kathleen Turner, actress

Marshall McLuhan, writer

Nelson Mandela, South African statesman and Nobel Peace Prize winner

Robin William, comedian and actor

Rosalyn S. Yalow, Nobel Prize winner in medicine

Rudolph A. Marcus, Nobel Prize winner in chemistry

COLOR HARMONIZATION

Navy blue / Beige-cream / Forest green / Spots of orange / Specks of sky blue / Lots of white and pastel yellow

Guardian Angel Nith-Ha-Yah

In Akkadian language, the name Nith-Ha-Yah literally means, "Energy centers, separated by the principle of time, converge into the original Unity by the grace of universal love that penetrates everything."

Clashing nations. Twenty co-workers, one available promotion. Grumbling family members. What's going on here? The perceptive men and women born from July 18 to 22 know! The harmonies of Angel Nith-Ha-Yah lead the minds of those under her/his care directly to the center, to the essence of all beings, the nucleus of all things. And because Nith-Ha-Yah inspires a deep love of the truth based on the unity of the universe, this Angel leads his/her friends to a profound understanding of the complex actions and reactions that guide all of the events in the world.

The most well connected Angel, Nith-Ha-Yah links his/her protégés to the invisible forces that weave together all the lives in the universe and connect them to the centers of cosmic energy. The result is a vast network of universal movement that the human mind experiences as space and time. Those close to Nith-Ha-Yah, therefore, have an acute awareness of time, the cycles of nature, and temporal movements. This awareness gives them—and their inner visions—a prophetic, futuristic quality.

It sounds esoteric, we know—the ticking of the cosmological clock, sands through the universal hourglass. But with the help of Angel Nith-Ha-Yah, those in her/his kinship can use their powerful cosmic connection to analyze the trends that shape world events, immerse themselves in the spirit of their epoch, and anticipate the ideas, phenomena, and situations that will mold the future. Endowed with the ability to understand the connections between various dimensions, tangible and intangible, these natural communicators excel in establishing business, social, and technological networks, creating or improving organizational and educational systems, and implementing or adapting policy. Indeed, their unique ability to "reach out and touch someone," then link that person to countless others, can make them appear both current and ahead of their time.

And that's not all. Because the Angel Nith-Ha-Yah teaches men and women that pure truth is the ultimate value, the only acceptable

HARMONIC MATCHES FOR NITH-HA-YAH'S PROTÉGÉS

- The best matches for success in economic and practical achievements will be among men and women born March 10–14, under the care of Mova-Mi-Yah.
- The best matches for recognition, fame, personal charisma, and social fulfillment will be among men and women born October 1–5, under the care of Ye-Yaza-El.
- The best matches for romance, love, and artistic and intellectual achievements will be among men and women born October 26–30, under the care of Se-Ali-Yah.

reference for their research, their discoveries, their words, and their actions, those under the protection of this Angel can become dedicated and successful researchers, devoting their time to philosophical or theological investigation, the explication of poetry, the secrets of homeopathic medicine, or biochemical research. The friends of Nith-Ha-Yah are able to analyze life without stopping its movement. Such a gift is appreciated by organizations or individuals that employ them as strategic advisers, ethnological explorers, botanists, or consultants in any field related to ecology.

If you are in the care of Nith-Ha-Yah, you may find yourself living the life of a single-minded seeker: living in austere surroundings, more concerned with the holes in your research than with the empty spaces in your little black book. If you become troubled by the ascetic environment you have chosen, you can ask Nith-Ha-Yah for the necessary help. Your celestial guardian will clarify your intentions and encourage you to put the search for the Truth before anything else—but never to your detriment. Nith-Ha-Yah loves those who love to learn! Invoke your powerful ally, and Nith-Ha-Yah will activate the invisible celestial forces and nourish you, emotionally and intellectually, in sufficient quantity to sustain your body, bolster your heart, and satisfy your mind. Suddenly all the gifts of heaven will arrive at your door, including long-lasting relationships, ripe opportunities, life-changing associations, and fulfilling friendships.

Faced with the challenges of social life, of separations, trials, and betrayals, those who are sensitive to the harmonic vibrations of Angel Nith-Ha-Yah make an easy transition between life's passages. Instead of dwelling on what might have been, they slip from one cycle to another, focusing on the hurdles of the present and on building a positive future. Secure in the knowledge that every good intention affects everyone and everything, both in their world and the universe, those close to Nith-Ha-Yah move forward, unveiling mysteries, reflecting their times while dancing on the edge of the human progress, ahead of their era.

Angel HE-A-A-YAH

JULY 23–27

Increases cosmic consciousness. Stimulates travel and exploration through the imagination. Develops empathy and telepathy. Bestows the gifts of persistence and perseverance.

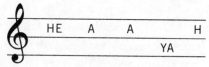

PHONETIC PRONUNCIATION

He as in Heraldic
A as in Arrow
A as in Arrow
Ya as in Yard
H Vocalize the final H as a soft exhalation

UNIVERSAL RESONANCE OF THE ANGEL'S NAME

He Spiritual life force. Love that underlies all things. Presence of the universal and all-encompassing spirit. Divine call, divine connection.

A The original and ultimate energy; before form, universal, infinite, unifying.

A The original and ultimate energy; before form, universal, infinite, unifying.

Yah Final vibration of the Angel's name. Receptivity and reflectivity. The presence of the deity; the abundance of the being.

Guardian Angel He-A-A-Yah

In Akkadian language, the name He-A-A-Yah literally means, "The principle that attracts the self to the Oneself, breathes the archetypal breath of all breaths, and resounds with the Verb of Creation."

What do Olympic figure skaters Dorothy Hamill and Peggy Fleming, Rolling Stones front man Mick Jagger, and irascible baseball

Aldous Huxley, *futurist and writer*
Alexandre Dumas Sr., *writer*
Amelia Earhart, *aviation pioneer*
Anthony Kennedy, *U.S. Supreme Court justice*
Carl Jung, *psychiatrist*
Dorothy Hamill, *Olympic figure skater*
George Bernard Shaw, *playwright*
Kevin Spacey, *actor*
Leo Durocher, *baseball hall of famer*
Mick Jagger, *rock musician*
Peggy Fleming, *Olympic figure skater*
Raymond Chandler, *writer*
Sandra Bullock, *actress*
Stanley Kubrick, *film director*
Woody Harrrelson, *actor*

COLOR HARMONIZATION

Turquoise / Opalescent white / Marble white / Golden beige / Alabaster / Spots of ocher / Tones of warm, fertile soil

HARMONIC MATCHES FOR HE-A-A-YAH'S PROTÉGÉS

- *The best matches for success in economic and practical achievements will be among men and women born March 5–9, under the care of Ha-Ye-Ya-El.*
- *The best matches for recognition, fame, personal charisma, and social fulfillment will be among men and women born September 26–30, under the care of Re-Ha-Â-El.*
- *The best matches for romance, love, and artistic and intellectual achievements will be among men and women born October 31–November 4, under the care of Âri-Ya-El.*

hall of famer Leo Durocher have in common? They are among the scrappy, persevering protégés of Angel He-A-A-Yah.

More than any other guardian, this powerful guide impregnates those in his/her care with the high harmonic vibrations of the original breath of creation. Entirely spiritualized by these subtle and powerful waves, those born between July 23 and 27 inhabit the earth secure in the knowledge that their characteristic persistence, empathy, and deep desire to achieve are divinely inspired.

While others look to the tangible world for their rewards, those attuned to the harmonic vibrations of He-A-A-Yah are people who walk in faith. But that doesn't mean they're not down-to-earth. The friends of He-A-A-Yah climb each logical step that brings them closer to their goals like the rungs of a ladder that link the earthly and celestial worlds. They use their inborn capacity for empathy to draw partners that are appropriate to their needs. With the help of He-A-A-Yah, they uncover the evolving trends that can affect their success. Then, when reason will take them no further, the swirl of faith propels them to the heavens.

Angel He-A-A-Yah provides men and women with a gift for perseverance. Such a gift allows them to undertake long-term projects, maintain their concentration on a particular goal, renew their motivations when faced with difficulties, and, stimulated by the original breath of Angel He-A-A-Yah, bring their dreams within reach. When these men and women apply their natural stick-to-itiveness to lofty intellectual projects, when they open their thoughts to the breath of creation, when they find an enterprise that combines reason and faith, then, by the grace of Angel He-A-A-Yah, the synchronic powers of Providence are stirred. A rain of favorable answers, happy encounters, unexpected discoveries, large benefits, strokes of luck, surprising windfalls, and gifts from heaven fall upon them.

If you are among He-A-A-Yah's intimates, you may—depending on the specific circumstances of your life—be perceived as a messenger of new times and ideas, as is He-A-A-Yah protégé Aldous Huxley. Indeed, your capacity to build visionary strategies may lead you, with the help of your patron, to become an excellent adviser to companies, institutions, and individuals. Or you may follow your impulse for free thinking and throw off the yoke of someone else's business altogether. Many of your brothers and sisters under the protection of Angel He-A-A-Yah have discovered that they are happier if they are at the command of their own ships—or airships, as was the case for Amelia Earhart. You may even become the power behind the power, as was baseball manager Leo Durocher. The influence of Angel He-A-A-Yah leads some men and women into taking behind-the-scenes positions where they can bring to life the strategies that flow from their rich inner visions.

When faced with emergency and crisis situations, these men and women turn out to be excellent analysts of previously hidden or distorted information. Depending on circumstances, those under the protection of Angel He-A-A-Yah can succeed in occupations requiring secrecy, coding, and decoding, diplomacy, police work, or special missions. For them, the stars, the suns, the galaxies, and the infinite space have the same daily presence as hills, oceans, trees, and the atmosphere. Carried and penetrated by the eternal breath, their minds travel from earth to heaven and from heaven to earth, in a constant circular movement.

However you choose to use He-A-A-Yah's generous gifts, you will follow your path with a fierce and uncompromising will and the unflagging determination to stay the course you have chosen. This does not mean you'll be blissfully oblivious when times get tough. In the heat of the moment, an easy out may seem attractive to you. But He-A-A-Yah helps her/his friends resist the temptation to give in to easy solutions. By invoking your eternal guide, you will steel yourself to the subtle diversions that might lead you astray or divert you from your mission. You might even take up a sport to relieve the pressure of daily life. Many men and women protected by He-A-A-Yah find tremendous success in sports because they possess the perseverance, the breath, and the faith from which great champions are made.

When in deep harmony with Angel He-A-A-Yah, people respond to the call of the heavens with enthusiasm, elevate their minds to the most ideal abstract forms, and equate their thoughts and actions on earth with the pure principles of universal truth. Kinship with this dynamic Angel is truly a blessing.

Angel YERATHA-EL

JULY 28–AUGUST 1

Encourages action. Reinforces leadership abilities. Increases the power to create and finalize. Stimulates the exploration of new ideas and enlightening methods.

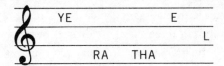

PHONETIC PRONUNCIATION

Ye as in Yes
Ra as in Rapid
Tha as in Tarot
El as in Elevation

UNIVERSAL RESONANCE OF THE ANGEL'S NAME

Ye Mastery. Dexterity, expertise; human action aligned with divine universal principles.

Ra Rotation, return, renewal; the natural cycles of existence. Radiance. Charisma. Inner vision and foresight on a universal scale. Princely leadership.

Tha Experience of time. Evolving temporal cycles eternally recurring. Mutation coupling mortality with immortality.

El Ending vibration of the Angel's name. Principle of excellence; chosen; elite. Elevating force. Source of perpetual transformation and evolution.

Guardian Angel Yeratha-El

In Akkadian language the name Yeratha-El literally means, "The Divine Verb, which sublimates and radiates the light rays of the cycles of time."

We all struggle to do the right thing. Those men and women in the care of guardian Angel Yeratha-El can't help it! Angel Yeratha-El

NOTABLE PEOPLE BORN UNDER THE INFLUENCE OF YERATHA-EL

Arnold Schwarzenegger, *actor*

Beatrix Potter, *author and illustrator*

Emily Brontë, *writer*

Henry Ford, *inventor of the automobile*

Herman Melville, *writer*

J. B. Lamarck, *scientist and naturalist*

Jacqueline Kennedy Onassis, *former U.S. first lady*

James Baldwin, *writer*

Lisa Kudrow, *actress*

Melvin Belli, *attorney*

Peter Jennings, *television journalist*

Yves Saint Laurent, *fashion designer*

COLOR HARMONIZATION

Ocher / Red / Yellow

endows her/his friends with the power of enlightened and enlightening actions. Such men and women are often recognized as natural leaders and prized for their ability to launch powerful efforts—professionally or culturally—that produce influential results.

To understand the commanding presence of those in tune with Yeratha-El, consider some of the compelling, charismatic people in his/her care: Arnold Schwarzenegger. Henry Ford. Jacqueline Kennedy Onassis. These aren't just icons; they are real characters invested with the power and ability to change the world around them and guide others with justice and precision. Thanks to the inner fire that brings light to their inner visions, those under the protection of Angel Yeratha-El have an intuitive knowledge of the impact and consequences of their actions. They are also able to pinpoint, without hesitation, the strategy that will bring about the results they desire, as quickly as possible.

It's not every day we come across this mix of can-do efficiency and personal magnetism. It is no surprise then that the men and women close to Yeratha-El are often appointed to positions of leadership. Depending on circumstances, they might be the strong and inspirational heads of families (like Jacqueline Kennedy) or the leaders of expeditions, governments, and religious or spiritual groups. They could be explicators of the news (like Peter Jennings) or the center of media focus. If they become involved in sculpture, pottery, or other transformative arts, they could change the look of the world, as did Yves Saint Laurent. Those who take their inspiration from Yeratha-El become powerful and daring achievers, able to mold matter and move hearts.

If you are close to Angel Yeratha-El, you have been given the organizational and motivational talent to attain positions of leadership. Once you've made your way to the top, you will enjoy an enduring popularity, thanks to your personal charisma, your progressive vision, and your ability to create solid consensus. Men and women protected by Angel Yeratha-El always endeavor to enlighten the world. You may find yourself reaching out to your fellow humans through the sciences, arts, technological arts, or through humanitarian organizations that reinforce social and political liberty. If circumstances allow, you may bring the brilliance of Yeratha-El into your life by choosing a career or hobby that is related to light, such

HARMONIC MATCHES FOR YERATHA-EL'S PROTÉGÉS

- *The best matches for success in economic and practical achievements will be among men and women born February 28–March 4, under the care of Yaba-Mi-Yah.*

- *The best matches for recognition, fame, personal charisma, and social fulfillment will be among men and women born September 21–25, under the care of Ha-Âmi-Yah.*

- *The best matches for romance, love, and artistic and intellectual achievements will be among men and women born November 5–9 under the care of Â-Sali-Yah.*

as glass work, stained-glass design, work with crystals, optical instruments, photography, or the visual arts. Your talents could also illuminate the political arena. Through the grace of Angel Yeratha-El, you know the secret of creating powerful images that appear to be new yet are drawn from a long-held historical or cultural tradition. Any cause you espouse will seem, at once, innovative and familiar to your audience.

Angel Yeratha-El opens up a channel to a permanent source of compassion, from which those in her/his care are invited to draw from abundantly. This reservoir of affection protects you from any tendency to become a tyrannical or dogmatic leader. It also awakens within you the celestially inspired power to heal. By melding your energies with the harmonic vibrations of Angel Yeratha-El, you become the channel for a profound gift of healing, which can apply to physical, psychological, moral, legal, or social illnesses and crises.

Of course, all these wonderful talents and abilities, in combination with your very visible presence, can make you vulnerable to the hostility of jealous enemies. If that happens, you should immediately invoke Angel Yeratha-El and focus your awareness on his/her nearness. The protection of this Angel allows you to avoid earthly battles and conflicts, the violence of which could diminish your positive energy and divert you from your mission as a bearer of light.

To sum up: the men and women under the harmonic influence of Angel Yeratha-El are the messengers of the future, the bringers of a new realm. Through their actions, they seek to awaken, organize, and aid the forces of benevolent justice through which the world is peacefully enlightened. When inspired by such a lofty mission, those under the protection of Yeratha-El bring together earthly and celestial beings alike and lead them to the heart of their true homeland, their motherland, their universal home.

Angel SE-A-HE-YAH

AUGUST 2–6

Stimulates mental and intellectual capacities. Increases the ability for logical reasoning. Provides a gift for caution and circumspection. Brings harmony between emotions and reason.

```
        A      HE      H
                  YA
   SE
```

PHONETIC PRONUNCIATION

Se as in Separate

A as in Arrow

He as in Hebrew

Ya as in Yard

H Vocalize the final H as a soft exhalation

UNIVERSAL RESONANCE OF THE ANGEL'S NAME

Se Diffusion, radiation. Extraction of all the energies enclosed in the nucleus. Birth of science, sentience, and sapience. Radiating knowledge. Cosmic fire, archetype of every sun in the universe.

A The original and ultimate energy; before form, universal, infinite, unifying.

He Spiritual life force. Love that underlies all things. Presence of the universal and all-encompassing spirit. Divine call, divine connection.

Yah Final vibration of the Angel's name. Receptivity and reflectivity. The presence of the deity; the abundance of the being.

COLOR HARMONIZATION

Dark maroon / Red / Dark gray / Light gray / Luminous green

HARMONIC MATCHES FOR SE-A-HE-YAH'S PROTÉGÉS

- *The best matches for success in economic and practical achievements will be among men and women born February 23–27, under the care of Ro-A-Ha-El.*
- *The best matches for recognition, fame, personal charisma, and social fulfillment will be among men and women born September 16–20, under the care of Ani-Ya-El.*
- *The best matches for romance, love, and artistic and intellectual achievements will be among men and women born November 10–14, under the care of Mi-Ya-Ha-El.*

Guardian Angel Se-A-He-Yah

In Akkadian language, the name Se-A-He-Yah literally means, "The radiating science that spreads universal energy in accordance with the law of love of the Supreme Being."

Some people are busiest when they're sitting in a chair. Such is the case for the intellectual adventurers who are protected by Angel Se-A-He-Yah. For them, intellectual activity is a priority. They exercise their minds with passion, producing enlightening ideas that project their creativity and enthusiasm.

Exuberant and zealous, but also levelheaded and logical, these are men and women whose hearts are always guided by the enlightenment of reason. It is best not to try to hide anything from those born between August 2 and 6. These are natural sleuths who can use their innate ability to draw out knowledge and information to their advantage. If they choose to develop that ability, they can excel in the fields of scientific research, police investigation, or journalism. With the help of Angel Se-A-He-Yah, they can develop a unique investigative style characterized by solid research, cautious and circumspect techniques, and intuitive, original conclusions.

If you are guided by Angel Se-A-He-Yah, you temper your feelings, desires, and emotions with logic and intellect. This doesn't mean you do not feel deeply. Because your mind and heart balance—not cancel!—each other out, you are protected against both the blindness of passion and the coldness of reason. Your brand of logic, then, is deliberation fed by strong intuition; your passions are illuminated by the light of reason.

People influenced by the harmonic vibrations of Angel Se-A-He-Yah have personalities that are placid and warm. That means you stay calm even when there is an emotional volcano erupting in your heart. This increasingly rare quality is highly valued by your friends and employers. You may be called upon often to help overcome obstacles, mediate conflicts, and resolve social or interpersonal tensions.

You are also endowed with common sense and stability, two other characteristics that will endear you to your managers and clients alike. You are cautious and prudent without being skeptical. And you know to question and analyze a situation before drawing conclusions. With such gifts, added to your inborn capacity for accurate observation, you are capable of managing substantial material and financial assets for yourself, your family, your friends, or clients. Angel Se-A-He-Yah will help you see to it that your books are always in balance and that your investments are as productive and stable as your personality.

For you and all of those born under the protection of this solid and dependable Angel, thinking before acting is of vital importance. You don't like to go off half-cocked or have your own hasty words used against you. While others jump headlong into a fray, you step back, consider the situation, and clarify your perceptions before acting or speaking. That's because those under the influence of Se-A-He-Yah understand that, for them, the most productive path to wealth and happiness is through reflection and introspection. Those who are attuned to those vibrations must always connect their actions and decisions to a well-founded and mature analysis; otherwise their decisions do not feel complete. Moreover, their impulsive, spur-of-the-moment decisions rarely produce successful results.

Although those guided by Se-A-He-Yah tend not to disperse their emotional energy without reason, these men and women enjoy good physical health and a robust stamina that can even increase as they grow older. If circumstances in their lives provide them with the opportunity to act out of the goodness of their hearts, these men and women may develop a gift for healing and could be essential in increasing the pool of knowledge in the fields of physical or mental health.

When in deep harmony with Angel Se-A-He-Yah, the minds of men and women overcome the obstacles of time and fearlessly go to the burning cosmic source of all knowledge and of all love. By allowing their hearts and souls to bask in celestial light, those under the protection of Angel Se-A-He-Yah will refine their thoughts, enlighten their feelings, and transform all they have learned on earth into the eternal wisdom of the heavens.

INVOCATION

O Angel Se-A-He-Yah,
Your immense light
Spirals in the universe
And transmits to humans
The vision of future worlds.
O Se-A-He-Yah,
Help me, help my mind
Discern the knowledge
That guides across time
Memories and thoughts.
O Se-A-He-Yah,
Procure me the divine surge
That will project
My soul
To the heavens of Angels.

Angel RE-YI-YA-EL

AUGUST 7–11

Stimulates visionary inspiration. Enhances spiritual life. Increases personal radiance, inwardly and outwardly. Opens to guidance by the celestial forces. Provides social protection and material riches.

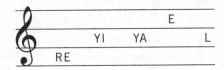

PHONETIC PRONUNCIATION

Re as in Ray

Yi as in Yin

Ya as in Yard

El as in Elevation

UNIVERSAL RESONANCE OF THE ANGEL'S NAME

Re Return, rotation, renewal. The natural cycles of existence. Radiance, charisma. Inner vision and foresight on a universal scale. Princely leadership.

Yi Mastery. Dexterity, expertise; human action aligned with divine universal principles.

Ya Mastery. Dexterity, expertise; human action aligned with divine universal principles.

El Ending vibration of the Angel's name. Principle of excellence. Chosen; elite. Elevating force. Source of perpetual transformation and evolution.

Guardian Angel Re-Yi-Ya-El

In Akkadian, the name Re-Yi-Ya-El means, literally, "The radiant vision is transformed into action and inspired by the celestial voice."

When in harmony with Angel Re-Yi-Ya-El, men and women are impregnated with the radiance of the divine Light and energized

NOTABLE PEOPLE BORN UNDER THE INFLUENCE OF RE-YI-YA-EL

Andy Warhol, painter and filmmaker

Angelica Huston, actress

Charlize Theron, actress

David Duchovny, actor

Dustin Hoffman, actor

Eiji Yoshikawa, writer

Gillian Anderson, actress

Herbert Hoover, former U.S. president

Mata Hari, infamous spy

Melanie Griffith, actress

Paul A. M. Dirac, physicist

Rosanna Arquette, actress

Whitney Houston, pop singer

Wolfgang Pauli, Nobel Prize winner in physics

COLOR HARMONIZATION

Green / Warm maroon / Black on silver / Neutral beige / Eggshell white

by the celestial Verb. Those under the protection of Angel Re-Yi-Ya-El may experience this cosmic radiance as visions that inspire their minds and dominate their intellectual processes. Because they are, above all else, intuitives and visionaries, they instinctively concentrate their focus on the spiritual source of their inspirations. As a result, they often appear to be in a state of grace.

The harmonic vibrations of Angel Re-Yi-Ya-El inspire in this Angel's protégés a talent for action and achievement in both the spiritual and social realms. When in resonance with Re-Yi-Ya-El, men and women are endowed with the ability to foresee the future and to help others see what they are looking for but do not discern. This talent can easily transport them to the head of any social or spiritual movement that attracts them.

If you are close to Re-Yi-Ya-El, you are inhabited by the cosmic light generated by your loving guardian. If you are placed by your Angel in the middle of a group, network, or association where others can glimpse your radiant light, you can exert a positive spiritual influence on everyone around. Depending upon your personal circumstances, you might excel as a speaker, preacher, religious leader, writer, lecturer, or at any calling requiring a distinct inner vision and personal style. In the social arena, you may become known as a visionary, diplomat, inspired businessperson, or as a civic leader who is known as an extraordinary guide and achiever.

Dynamic, charismatic, and bright, you and all those under the protection of Angel Re-Yi-Ya-El are more than qualified to forge your own future—but you won't have to go it alone. Your thoughtful guardian has provided you with influential and prestigious friends who are always in the right place at the right time. These powerful allies will smooth your path and do everything they can to ensure your success. In fact, with the aid of Re-Yi-Ya-El and your earthly boosters, the projects you care most about are guaranteed to succeed against all odds and in spite of all logic. You may even become known as someone with a magic touch. In your case, that assessment happens to be right on! Re-Yi-Ya-El opens a channel between earth and the swirling celestial powers for those in her/his care. You are on the receiving end of limitless love and support from invisible sources but with very clear and tangible results.

HARMONIC MATCHES FOR RE-YI-YA-EL'S PROTÉGÉS

- *The best matches for success in economic and practical achievements will be among men and women born February 18–22, under the care of Ha-Bovi-Yah.*
- *The best matches for recognition, fame, personal charisma, and social fulfillment will be among men and women born October 21–25, under the care of Yela-Hi-Yah.*
- *The best matches for romance, love, and artistic and intellectual achievements will be among men and women born October 6–10, under the care of He-He-Ha-El.*

In order to take full advantage of the cosmic light Angel Re-Yi-Ya-El projects, the protégés of this illuminating Angel must always be ready to convert their celestial energies into actions and undertake the projects designated by their visions. Ask, and Angel Re-Yi-Ya-El will help you to do this. To further ensure Re-Yi-Ya-El's guidance, it is important that you always act out of pure intentions—that is, those aspirations anchored within the self, deep in the state of being. In fact, when your desire to reach the highest altruistic goals overrides your wish for personal gain, then you will project your desires into the cosmic dimensions, and great material and spiritual abundance will be yours.

Whatever career path you choose, you and your sisters and brothers in the care of Angel Re-Yi-Ya-El will turn your thoughts and talents to humanitarian missions when you reach middle age. With the help of your illuminating guardian, you will share with others the celestial source of your inspiration and prophetic visions. Re-Yi-Ya-El will give you the words to communicate your deepest feelings about the meaning of faith, the value of poetry, and the transformational power of the state of grace that has motivated your highest aspirations.

In the past, men and women who were strongly inspired by Angel Re-Yi-Ya-El were called prophets and visionaries and had many followers. In contemporary life, they are sought out for their ability to predict and provoke events, and they often find work in government or private organizations as members of strategic staffs or important participants in business or financial groups.

With the help of Angel Re-Yi-Ya-El, you will always be able to inspire your contemporaries and reveal to them, through your thoughts and example, the celestial origin of all worldly wealth and riches.

Angel OVA-MA-EL

AUGUST 12–16

Fertilizes ideas and actions. Reinforces creative abilities. Encourages maternity and paternity. Transforms abstract thoughts into concrete reality. Provides the ability to heal.

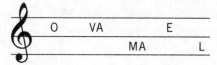

PHONETIC PRONUNCIATION

O as in Orange
Va as in Varsity
Ma as in Master
El as in Elevation

UNIVERSAL RESONANCE OF THE ANGEL'S NAME

O Original, ultimate energy; before form, universal, infinite, unifying.

Va Vitalizing factor. Fruitfulness and productivity. Catalyst of variety, vitality, verity, will, and vigor.

Ma The matrix; the model upon which creation is based. Manifestation in the material world. Loving maternal protection.

El Ending vibration of the Angel's name. Principle of excellence. Chosen; elite. Elevating force. Source of perpetual transformation and evolution.

Guardian Angel Ova-Ma-El

In Akkadian language, the name Ova-Ma-El means, literally, "The matrix egg of the Universal Mother fertilized by the evolving Principle."

The harmonic vibrations of Angel Ova-Ma-El activate in this world the most essential and primal vitalizing substances. Touched by the light emanating from the cosmic egg, the principle of eternal

COLOR HARMONIZATION

Creamy white / Beige / Dark maroon / A circle of golden yellow in front of each of those background colors

HARMONIC MATCHES FOR OVA-MA-EL'S PROTÉGÉS

* *The best matches for success in economic and practical achievements will be among men and women born February 13–17, under the care of A-Ya-Â-El.*
* *The best matches for recognition, fame, personal charisma, and social fulfillment will be among men and women born October 16–20, under the care of Vavali-Yah.*
* *The best matches for romance, love, and artistic and intellectual achievements will be among men and women born October 11–15, under the care of Mi-Yi-Ca-El.*

creation, those under the protection of Angel Ova-Ma-El are warmed, awakened, and enlightened. They welcome this celestial, sublime, and fertilizing light and let it vibrate in their minds. This shimmering brilliance will give life and color to their most abstract ideas.

Because Angel Ova-Ma-El focuses the constant flow of the Universe's radiance on those under her/his protection, this Angel's protégés receive as a gift the ability to conceptualize and create, to give life to their dreams, and to nurture their ideas from abstract concept to their visible and tangible realization. Those who enjoy a deep connection with the vibrating harmonies of Angel Ova-Ma-El are true self-starters who know how to begin a project from nothing, create a sound foundation to support it, give birth to a new reality, and sustain it to its ultimate completion. If, like Madonna, comedian Steve Martin, or poet Charles Bukowski, they cultivate the opportunities they encounter in an artistic way, those under the protection of Angel Ova-Ma-El will bring their ideas to life in print or song on the stage, screen, or canvas. Those of a more scientific bent may excel in areas that allow them to translate the abstractions of cosmic structures into understandable living ideas. They may be innovators in such areas as speculative mathematics, astronomy, particle physics, and bioelectronics.

Whether in their personal, social, or professional lives, the men and women guided by Ova-Ma-El can find success in any occupation that requires the combined qualities of a father and a mother. In other words, these men and women find in their relationship with Angel Ova-Ma-El the paternal resources necessary to fertilize or activate their ideas as well as the profoundly nurturing mother power necessary to establish models and matrixes and provide them with the nourishment they need to grow and evolve. By cultivating and reinforcing their affinity with their guardian, anyone born between August 12 and 16 can become a good Father-Mother or Mother-Father.

If you are born under the protection of Angel Ova-Ma-El, you are a source of amazement to everyone around you. While their dreams may be castles in the sky, yours become real! Creative yet practical, completely indefatigable, you can bring an innovative idea to life despite any obstacle. For that reason, you would thrive at a start-up company or working within an emerging sector. Given the right financial backing, you would also be a particularly prolific entrepreneur, creating brand new projects and products nearly as quickly as you could conceive of them.

But don't think for a moment that you and everyone born under the guidance of Ova-Ma-El are "all work and no play" personalities. This Angel is sensitive and nurturing, inventive and energizing. He/She is the embodiment of the primal forces that create life. You, consequently, are a natural-born nurturer, a simultaneously maternal and paternal spirit with strong shoulders others can cry on and a sensitive yet solid spirit. Those closest to you not only *have* your number but use it—frequently!—whenever they need consoling, yearn for an emotional presence, or just need a hug. In your personal, family, and social life, you not only get the emotional goodies, you generously distribute them to others. The harmonic tonalities of Angel Ova-Ma-El encourage you to give unselfishly of yourself.

Angel Ova-Ma-El provides a healing energy that allows for success in the caring professions. You may find your calling within the health care field or in social assistance, psychological counseling, guidance, child care, or early-childhood education. The presence of Angel Ova-Ma-El can also be invoked to cure the physical imbalances that are created by emotional trauma.

Because he/she represents the essential fertilizing force of life, Angel Ova-Ma-El can provide to those who call upon her/him both material and emotional wealth. Angel Ova-Ma-El deepens friendships, enhances marriages, and strengthens family ties.

When in deep harmony with Angel Ova-Ma-El, people's minds rise up to meet the original sources of Creation. There, in the heavens, they discover the ideal form of all things—crystals, stars, drops of water, flowers, birds, Angels, and everything in creation. Then, in awe of the purity of the cosmos, those under the protection of the infinite mother/father set out to reveal the infinite brilliance of the Divine spirit to everyone on earth.

Angel LE-CABA-EL

AUGUST 17–21

COLOR HARMONIZATION

Violet / Burgundy red / Ocher / Orange

Connects with invisible forces. Increases knowledge and the ability to learn. Stimulates poetic inspiration. Reinforces the courage to confront the truth. Provides a gift for simplifying and clarifying.

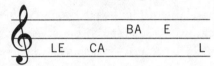

PHONETIC PRONUNCIATION

Le as in Leisure

Ca as in Cabala

Ba as in Bard

El as in Elevation

UNIVERSAL RESONANCE OF THE ANGEL'S NAME

Le Dynamic learning. The ability to make mental links. Intellectual elevation. An evolving, ascending movement of the mind. Lucidity and enlightenment.

Ca The practical, physical, and material manifestation of ideas and thoughts. A solidifying, coalescing force within the fluid substances of the universe. Energies of cohesion and collusion, connivance, collaboration, cooperation. A force of strength and power.

Ba The universal, paternal force; that which contains the code of all codes. The formative energy generating all data and shapes. The generic code that begins all lives, all manifestations, all experiences.

El Ending vibration of the Angel's name. Principle of excellence. Chosen; elite. Elevating force. Source of perpetual transformation and evolution.

Guardian Angel Le-Caba-El

In Akkadian language the name Le-Caba-El means, literally, "The good one sends to heaven is returned, in equal measure, from heaven." Or, "Opening the mind in order to receive the divine knowledge of living codes."

The harmonic tonalities of Angel Le-Caba-El penetrate the minds of men and women with liberating knowledge that encourages them to spend their lives questioning the very foundations of what we know to be true. Those under the influence of Angel Le-Caba-El learn, not from study but from the spontaneous understandings, intuitive truths, poetic and spiritual inspirations, and sudden insights that spring, unbidden, to their consciousness. The fundamental questions that fertilize their minds and cause them to think and rethink the structure of their internal and external worlds appear to come from nowhere. In fact, they are Le-Caba-El's calling card.

Although the constant questioning of every aspect of existence might frustrate more literal-minded friends and co-workers, such curiosity is a gift. More specifically, it's a gift without any strings attached. Angel Le-Caba-El not only prompts the questioning, he/she then provides the answer in a single inspirational, shocking, wonderful "aha!" moment. Hence, while the rest of us ponder, read, and study, those close to this wise Angel are blessed with an intuitive knowledge of the answers to life's most profound questions. No matter how difficult the test, they get an A—and they don't have to study for it, either.

If you are inspired by Angel Le-Caba-El, you are just as comfortable traveling through the celestial dimensions, drawing your thoughts and ideas from above, as you are walking the earthly paths and culling your perceptions from below. Wherever you seek your answers, you are always trying to get to the bottom of some issue. What is the meaning of life? What is the meaning of the word *meaning*? Whether you phrase your questions like the premise of a Ph.D. dissertation or in the simplest possible language, your queries always aim for the very center of your spiritual quest or the latest scientific research.

When an answer comes, you will take it in without prejudice. The curious, intelligent men and women inspired by Angel

O Angel Le-Caba-El,
On my thirsty soul
In its earthly vase,
You pour eternally
The celestial truths.
Angel Le-Caba-El,
Thank you for the living knowledge
That shines under your clear sight.
Filled with new courage,
Under the rain of stars,
I tune in.
O Le-Caba-El,
I tune in
The chant of Angels,
And I pursue the immense rainbow
That propels to divine domains.

HARMONIC MATCHES FOR LE-CABA-EL'S PROTÉGÉS

- *The best matches for success in economic and practical achievements will be among men and women born February 8–12, under the care of Mana-Qua-El.*
- *The best matches for recognition, fame, personal charisma, and social fulfillment will be among men and women born October 11–15, under the care of Mi-Yi-Ca-El.*
- *The best matches for romance, love, and artistic and intellectual achievements will be among men and women born October 16–20, under the care of Vavali-Yah.*

Le-Caba-El are open to all forms of knowledge. They possess a powerful ability to confront the truth, no matter how pleasant or unpleasant it may be. And they are fearless enough to travel all of the roads open to them in pursuit of their quest, wherever they may lead. While searching for the truth, those under the protection of Angel Le-Caba-El know how to use all the intellectual and spiritual means at their disposal: analysis, reasoning, imagination, synthesis, analogy, and faith. No wonder so many writers and journalists are born under the care of this Angel!

Depending on their personal circumstances, men and women who receive knowledge and courage from Angel Le-Caba-El can be Heroes of Knowledge, those special people who are willing to use their considerable intellectual gifts in the pursuit of esoteric studies. They can also successfully apply their intellectual audacity in areas such as astronomy, mathematics, or theoretical geometry. Whatever occupation they choose, they will be a welcome addition to any staff. They are able to resolve difficult and dense problems, untie complicated knots, and accurately assess facts, people, and things at a glance. Consequently, they excel in activities that call for clarification of data or tasks.

Make no mistake: these are people who appreciate secrets. And it's a good thing, too. Angel Le-Caba-El has a compelling secret to share with them: how to shift weight and create balance in their lives, in their work, in their relationships, and in the cosmos. Through this natural gift for evaluating, estimating, and quantifying, these men and women ensure the stability, coherence, and permanence of everything they create, think, and do. Depending on their personal preferences, those who have established kinship with Angel Le-Caba-El know, for example, how to create new textile fibers, design gardens or public spaces, analyze complex processes, synthesize results in computer programs, conceive of new industrial organizations, modify technical procedures, and propose new axiomatic theories. They can boldly go where no one has gone before, like Gene Roddenberry—and Orville Wright.

If you are in harmony with the vibrations of Angel Le-Caba-El, you are open-minded about the cosmic dimensions. You know how to transfer your celestial knowledge to earthly domains and how to translate it into either mystical, technical, or practical everyday use.

However you choose to use this information, it will be in alignment with your specific mission or the way you choose to direct your life.

The harmonies of Angel Le-Caba-El grant you and everyone in this Angel's care both a celestial knowledge and a dynamic method that allows you to generate new and astonishing understanding. By keeping close to Le-Caba-El, you can welcome and recognize the celestial lights and use them to enlighten others, paving the way on earth to the heavens. By invoking your guardian, you ensure that you will receive divine communications, know just how to decode and translate them, and transmit them to others without diminishing or flattening them.

As translators and interpreters from one language or science to another, skilled in hermeneutics, moving back and forth between cultures and worlds, astronomers, creators of cohesive social, economic, and family structures, spiritual communicators and decoders, cabalists, quick analysts, dazzling synthesizers, and astrologers, men and women in full awareness of the harmonies of Angel Le-Caba-El are able to enrich all areas of knowledge. They stand as examples of what can happen to us all once we stop fearing the pure expression of the truth.

Angel VA-SARI-YAH

AUGUST 22–26

Creates associations and unions. Stimulates vitality and growth. Promotes preeminence through merit. Increases wealth. Promotes the dissemination of ideas and of material goods.

NOTABLE PEOPLE BORN UNDER THE INFLUENCE OF VA-SARI-YAH

Barbara Eden, *actress*

Cal Ripken Jr., *baseball player*

Clara Bow, *actress*

Claude Debussy, *composer*

Dorothy Parker, *writer*

Duke Kahanamoku, *swimmer*

Frederick Forsyth, *writer*

Gene Kelly, *dancer and actor*

Geraldine Ferraro, *politician*

Guillaume Apollinaire, *poet*

Jonathan Wainwright, *soldier*

Jorge Luis Borges, *writer*

Macaulay Culkin, *actor*

Norman Schwartzkopf, *army general*

Peggy Guggenheim, *art collector and patron*

Ray Bradbury, *writer*

Regis Philbin, *television personality*

Sean Connery, *actor*

COLOR HARMONIZATION

Black / White / Red / French blue

PHONETIC PRONUNCIATION

Va as in Value

Sa as in Sarah

Ri as in Riga

Ya as in Yard

H Vocalize the final H as a soft exhalation

UNIVERSAL RESONANCE OF THE ANGEL'S NAME

Va Vitalizing factor. Fruitfulness and productivity. Catalyst of variety, vitality, verity, will, and vigor.

Sa Diffusion, radiation. The ability to comprehend and use the forces enclosed in the nucleus. Birth of science, sentience, and sapience. Radiating knowledge. Cosmic fire, archetype of every sun in the universe.

Ri Rotation, return, renewal; the natural cycles of existence. Radiance. Charisma. Inner vision, and foresight on a universal scale. Princely leadership.

Yah Final vibration of the Angel's name. Receptivity and reflectivity. The presence of the deity; the abundance of the being.

Guardian Angel Va-Sari-Yah

In Akkadian language, the name Va-Sari-Yah means, literally, "The fertilizing and productive union of the Prince/Princess at the service of the Supreme Power of Creation."

Think back to the charming, noble princes and princesses that rode out of the pages of your favorite childhood storybooks. These weren't socialites and celebrities, like some royals today. They were attractive, sensitive, intelligent men and women who could really shake up a ball and bring harmony to a kingdom. Moreover, they shared their gifts generously and were even willing to take on a quest, even a perilous one, if it might bring peace, wisdom, or spiritual enlightenment to others. Such magnanimous men and women can be hard to find—unless you look to those generous, enlightened souls born under the influence of guardian Angel Va-Sari-Yah.

The harmonic tonalities of Angel Va-Sari-Yah infuse those born between August 22 and 26 with the principles of universal attraction and of fertilizing union. This powerful Angel's vibrations also enlighten the minds of those he/she guides with cosmic awareness and illuminates their hearts with the radiant flame of celestial intelligence. Endowed with the life-giving power of an eternal spring, those under the protection of this Angel of regeneration and renewal are able to engender productive unions, encourage growth, and promote fruitful associations.

When invoked sincerely, Angel Va-Sari-Yah bathes all projects in the universal vital flow that brings life to all things. Whether the project is a flower garden or an orchard, whether it is a love letter, a master's thesis, or an elaborate intellectual or artistic production, it is bound to thrive and bear delectable fruit. When invited to share in one's personal life, Angel Va-Sari-Yah can enlighten emotional impulses, create a link between action and emotions, and inspire creative choices and harmonious decisions.

Most of all, if you were born into this Angel's care, the harmonies of Va-Sari-Yah encourage and reinforce your abilities to occupy the position of the ideal prince or princess in your social circle, professional group, or in the world. Bear in mind, this doesn't mean that UPS will be dropping off a scepter at your door. It does mean that when you tune in to this Angel's vitalizing sensibility and

INVOCATION

O Angel Va-Sari-Yah,
Every star knows your name
And you know each and all suns,
That illuminate eternally
The great mornings of the universe.
O Va-Sari-Yah,
Of my soul you know the age,
And my story is told to you
In the great book of eternity.
O Va-Sari-Yah,
I invoke your name,
Every vowel is a star
That pulses in the heavens' heart.

radiant intelligence, you will be led to discover unsuspected wealth and hidden beauties; you will resolve conflicts and unite opposing parties; you will successfully make difficult or unlikely alliances; you will find yourself in a position of prominence without having to conquer or displace others to achieve that position; and you will create and share abundance, much like a benevolent ruler.

Let others generate cash-flow, products, or spin; those who seek deep harmony with Angel Va-Sari-Yah are capable of generating fervor and hope, of crossing national and racial boundaries, and transforming social groups, institutions, and even nations using only the strength of their formidable personal charisma.

In the past, those born under the influence of this empowering Angel have acquired notoriety thanks to their celestially given skills in agriculture or engineering, in creating irrigation networks that provide the earth with water, or in devising brilliantly organized food distribution systems that sustain nations. In contemporary societies, these men and women may excel in agriculture or fields analogous to land irrigation and also in professions that direct the flow of money or circulate the vital goods that enrich personal, family, communal, national, or global life.

If you are protected by Angel Va-Sari-Yah, you may have a sense that you are uniquely blessed or that the talents and gifts that have brought you success are of celestial origin, but you won't be broadcasting these beliefs to others. You prefer to reveal your spiritual side through your concrete actions in the world. Whether you become a teacher, farmer, journalist, doctor, a CEO of an industrial or financial conglomerate, a social, union, or political leader, a judge, or a member of a religious order, you will use your regal bearing and noble influence to spread knowledge, promote harmony, bring about unity, and promote the physical, mental, and spiritual well-being of everyone around you.

In your inner life, you, like all of the friends of Va-Sari-Yah, know how to express strong emotions and control them at the same time. Aware of your connection with the heavens and eager to master knowledge in its entirety, you and all of your brothers and sisters under Va-Sari-Yah's protection can avoid the obstacle of tyrannical pride and grasp the authentic spiritual nobility that is the prerogative of true princes and princesses.

HARMONIC MATCHES FOR VA-SARI-YAH'S PROTÉGÉS

- *The best matches for success in economic and practical achievements will be among men and women born February 3–7, under the care of Damabi-Yah.*
- *The best matches for recognition, fame, personal charisma, and social fulfillment will be among men and women born October 6–10, under the care of He-He-Ha-El.*
- *The best matches for romance, love, and artistic and intellectual achievements will be among men and women born October 21–25, under the care of Yela-Hi-Yah.*

Angel YE-HOVI-YAH

AUGUST 27–31

Stimulates creativity, fertility, and fecundity. Increases the power of realization. Amplifies mental power. Leads past obstacles, straight to desired goals. Inspires flawless and effective strategies.

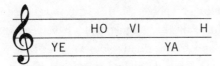

	HO	VI		H
YE			YA	

PHONETIC PRONUNCIATION

Ye as in Yes
Ho as in Holiday
Vi as in Victory
Ya as in Yard
H Vocalize the final H as a soft exhalation

UNIVERSAL RESONANCE OF THE ANGEL'S NAME

Ye Mastery. Dexterity, expertise; human action aligned with divine universal principles.

Ho Spiritual life force. Presence of universal love and the all-permeating spirit. Divine call, divine connectivity.

Vi Vitalizing factor. Fruitfulness and productivity. Catalyst of variety, vitality, verity, will, and vigor.

Yah Final vibration of the Angel's name. Receptivity and reflectivity. The presence of the deity; the abundance of the being.

Guardian Angel Ye-Hovi-Yah

In Akkadian language, the name Ye-Hovi-Yah means, literally, "The power of attraction of Universal Love enters into a fertile union with the eternal presence of the Supreme Being."

The harmonic tonalities of Angel Ye-Hovi-Yah encourage those in this Angel's care to enter into an intimate alliance with the forces

COLOR HARMONIZATION

Yellow gold / Cobalt blue / Dark violet / Apple green

HARMONIC MATCHES FOR YE-HOVI-YAH'S PROTÉGÉS

- *The best matches for success in economic and practical achievements will be among men and women born January 29–February 2, under the care of Me-He-Ya-El.*
- *The best matches for recognition, fame, personal charisma, and social fulfillment will be among men and women born November 10–14, under the care of Mi-Ya-Ha-El.*
- *The best matches for romance, love, and artistic and intellectual achievements will be among men and women born September 16–20, under the care of Ani-Ya-El.*

of creation and perpetual evolution that emerge from the stable, eternal universal Spirit. With the help of Ye-Hovi-Yah, their thoughts align with the vibrant energies of the Spirit. Their creative dreams come to life and transform the world.

We have all seen a small child walking a large and powerful dog. Although the child is the only one of the pair who actually knows where they are going, the dog soon realizes that he or she is stronger. At that point, the dog begins to walk the child—and intellect is pulled along by power. So it is with those born into the care of Angel Ye-Hovi-Yah. Late August babies have been entrusted with great creative and transformative powers that they must learn to control—through force of will and awareness of purpose—in order to achieve their potential.

There is a great deal to be said for going with the flow when the flow in question is the current of celestial wisdom that carries us to our destinies. We are bathed in grace, open to serendipitous fortune. Consequently, when those close to Ye-Hovi-Yah apply their will and awareness in conformity with the divine law of love, they are provided by their loving guardian with fecundity and fertility. They are able to transform the environment, move minds and mountains, accomplish miracles, and even create masterworks that defy logic or reason. Under the influence of this inspiring Angel, men and women develop the power to create, transform, and intervene, and that power propels them to the highest positions of leadership in their personal, professional, or social spheres.

Of course, achievement has its rewards—and its responsibilities. Those under the protection of Angel Ye-Hovi-Yah are given the means to fulfill their potential, but they are also encouraged to magnify the inner light of their awareness in order to ensure the purity of their undertakings. The enlightened friends of Ye-Hovi-Yah always align their actions with the highest truths. In exchange, Ye-Hovi-Yah provides them with the ability to give their dreams roots, to make sure the life-giving sap circulates freely from root to bud, and to do everything necessary to reap an abundant harvest. Indeed, if they enlighten themselves with Ye-Hovi-Yah's essential principles and refuse to settle for illusions and half-truths, those under the protection of this bountiful Angel will see obstacles disappear before their eyes, knots untie in their own hands, and seemingly impenetrable walls open to them.

If, on the other hand, those under the care of Angel Ye-Hovi-Yah succumb to temptation and use their powers for selfish gain, the result will not be so rosy. Men and women who are in kinship with Ye-Hovi-Yah reach the top of their creative ability. Surrounded by their great achievements, admired by many followers, they can begin to fall in love with their own words. Blinded by their brilliant achievements in this world, they can forget the divine sources of their power. When they do—when their actions are based, not on celestial guidance, but on satisfaction in the here and now—their actions can bring catastrophic results. Even when these consequences are short-lived, they can have widespread effects.

Ye-Hovi-Yah richly rewards the pure of heart. Surely, Mother Teresa and spiritual seeker Richard Gere have discovered this Angel's profound power. When in sincere and harmonious resonance with Angel Ye-Hovi-Yah, men and women are able to preserve the sacred union between human willpower and the universal spirit and wield the power that can transform the world. Those who sincerely desire to be guided by the Verb of Creation and invoke the protection of this Angel must, in return, conduct their lives according to the principles of authenticity, purity, and truth. Their efforts will be richly rewarded with successful undertakings, true love, and loyal friendships.

Angel LE-HA-HI-YAH

SEPTEMBER I–5

Develops intuition. Increases the ability to link, unite, and converge. Amplifies intellectual and emotional flexibility. Enlightens and clarifies thoughts and goals. Encourages helping others on the way to change and evolution.

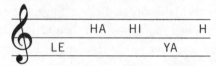

PHONETIC PRONUNCIATION

Le as in Lee
Ha as in Habit
Hi as in History
Ya as in Yard
H Vocalize the final H as a soft exhalation

UNIVERSAL RESONANCE OF THE ANGEL'S NAME

Le Dynamic learning. The ability to make mental links. Intellectual elevation. An evolving, ascending movement of the mind. Lucidity and enlightenment.

Ha Spiritual life force. Presence of universal love and the all-permeating spirit. Divine call, divine connection.

Hi Spiritual life force. Presence of universal love and the all-permeating spirit. Divine call, divine connection.

Yah Final vibration of the Angel's name. Receptivity and reflectivity. The presence of the deity; the abundance of the being.

Guardian Angel Le-Ha-Hi-Yah

In Akkadian language, the name Le-Ha-Hi-Yah means, literally, "The awareness: knowledge moves forward enlightened by the breath of divine love."

The harmonic vibrations of Angel Le-Ha-Hi-Yah motivate men and women to seek out connections between beings and the things

NOTABLE PEOPLE BORN UNDER THE INFLUENCE OF LE-HA-HI-YAH

Arthur Koestler, writer and journalist

Charlie Sheen, actor

Darryl Zanuck, film executive and producer

Edgar Rice Burroughs, writer

Ferdinand Porsche, automotive designer

Henry Ford II, automotive entrepreneur

Jimmy Connors, tennis champion

Keanu Reeves, actor

Raquel Welch, actress

Richard C. Trench, clergyman and poet

Richard Wright, writer

Rocky Marciano, boxing champion

Rose McGowan, actress

Salma Hayek, actress

COLOR HARMONIZATION

Red / Yellow / Orange / Dark gray / Warm maroon / Touches of indigo blue

around them and to uncover meeting points, fruitful convergences, causes and effects, and unifying structures.

The quick-thinking men and women in harmony with Angel Le-Ha-Hi-Yah would best be illustrated with a lightbulb over their heads. That's because this inspiring Angel bestows upon those in her/his care the ability to acquire knowledge by intuitive bursts and sudden transcendent thoughts that lead to breakthrough discoveries in spiritual, scientific, or practical areas. With the help of Angel Le-Ha-Hi-Yah, men and women are able to find the common points that bring seemingly disparate elements together. They can also act as the intellectual trailblazers who point out to the rest of us the shortcuts leading to new and exciting conclusions. Endowed with quick minds that can produce enlightening syntheses, these men and women can also be excellent guides in periods of transition. Having received the benefit of their guardian's help, they know how to help others go through periods of crisis, overcome emotional and intellectual inhibitions, and neutralize their fear of change.

Faced with a seemingly complex situation, or confronted with the density and intricacy of the natural and physical world, those under the protection of Angel Le-Ha-Hi-Yah elevate their thoughts, like a kite, into the flow of universal transparency, where everything is clear, possible, flowing from oneness. Then, from the intelligence that is communicated to them from above, they are able to see the simple pattern that makes up the complexities of the world below. For them and everyone who has been touched by the brilliance of Angel Le-Ha-Hi-Yah, imagination transcends the limits of fixed logic, intuitive knowledge elevates the mind, and thoughts and emotions are fluid and always renewed.

If you have made a connection with Angel Le-Ha-Hi-Yah, you draw your intellectual abilities from the source of the inexhaustible energy of the divine love. Consequently, you have a tendency to think first before acting. This is because, to you, the richest and most productive work is achieved by elevating the intellect and maintaining its fluidity.

Depending on your personal circumstances, you and everyone under the protection of Angel Le-Ha-Hi-Yah may excel in occupations related to teaching, particularly if your position does not limit

HARMONIC MATCHES FOR LE-HA-HI-YAH'S PROTÉGÉS

- *The best matches for success in economic and practical achievements will be among men and women born January 24–28, under the care of Ânava-El.*
- *The best matches for recognition, fame, personal charisma, and social fulfillment will be among men and women born November 5–9, under the care of Â-Sali-Yah.*
- *The best matches for romance, love, and artistic and intellectual achievements will be among men and women born September 21–25, under the care of Ha-Âmi-Yah.*

your freedom of thought and expression. Le-Ha-Hi-Yah's friends are endowed with a gift for analyzing and synthesizing—and that talent carries with it a strong impact. By invoking Angel Le-Ha-Hi-Yah, you will be able to uncover the unifying similarities in everyone and everything around you and propose mutually productive solutions to the difficulties that separate people. This means that you could have a positive effect on interethnic and intercultural relations and become a much-needed unifying force in today's world.

By reinforcing your conscious spiritual resonance with the vibrating harmonies of Angel Le-Ha-Hi-Yah, you could excel in positions of mediation, arbitration, and conciliation, whether you act as peacemaker in professional or personal arenas. You could aspire to become a diplomat, judge, ecumenical delegate, marriage or family counselor, language teacher, psychologist, or school principal. You could also become a particularly positive and inspiring parent, one who is able to overcome any sibling rivalry to create a remarkably warm and harmonious home life. Thanks to your ability to understand without judging and to accept differences without prejudice, you and all of those under the protection of Angel Le-Ha-Hi-Yah could rise to powerful positions, becoming beloved leaders who unite instead of divide and projecting light upon all so that no one is left in the shadows.

But before you find a pedestal to climb on, consider this: despite, or perhaps because of, the fluidity of your intellect and your brilliant intuitions, you may find it difficult to apply certain practical and necessary strategies in your own life. Specifically, you may find it difficult to manage your own material and economic affairs. In those instances, it is best to invoke the grace of Angel Le-Ha-Hi-Yah. In return for your constant and generous work for the benefit of others, your loving guardian will see to it that you receive abundant financial and emotional help, material and intellectual gifts, and feelings of love and friendship.

Angel Le-Ha-Hi-Yah connects those close to him/her with the harmonizing energies of universal love. With the help of this unifying Angel, these men and women are able to progress quickly toward a goal, bypass the usual stages of development, never miss the best opportunities, and follow their creative impulses. By amplifying their empathy with Angel Le-Ha-Hi-Yah, these men and women are able, if they have the desire to do so, to seek out notoriety and reach fame in whatever intellectual and artistic fields they choose.

If circumstances put them at the center of disputes, discords, and hostile situations, those under the protection of Angel Le-Ha-Hi-Yah may see their vital energies strongly diminished, and they may encounter periods of discouragement and psychological depression. It is then that they must, through invocation, reinforce their connection with their celestial guide. He/she will elevate their minds toward the ultimate source of all unions and illuminate their souls with the light of universal consciousness.

INVOCATION

O Angel Le-Ha-Hi-Yah,
I invoke you,
Help me.
O Le-Ha-Hi-Yah,
You condense hours,
Expand spaces,
You ally all hymns,
And the harmony of your presence
Revives the song of my soul.
O Angel Le-Ha-Hi-Yah,
Take me now,
Instantly
To the eternal light.

Angel CHAVA-QUI-YAH
SEPTEMBER 6–10

Increases perception and observation. Helps identify the sources of wealth. Activates a capacity for calculation and evaluation. Amplifies the spreading of goods and ideas. Bestows generosity and tolerance.

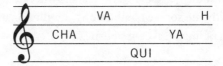

PHONETIC PRONUNCIATION

Cha as in Javier (Spanish) or Ach (German)
Va as in Value
Qui as in Quit
Ya as in Yard
H Vocalize the final H as a soft exhalation

UNIVERSAL RESONANCE OF THE ANGEL'S NAME

Cha Cohesive substance that unifies the universe. Capability, analysis; breaking down, then reassembling components to a new coherence.

Va Vitalizing factor. Fruitfulness and productivity. Catalyst of variety, vitality, verity, will, and vigor.

Qui The ability to define, structure, and configure; knowledge of the principles of calculation, evaluation, quantification. Equilibrium and balance. Multiplication of natural riches and material abundance. Cosmic consciousness.

Yah Final vibration of the Angel's name. Receptivity and reflectivity. The presence of the deity; the abundance of the being.

NOTABLE PEOPLE BORN UNDER THE INFLUENCE OF CHAVA-QUI-YAH

Adam Sandler, comedian and actor

Angie Everhart, actress

Antonín Dvořák, composer

Arnold Palmer, golf champion

Billy Preston, musician

Cardinal de Richelieu, first minister of France

Elia Kazan, film director

J. P. Morgan, financier

Jane Adams, actress

Karl Lagerfeld, fashion designer

Leo Tolstoy, writer

Marquis de Lafayette, French general and statesman

Michael Keaton, actor

Queen Elizabeth I, queen of England

Richard the Lion Hearted, king of England

COLOR HARMONIZATION

Dark gray / Green-yellow / Rust / Rusty brown / Indigo

Guardian Angel Chava-Qui-Yah

In Akkadian language, the name Chava-Qui-Yah means, literally, "The empirical comprehensive intelligence fertilizes the production of wealth in the visible and physical world."

The harmonic vibrations of Angel Chava-Qui-Yah give those in this generous Angel's care great powers of perception and observation. Stimulated by Angel Chava-Qui-Yah, these men and women take in all of the vivid details of their world and rapidly comprehend the complexities of the relationships around them. With the help of Chava-Qui-Yah, who magnifies the power of the mind, people's perceptions can become so astute that they understand not only details but also the subtle movements that shape the details. As with the people who see not only the current in the river but also the placement of the bedrock that quickens or turns the current, the sharp eyes of those close to Chava-Qui-Yah perceive movement in stillness and uncover differences in what is seemingly similar.

When in harmony with Angel Chava-Qui-Yah, those born between September 6 and 10 live in a state of heightened consciousness. Their minds drop veils and remove masks, revealing dimensions that escape most of us. Thanks to this receptive Angel, those in her/his care can draw from the creative source, gather inspiration from the world's rich diversity, and create new and exciting vehicles for their imaginative, innovative ideas.

If you are close to Chava-Qui-Yah, you may use your keen powers of observation as the head of a pharmaceutical laboratory, a consultant for a company that produces wealth and goods, the publisher of books related to new discoveries, a research director of a university, a participant in a think tank, or a trend analyst in the financial or high technology sector or intelligence service.

With the assistance of Angel Chava-Qui-Yah, who bestows a talent for evaluation and calculation, you can become a quick and level-headed organizer—or reorganizer. A person who can establish at a glance the "what" (the nature of things), the "how many" (quantity) and the "how much" (proportion) required in any situation, you can quickly calculate the "how." That means you can suggest just the right solution to implement, whether it is distributing rewards, organizing the production of a new product, delegating

HARMONIC MATCHES FOR CHAVA-QUI-YAH'S PROTÉGÉS

- *The best matches for success in economic and practical achievements will be among men and women born January 19–23, under the care of Ye-He-Ha-El.*
- *The best matches for recognition, fame, personal charisma, and social fulfillment will be among men and women born October 31–November 4, under the care of Âri-Ya-El.*
- *The best matches for romance, love, and artistic and intellectual achievements will be among men and women born September 26–30, under the care of Re-Ha-Â-El.*

tasks within a professional team or a family, or preparing a military or scientific expedition.

But you're not just a problem solver for others; you can even troubleshoot in your own life! The harmonic vibrations of Angel Chava-Qui-Yah help you to bypass psychological obstacles like denial. Because you are so open-minded, you are free to discover veiled truths, hidden motives, and shadow beliefs. Once they are revealed, you are able to share the truth with others with such charm and honesty that others can't help but become fans. In fact, Angel Chava-Qui-Yah provides you with a constant and devoted entourage of people who will help you fight for your favorite causes or carry out your plans.

If circumstances allow, you and all those under the protection of Angel Chava-Qui-Yah may successfully use your mental abilities to resolve conflicts, disputes, and controversies. Your mediation technique—overcoming sticky problems by affirming each party's original point of view—is invariably a source of lasting harmony, even when the dispute has been acrimonious. This technique was one of the secrets to the success of the Marquis de Lafayette, the great eighteenth-century French general and statesman.

The Angel Chava-Qui-Yah brings the sensorial and spiritual resources of the universe to the awareness of those he/she loves. Through this Angel's help, men and women can cultivate the qualities of generosity and tolerance and can, with the enthusiastic help of their loyal friends, reach positions of importance and renown. Wherever their dreams lead them, Angel Chava-Qui-Yah will always be at their side, constantly refining their awareness until, in a burst of joy, the wonderful details of the universe are illuminated in the eternal light of the infinite creation.

Angel MENA-DA-EL

SEPTEMBER 11–15

Increases the power of achievement. Develops the drive for perfection. Helps to understand what is important and essential. Allows for easy transition from one world to another. Stimulates capacities for transaction and transition. Provides the gift for discovery and revelation.

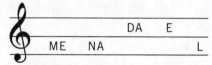

PHONETIC PRONUNCIATION

Me as in Maiden
Na as in Natural
Da as in Darling
El as in Elevation

UNIVERSAL RESONANCE OF THE ANGEL'S NAME

Me The matrix. The model upon which creation is based. Manifestation in the material world. Loving maternal protection.

Na Nucleus, center, the essential; identity, individuality. Penetration to the central core of every reality. Negation and rejection of superficial and perverse realities.

Da Revelation, discovery, challenge. Detachment from the center. Passage from one world to another. Conscious knowledge of distances, contrasts, and differences.

El Ending vibration of the Angel's name. Principle of excellence. Chosen; elite. Elevating force. Source of perpetual transformation and evolution.

COLOR HARMONIZATION

Forest green / Brown / Volcanic gray / Sparks of yellow and orange / Burgundy red

HARMONIC MATCHES FOR
MENA-DA-EL'S PROTÉGÉS

- *The best matches for success in economic and practical achievements will be among men and women born January 14–18, under the care of Vama-Ba-El.*

- *The best matches for recognition, fame, personal charisma, and social fulfillment will be among men and women born October 26–30, under the care of Se-Ali-Yah.*

- *The best matches for romance, love, and artistic and intellectual achievements will be among men and women born October 1–5, under the care of Ye-Yaza-El.*

Guardian Angel Mena-Da-El

In Akkadian language, the name Mena-Da-El means, literally, "What comes through the door of the Angelic dimension into our everyday world." Or, "From the matrix that envelops and nourishes the nodules of the divine presence springs the source of dynamic discoveries."

Does practice make perfect? Perhaps not. Still, the men and women in the care of guardian Angel Mena-Da-El make a practice of seeking perfection—in their work, their relationships, and every aspect of their daily lives.

Angel Mena-Da-El enhances the likelihood that the men and women in her/his care will achieve. Like manna nourishing both the intellect and the physical body, Angel Mena-Da-El's influence sustains both their desire for knowledge and their need for attainment. This generous Angel simultaneously offers those under his/her protection a deep understanding of universal principles that define the world and a great drive toward action, creation, and achievement.

Indeed, many of the doers in Mena-Da-El's care appear to others as achievers. Like Margaret Sanger, Oliver Stone, and Olympic runner Michael Johnson, they are certainly people who successfully undertake ambitious projects. It is important to note they are also people who tend to take on daunting challenges. Consequently, because of the visible and tangible results of their work, these men and women emerge from anonymity, garner recognition, and become known as special and irreplaceable participants in their social, professional, and personal spheres.

Of course, they are also known as people who will not settle for a mediocre performance, a halfhearted try, or a less-than-stellar effort. Those under the protection of Angel Mena-Da-El have taken the attempt to reach perfection as their personal quest. Although such a stickler is hardly apt to fail, a perfectionist is not always helpful in a work or group environment. For one thing, perfection is not attained in a day, but projects are often on a tight schedule. Detail-oriented people can appear to be slow; frustrated co-workers can even consider them a drag on a department. A persnickety attitude toward perfection can also appear to be excessive or have an elitist quality.

With the help of Angel Mena-Da-El, those in her/his protection are able to identify, without any doubt, the vital centers of any situation, complex structure, or living entity. This uncanny ability to zero in on what makes an organization—or even a friend—tick guarantees that any action they take goes straight to the heart of a problem. And since those born between September 11 and 15 are also blessed with an innate understanding of the passage points—or energy lines—that link separate systems or languages, they often demonstrate a talent for devising solutions that can streamline an entire department or group or corporation.

Those under the protection of Angel Mena-Da-El can, when circumstances give them the opportunity to do so, travel easily from one country to another, from one cultural environment to another. For these people, distances and differences are not obstacles. By focusing on what all people share, they can always communicate their desires and ideas.

If you are in kinship with Mena-Da-El, you tend to view each of your goals as a mission. Whether you are self-directed and define your own objectives or whether you accept the direction of others, you take your missions seriously and always finish what you have undertaken. Although you tend to be discreet and shy away from publicity or acclaim, you are a natural and skilled diplomat who can smooth out the wrinkles in any construction project, military operation, or scientific, literary, or theological research program. In fact, with your guardian's help, you could make a career out of being an itinerant problem solver. The harmonic vibrations of Angel Mena-Da-El encourage you to intervene in difficult situations, dissolve obstacles, and implement improvement. But once the problem is solved, you move on to the next project. Your work, as they say, is done.

Of course, it's one thing when Superman flies from crisis to crisis and quite another when mere mortals attempt the same. Too many entries on your résumé can make you appear to be unstable, particularly when you are judged by the standards that include a respect for permanence and familiarity. However, Angel Mena-Da-El generously provides those who call on her/him with the courage to face up to many new situations. You will confront each new experience the way an author faces a blank page—with excitement, optimism, and a good deal of respect. You know that your loving guardian will provide you with the energy to do your job with determination and aplomb. You also know that if you suddenly feel you've gotten in over your head or if you have lost your sense of balance due to the loss of your job, capital, a friend, or a spouse, all you need to do is call upon Angel Mena-Da-El. With prayer and invocation, your protector will lead you to a positive outcome.

Remember: those who are in deep harmony with Angel Mena-Da-El vault the fences of space and time and reach the ultimate truth. Ensure that your actions in everyday life reflect the celestial spiritual models, and you'll be guided to your highest destiny.

Angel ANI-YA-EL

SEPTEMBER 16–20

Develops individual and personal awareness. Amplifies willpower. Increases the desire to go beyond ordinary limits. Promotes access to preeminent positions. Encourages transformation. Promotes loyal and long-lasting relationships.

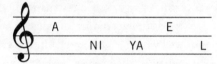

PHONETIC PRONUNCIATION

A as in Arrow
Ni as in Niche
Ya as in Yard
El as in Elevation

UNIVERSAL RESONANCE OF THE ANGEL'S NAME

A The original, ultimate energy. Before form, universal, infinite, unifying.

Ni Nucleus, center, the essential; identity, individuality. Penetration to the center of every reality. Negation and rejection of superficial and perverse realities.

Ya Mastery. Dexterity, expertise; human action aligned with divine universal principles.

El Ending vibration of the Angel's name. Principle of excellence; chosen; elite. Elevating force. Source of perpetual transformation and evolution.

Guardian Angel Ani-Ya-El

In Akkadian language, the name Ani-Ya-El means, literally, "I am the concentrated power of action, evolution, and elevation."

"Say what you mean and mean what you say." Communicating honestly, clearly, and deeply may be a challenge for some people, but for those who are inspired by the harmonic vibrations of Angel Ani-Ya-El the gift of meaningful gab comes naturally. While others

NOTABLE PEOPLE BORN UNDER THE INFLUENCE OF ANI-YA-EL

David Copperfield, *magician*
David Souter, *U.S. Supreme Court justice*
Edgar Mitchell, *astronaut*
Frankie Avalon, *pop singer*
Greta Garbo, *actress*
Hank Williams, *country singer*
Jennifer Tilly, *actress*
Jeremy Irons, *actor*
Lauren Bacall, *actress*
"Mama" Cass Elliot, *singer*
Peter Falk, *actor*
Robert B. Parker, *writer*
Sophia Loren, *actress*
Tommy Lee Jones, *actor*
Upton Sinclair, *writer*

COLOR HARMONIZATION

Yellow saffron / Turquoise / Ocher-orange / Brown-red / Apple green / Ebony black

HARMONIC MATCHES FOR ANI-YA-EL'S PROTÉGÉS

- *The best matches for success in economic and practical achievements will be among men and women born May 14–18, under the care of He-Ha-Â-Yah.*
- *The best matches for recognition, fame, personal charisma, and social fulfillment will be among men and women born August 2–6, under the care of Se-A-He-Yah.*
- *The best matches for romance, love, and artistic and intellectual achievements will be among men and women born August 27–31, under the care of Ye-Hovi-Yah.*

wallow in small talk, these people truly express *themselves*. Their personalities, their aspirations, even the strict quality standards they impose on everything they say and do—all comes through in their words and actions, gestures and expressions.

In brief: if you're looking to while away a blissfully uneventful, intellectually undemanding afternoon, it may be best if you look elsewhere for company. Indeed, the friends of Ani-Ya-El are not the lightweights of the world. Dynamic and intense, these are men and women with a powerful sense of self, a fascinatingly complex personality, and a profound understanding of what it means to be a unique person endowed with a robust and dauntless free will. Such people sometimes perceive themselves as being endowed with superior intellectual and spiritual powers that propel them to positions of authority or supremacy. They aren't wrong. Their strong egos prompt them to act in accord with only the highest standards. Their quest for excellence leads them, inevitably, to success.

Do those in kinship with Angel Ani-Ya-El sound like true individuals? They are. This remarkable guardian provides those in her/his care with a special awareness of individual uniqueness. Each of Ani-Ya-El's protégés understand that he or she is a separate entity, a complete being, a rich and powerful, indivisible and autonomous self. Consequently, those born between September 16 and 20 have a vivid awareness of their own power and no doubts about their ability to change the things and influence the beings around them.

In other peoples' eyes, those dear to Ani-Ya-El are portraits in courage. Angel Ani-Ya-El infuses in men and women the desire to go beyond the limits of fear and daring, to take on those tasks and projects that seem difficult or out of reach to others. This makes them natural competitors in all areas of life. These men and women don't need assertiveness training. They know very well how to assert themselves, thank you, and they put a good deal of effort into finding personal or social situations that allow them to experience challenges and surpass their previous goals. To them, daily life is a competition best viewed from the winner's podium.

If you are born under the protection of Angel Ani-Ya-El, you will excel in any endeavor that operates on the star system—that is, any business, profession, hobby, or lifestyle that glorifies personalities, rewards ability, and recognizes talent. While you and all those close to Ani-Ya-El are likely to garner success and fame in nearly any milieu, you may excel in such public forums as sports, industry, finance, art, sales, science, politics, medicine, communication, social services, or religion.

Those in the care of Angel Ani-Ya-El receive much, but they also give much in return. By calling upon your guardian, you may be blessed with the ability and strength to deeply transform the industry you work in, your neighborhood, or even the world. If you put your prodigious effort and stellar persona behind the right cause, you may produce results so remarkable that people will say that the world has changed because of you. What greater testimony could there be to your effort, your unselfishness, and your humanitarianism?

Of course, restraining a powerful ego is a bit like holding a tiger by the tail: allow it to slip from your grasp, and it can pose a danger to yourself and others. Left unchecked, your bold individuality and will to transform the world could turn you into an overly ambitious drag, with no humanizing doubts and no sense of humor. You may even become convinced that you have a privileged and intimate relationship with divine forces and become extremely arrogant, fanatically religious, tyrannical, or mad with power. It will help to remind yourself that Angel Ani-Ya-El has generously shared his/her courage with you so that you can be a powerful force for good on earth. Your generous guardian will continue to provide for you as long as you share the same altruistic goals.

The harmonic vibrations of Angel Ani-Ya-El encourage men and women to cultivate deep, long-lasting, committed, loyal, and faithful emotional relationships, both in love and friendship. When they reach maturity, these men and women are often invested with authority and trust based upon the image of competence they exude and the sense of security they spread to those around them. If they avoid arrogance and pride, Angel Ani-Ya-El will surely provide them with guidance (if and when they ask for it!) and lead them toward the source of the luminous rivers that have irrigated their minds, nourished their hearts, and refreshed their souls since the day of their birth.

Angel HA-ÂMI-YAH

SEPTEMBER 21–25

Increases the sharpness of senses and emotions. Amplifies feelings of love and friendship. Opens the pathways to the heart. Reinforces the sense of community and collective togetherness. Helps in discovering hidden riches and treasures.

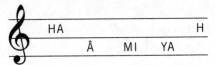

PHONETIC PRONUNCIATION

Ha as in Habit
Â as in Arrow, ending with a soft breath out
Mi as in Mirror
Ya as in Yard
H Vocalize the final H as a soft exhalation

UNIVERSAL RESONANCE OF THE ANGEL'S NAME

Ha Spiritual life force. Presence of universal love and the all-permeating spirit. Divine call, divine connection.

Â The origin of the sensory world; the foundation of human emotions and passions. Enhancement of visual senses and hearing acuity. Supersensitivity.

Mi The matrix; the model upon which creation is based. Manifestation in the material world. Loving maternal protection.

Yah Final vibration of the Angel's name. Receptivity and reflectivity. The presence of the deity; the abundance of the being.

Guardian Angel Ha-Âmi-Yah

In Akkadian language, the name Ha-Âmi-Yah means, literally, "The breath of the divine love is the source and origin of the matrix of manifestations."

NOTABLE PEOPLE BORN UNDER THE INFLUENCE OF HA-ÂMI-YAH

Bill Murray, *actor*

Bridgette Wilson, *actress*

Bruce Springsteen, *singer and musician*

Catherine Zeta-Jones, *actress*

Christopher Reeve, *actor*

F. Scott Fitzgerald, *writer*

Faith Hill, *singer*

H. G. Wells, *writer*

Heather Locklear, *actress*

Julio Iglesias, *singer*

Liam Gallagher, *singer*

Mark Hamill, *actor*

Michael Douglas, *actor*

Phil Hartman, *comedian and actor*

Ray Charles, *singer and musician*

Stephen King, *writer*

Will Smith, *actor and singer*

William Faulkner, *writer*

COLOR HARMONIZATION

Lavender / Violet / Pastel yellow / Ocher / Mustard / Peach-pink / Creamy white and golden beige

From a book one gets information; but from the heart one gets an education. This insightful sentiment is central to the men and women born under the protection of Angel Ha-Âmi-Yah, a sensitive guardian who endows those within his/her care with acute senses and an equally strong gift for mental perception. With the help of Ha-Âmi-Yah, those who have won this Angel's heart hear, see, and feel the depth of everything around them, successfully penetrate the mysteries of the world, and wrap themselves in the warm and luminous truths that illuminate the universe.

Although they are good and interested students, those in Angel Ha-Âmi-Yah's care are predisposed to learning—about life, humanity, and the universes beyond this one—through the heart rather than through intellect alone. Perceptive and curious, these sensitive souls draw their energies and conclusions directly from the currents of love that carry us all to our destiny. Trusting, self-assured, and intuitive, these unique men and women are attuned to the calls of love and willing to plunge headlong beneath the smooth surface of reality just so they can better understand the vital forces of attraction that link us all.

The harmonic vibrations of Angel Ha-Âmi-Yah promote the virtues of generosity and love of others, and those in kinship with Angel Ha-Âmi-Yah generously pour their emotional gifts on those around them: relatives, friends, community groups, nations. If this description conjures up images of an affable host and a merry, even somewhat boisterous party, then you're getting the right idea. Angel Ha-Âmi-Yah endows men and women with a strong sense of convivial friendliness, of collective good, of common interest and mutual benefit, and those values form the foundation of their emotions, thoughts, and actions. Because they perceive themselves empathetically, as part of a whole, these generous, gregarious personalities find it easy to share. They live to give back the emotional and material wealth they have acquired, which they believe has been generated by everyone and therefore belongs to everyone.

Those under the protection of Angel Ha-Âmi-Yah have a strong sense of social ecology; this is, they always view the interests of the human group as the primary foundation for all the benefits received by individuals. Depending on circumstances in their lives, these men and women may be instrumental at resolving crises and rivalries

HARMONIC MATCHES FOR HA-ÂMI-YAH'S PROTÉGÉS

- *The best matches for success in economic and practical achievements will be among men and women born May 9–13, under the care of Lo-Avi-Yah.*
- *The best matches for recognition, fame, personal charisma, and social fulfillment will be among men and women born July 28–August 1, under the care of Yeratha-El.*
- *The best matches for romance, love, and artistic and intellectual achievements will be among men and women born September 1–5, under the care of Le-Ha-Hi-Yah.*

within families, groups, or societies, not through judgment or decree (these are not Solomons who create resolution with a sword!) but through honest and friendly arbitration.

The best team makers are not managers or bureaucrats but active, involved members of the team. These special men and women are able to succeed in large-scale social, national, or even international projects, because their perception of the common good has no limit. True believers in the community of the human family, they see all children in each child, all women in each woman, and all oppressed people in a single slave. With such an enlightened vision, they are able to take on great human causes, often with revolutionary results. With the help of Angel Ha-Âmi-Yah, these men and women are also able to gather each person's resources and ideas for the benefit of all.

If your birthday falls between September 21 and 25, you may be the galvanizing point around which other politically and socially minded people gather. By invoking Angel Ha-Âmi-Yah, you can become a true peacemaker, diminishing rivalries between seeming opposites—men and women, spirit and matter, humans and nature, leaders and followers, individuals and nations, nations and world-wide planetary interests—and unifying all forces for the common good.

And how will you recognize the common good? If you do not give in to simplistic selfishness, Angel Ha-Âmi-Yah will point the way, just as he/she did for Bruce Springsteen, whose songs continue to inspire philanthropic and political action, or for Christopher Reeve, a powerful spokesman for spinal cord injury research, and for countless others whose paths are illuminated by this luminous Angel.

Angel Ha-Âmi-Yah promotes, in those under this Angel's protection and in those who invoke him/her, the love of others and of the world that unites them. Ha-Âmi-Yah encourages them to explore the unexplored areas of matter, of nature, and of the mind and helps them perceive the unlimited resources to be eternally shared with all of their human brothers and sisters.

Angel RE-HA-Â-EL

SEPTEMBER 26–30

Provides visionary power. Stimulates ambitious ideas and actions. Leads to spiritual elevation. Encourages authentic simple relationships. Provides the necessary push for carrying out great projects.

PHONETIC PRONUNCIATION

Re as in Regal

Ha as in Habit

Â as in Arrow, ending with a soft breath out

El as in Elevation

UNIVERSAL RESONANCE OF THE ANGEL'S NAME

Re Rotation, return, renewal; the natural cycles of existence. Radiance. Charisma. Inner vision and foresight on a universal scale. Princely leadership.

Ha Spiritual life force. Presence of universal love and the all-permeating spirit. Divine call, divine connection.

Â The origin of the sensory world; the foundation of human emotions and passions. Enhancement of visual senses and hearing acuity. Supersensitivity.

El Ending vibration of the Angel's name. Principle of excellence; chosen; elite. Elevating force. Source of perpetual transformation and evolution.

Guardian Angel Re-Ha-Â-El

In Akkadian language, the name Re-Ha-Â-El means, literally, "The radiating spirit of love is the source of the evolutionary forces."

Thanks to the qualities and talents provided by the harmonic vibrations of Angel Re-Ha-Â-El, men and women whose birthdays

COLOR HARMONIZATION

Golden pastels / Pastel blues / Pale lavender-rose / Pastel greens / Pale yellows and very light orange

HARMONIC MATCHES FOR RE-HA-Â-EL'S PROTÉGÉS

- *The best matches for success in economic and practical achievements will be among men and women born May 4–8, under the care of Aladi-Yah.*
- *The best matches for recognition, fame, personal charisma, and social fulfillment will be among men and women born July 23–27, under the care of He-A-A-Yah.*
- *The best matches for romance, love, and artistic and intellectual achievements will be among men and women born September 6–10, under the care of Chava-Qui-Yah.*

fall between September 26 and 30 are able to successfully undertake vast long-term projects and ambitious plans with clear visions of the future. Angel Re-Ha-Â-El enhances inner vision, activates and purifies emotions, reinforces the sharpness of all the senses, and encourages those under her/his protection in their search for a deep understanding of the world around them. With the help of Angel Re-Ha-Â-El, those in his/her care apprehend every situation that arises in their lives, their society, and their social world. Those in Re-Ha-Â-El's care are inspired to undertake a lifelong search for the basic and primary truths that turn the world. Discerning and swift, these men and women are the first to dismiss those half truths that only serve to reassure timid and lazy minds.

Of course, there is no minimum mileage requirement on a search for truth. It can take one no further than the book on one's lap, or it can transport seekers beyond the limits of their wildest dreams. Angel Re-Ha-Â-El endows those under his/her protection with a powerful breadth of life, which encourages them to widen their intellectual perspectives, embrace vast horizons, and go beyond the bounds of time while at the same time reinforcing their abilities to understand realities that, hardly visible today, will emerge as determining factors for events in the future. When under the guidance of Angel Re-Ha-Â-El, these men and women perceive the movements that orchestrate the world, experience the successive cosmic inhalations and exhalations, and understand the cycles of contraction and expansion.

If you are a protégé of this exhilarating Angel, you feel happiest where the air is pure and invigorating. You also like to breathe deeply and freely in the figurative sense, preferring to roam—physically, intellectually, or spiritually—where the spirit moves you. In your professional or private occupations, you always look for ways to get things done by the most direct means, with simplicity, without manipulation, in full light, and with rectitude. Depending on your personal circumstances, you may put your celestially endowed abilities to work for you in the field of sports, health counseling, project development, conflict resolution, or financial or economic expansion. You may even become a psychological, sociological, or spiritual source of inspiration for those who are embarking on a search for truth of their own.

Because those inspired by Angel Re-Ha-Â-El are not inclined to act directly and personally, those under this guardian's influence are often integrated in the social world at the request of others who appreciate their flawless integrity and talents as predictors of the future. This means that, whether you planned such a career or not, you may find yourself in demand as a research consultant or trend analyst within a social or political institution, a large commercial company, or a research center. Nevertheless, the pursuit of personal wealth and material goods will always be secondary to your intellectual and spiritual achievements. Through your kinship with your guardian, you have come to understand that what you do for others—whether those in your family or in your community—will almost always bring you economic and personal comfort.

Those under the protection of Angel Re-Ha-Â-El sincerely aspire to a communal life dictated by clarity, simplicity, simple love, and honesty. When they are temporarily stumped by a complex question or situation, they look to history. By studying the way the progressive dreams of the past were made real, they can chart a thoughtful and broad-minded course for the future.

By the grace of Angel Re-Ha-Â-El, men and women do not fear the devastating forces of ignorance, the withering of the heart, or the stagnation of hope, because, when they call on Angel Re-Ha-Â-El, a divine life breath stirs their vision, inflames their love, and elevates, infinitely, their spirit.

Angel YE-YAZA-EL

OCTOBER 1–5

Provides the ability to act and react quickly. Increases mental and physical energy. Clarifies intents and enlightens goals. Amplifies intellectual agility and manual dexterity. Promotes spectacular and heroic actions.

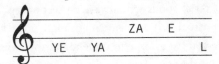

PHONETIC PRONUNCIATION

Ye as in Yes
Ya as in Yard
Za as in Zap
El as in Elevation

UNIVERSAL RESONANCE OF THE ANGEL'S NAME

Ye Mastery. Dexterity, expertise; human action aligned with divine universal principles.

Ya Mastery. Dexterity, expertise; human action aligned with divine universal principles.

Za The seed of life; the energy that bestows vitality and nourishment. Light of life. Sexual energy. High velocity. Power of simultaneity and instantaneity. Zen powers.

El Ending vibration of the Angel's name. Principle of excellence; chosen; elite. Elevating force. Source of perpetual transformation and evolution.

Guardian Angel Ye-Yaza-El

In Akkadian language, the name Ye-Yaza-El means, literally, "The power of the divine Creator enters into symbiosis with the operating power of her/his creations and undulates perpetually across the universal space at a dazzling speed."

For the men and women who welcome the harmonic influence

NOTABLE PEOPLE BORN UNDER THE INFLUENCE OF YE-YAZA-EL

Alicia Silverstone, actress

Charlton Heston, actor

Donna Karan, fashion designer

Gore Vidal, writer

Graham Greene, writer

Groucho Marx, comic and actor

Jackie Collins, writer

Jimmy Carter, former U.S. president

Julie Andrews, actress and singer

Kate Winslet, actress

Mahatma Gandhi, Indian reformer and leader

Mark McGuire, baseball player

Robert Kieffer, gymnast

Susan Sarandon, actress

William Rehnquist, U.S. Supreme Court justice

COLOR HARMONIZATION

Red / Creamy white / Brown / Navy blue / Dark green / Yellow-ocher of Angel Ye-Yaza-El, life can seem like a feast-or-famine proposition. They experience intense periods of activity followed by long periods of inactivity. However, because these individuals act fast, they accomplish, resolve, achieve, and transform a great deal in a remarkably short time. Those close to them, their friends and colleagues, are often relieved to see them stop for a while, fearing that such intensity might deplete them.

Wait—what was that blur? Chances are, it was a protégé of Angel Ye-Yaza-El. These dazzlingly efficient men and women act as fast as they think. In fact, they move so quickly that their activities are likely to blur. They are able to complete several actions in what looks to other people like one simple movement. Although it isn't always easy for others to keep track of what these busy people are doing, the result is so clear and immediate that others would swear that the friends of Ye-Yaza-El always go straight to the end result without any interim steps. The truth is that Angel Ye-Yaza-El encourages pauses. However, his/her protégés are so adept and their execution so dazzling that they appear to be engaging in sleight of hand. Interestingly, the influence of Angel Ye-Yaza-El is well represented by the actions of a Zen master, who can sit for hours, days, even years, and then, in one single, fluid movement, pick up a bow and arrow, close his eyes, pull back the string, listen for the impact of the arrow on its target, bow to the universe, then sit down to resume his meditation.

If you have developed a relationship with Angel Ye-Yaza-El, you may have a gift for manual dexterity or intellectual agility that is noticed by others. Indeed, this ability could even lead you to public notoriety. A skillful magician, no matter what the situation, you are able to pull the rabbit out of the hat—and even perform a few tricks to further impress your friends and colleagues. If you try your agile hand at another career, you may find success in such fields as arts and crafts or industrial art or in occupations that require a talent for quick, pithy writing, such as journalism or speech writing.

The harmonic vibrations of Angel Ye-Yaza-El encourage vast and ample detours in life, with no limits in time and space. These side trips allow you to indulge in analogical thinking and unexpected experiences. Depending upon your personal circumstances, you may use these time-outs to develop the skills necessary to

HARMONIC MATCHES FOR YE-YAZA-EL'S PROTÉGÉS

- The best matches for success in economic and practical achievements will be among men and women born April 29–May 3, under the care of Hazi-Ya-El.
- The best matches for recognition, fame, personal charisma, and social fulfillment will be among men and women born July 18–22, under the care of Nith-Ha-Yah.
- The best matches for romance, love, and artistic and intellectual achievements will be among men and women born September 11–15, under the care of Mena-Da-El

becoming authors of great discoveries in physics, biology, or high technology or, more specifically, in sectors related to communications and wave-related phenomena.

Be aware: you and all those in the care of Ye-Yaza-El are extremely good at taking shortcuts to achieve what you want. You may come to feel distanced, cut off, or even bored by a world that sometimes moves at the speed of a snail. In the long term, you may even come to believe that your slower-functioning colleagues are not worthy of your attention. This may lead you to develop a misanthropic, isolated, dark, and disconnected character. Remember that when you allow yourself to become carried away by your own brilliance, you make the mistake of ignoring the true origins of your talents. Cut off from their source, your talents gradually diminish, and you will be guided only by your feelings of superiority. When that happens, you will be like an illusionist who sets out to trick others but in the end only deceives the self.

By invoking Angel Ye-Yaza-El, you can recapture your agility and dexterity, your ability to act, achieve, and discover beyond the obstacles of space and time. Most of all, you will be directed back to the enlightened path from which you have strayed and will use the gifts provided by Angel Ye-Yaza-El to elevate humankind as well as yourself.

Angel HE-HE-HA-EL

OCTOBER 6–10

Stimulates and enriches inner life. Provides harmony of the soul. Opens the way to serenity and peace. Enables intimate relationships and love. Helps overcome conflicts.

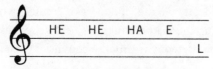

HE HE HA E L

PHONETIC PRONUNCIATION

He as in Heritage
He as in Heritage
Ha as in Habit
El as in Elevation

UNIVERSAL RESONANCE OF THE ANGEL'S NAME

He Spiritual life force. Presence of universal love and the all-permeating spirit. Divine call, divine connection.

He Spiritual life force. Presence of universal love and the all-permeating spirit. Divine call, divine connection.

Ha Spiritual life force. Presence of universal love and the all-permeating spirit. Divine call, divine connection.

El Ending vibration of the Angel's name. Principle of excellence; chosen; elite. Elevating force. Source of perpetual transformation and evolution.

Guardian Angel He-He-Ha-El

In Akkadian, the name He-He-Ha-El means, literally, "Love, unity, and the irresistible attraction of the spiritual and originating life force form the unique source of all evolving movements."

There's no place like home, especially for those peace-loving men and women born between October 6 and 10. Surrounded by

Archbishop Desmond Tutu, Nobel Peace Prize winner
Frank Herbert, writer
Giuseppe Verdi, composer
Helen Wills Moody, tennis champion
Jackson Browne, musician
Jesse Jackson, religious and political leader
Jody Williams, Nobel Peace Prize winner
John Lennon, musician
Martina Navratilova, tennis champion
Matt Damon, actor
Maya Lin, designer of the Vietnam Veterans' War Memorial
Niels Bohr, Nobel Prize winner in physics
Orville Moody, professional golfer
Sigourney Weaver, actress
Thelonious Monk, jazz musician
Thor Heyerdahl, explorer and anthropologist

COLOR HARMONIZATION

Warm coral / Ocher-orange / Creamy white / Straw yellow / Blue veiling / Soft green like emerging spring grass

the harmonic vibrations of Angel He-He-Ha-El, these fortunate souls have a unique opportunity to create an inner life that is filled with love, simplicity, authenticity, and intense joy. Make no mistake: what they are offered by their guardian are the seeds of consciousness, the same seeds that for monks, cloistered clerics, ascetics, and visionaries take root within the silence of the soul. The friends of He-He-Ha-El do not abandon their normal social and professional lives. They are offered the option of blooming where they are planted, creating and maintaining the necessary conditions for solitude, peace, and harmony within the bounds of what they consider to be real life.

So where are we likely to find these enlightened souls? Anywhere they can think clearly, live modestly, and enjoy the simple riches of life. When in harmony with Angel He-He-Ha-El, men and women avoid, as much as possible, restless and noisy social situations, and they reduce to a strict minimum their search for status, prestige, and money. Whatever activities they choose, privately or professionally, must be linked to a spiritual source, must pave the way for feelings of togetherness, and, most of all, must provide a buffer against the world of pretense. If these people can maintain harmony within their souls, simplify their desires, and enlighten their minds until their thoughts become clear as crystal, they will receive the riches of love, friendship, and family warmth and an abundance of financial stability.

Wouldn't these extroverted introverts really rather be alone? Certainly, they are able to weather long periods of relative isolation. Explorer Thor Heyerdahl spent months on the sea; Desmond Tutu was often ostracized by his government for his antiapartheid rhetoric, and even John Lennon retreated from his fame. Yet, though these quiet types draw strength and knowledge from silence, their need for isolation is balanced by their deep love for all the beings with whom they share the universe. Free from prejudice, secure in the knowledge that every person, creature, and thing contributes equally to the majesty of the universe, these are people who believe deeply in Jesse Jackson's "beautiful mosaic."

If you were born under the protection of Angel He-He-Ha-El, you will feel most successful when you are allowed to express your gift for bringing people together and creating links and alliances for the common good. But don't expect to be a successful mediator if it means stretching the facts or bringing people together under false pretenses. Angel He-He-Ha-El encourages those under her/his protection not to compromise the truth. Unless you are guided by the highest spiritual and ethical principles, the unions you form will not endure and will not profit you or anyone else.

Although you are a welcome addition to any party or professional group—who wouldn't want a peacemaker in residence, just in case?—you and all those born under the protection of Angel He-He-Ha-El prefer one-on-one or small-group relationships that allow for authentic intellectual exchanges. You may even seek out professional and social liaisons that limit your contact with crowds and that do not require you to be in direct competition with others or devise strategies to weaken your rivals. The harmonic vibrations of Angel He-He-Ha-El encourage in those that accept them a true longing for unity and universal love. These values can become frayed in the dog-eat-dog world.

Depending on your personal circumstances and potential, you and your sisters and brothers in kinship with He-He-Ha-El may succeed in creating literary works, such as poetry, philosophical meditation, or ethical and theological theories; you may also compose music or create sculpture, painting, architecture, or other art forms. You could even become adept at the performing or physical arts such as martial arts, archery, or dance. But before you buy those tap shoes, please note: your success in the arts is contingent upon your openness to the guidance of peace and harmony. Unless you separate your aspirations from the constraints of intense competition, unless you are motivated by something other than fashion, trends, or an avant-garde posture, your success will be short-lived. In other areas of professional practice, such as law or medicine, your success is assured as long as you propagate a sense of equity for all and promote the unifying aspects of caring for others. Your loving guardian does not provide prestige for prestige's sake.

In short, the harmonic vibrations of Angel He-He-Ha-El nourish the souls and hearts of men and women who, through their deep

HARMONIC MATCHES FOR HE-HE-HA-EL'S PROTÉGÉS

- *The best matches for success in economic and practical achievements will be among men and women born April 24–28, under the care of Ca-Hetha-El.*
- *The best matches for recognition, fame, personal charisma, and social fulfillment will be among men and women born August 22–26, under the care of Va-Sari-Yah.*
- *The best matches for romance, love, and artistic and intellectual achievements will be among men and women born August 7–11, under the care of Re-Yi-Ya-El.*

connection with the subtle energies of the universe, become the centers of attraction for the souls and hearts of others. Their enlightening thoughts, merged with those of their brothers, sisters, and friends, orbit the universe like a ball of fire carrying to celestial beings the message that humans, united under the eternal guidance of Angel He-He-Ha-El, long to reach the heavens and unite with the Angels.

Angel MI-YI-CA-EL

OCTOBER 11–15

Reinforces independence of character. Lightens the weight of everyday life. Encourages practical and prolific creative minds. Stimulates refinement of the mind. Provides qualities of coherence and coordination.

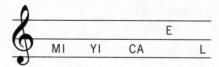

PHONETIC PRONUNCIATION

Mi as in Mirror
Yi as in Yield
Ca as in Car
El as in Elevation

UNIVERSAL RESONANCE OF THE ANGEL'S NAME

Mi The matrix; the model upon which creation is based. Manifestation in the material world. Loving maternal protection.

Yi Mastery. Dexterity, expertise; human action aligned with divine universal principles.

Ca The practical, physical, and material manifestation of ideas and thoughts. A solidifying, coalescing force within the fluid substances of the universe. Energies of cohesion and collusion, connivance, collaboration, cooperation. A force of strength and power.

El Ending vibration of the Angel's name. Principle of excellence; chosen; elite. Elevating force. Source of perpetual transformation and evolution.

Guardian Angel Mi-Yi-Ca-El

In Akkadian, the name Mi-Yi-Ca-El means, literally, "I am the mother spirit, creator of archetypal principles, from which come all of the beings that carry organized and organic life." Or "I am the

COLOR HARMONIZATION

Maroon / Rust / Black / Navy blue / Light gray / Spots of ocher

one who orders and oversees the living principles of generative and growing cohesion."

If there is a far-flung or twisting, turning spiritual path in the vicinity, those in kinship with Angel Mi-Yi-Ca-El will undoubtedly find it. If not, they will create it. That's because the exceptional men and women who unite harmoniously with this indulgent Angel strive to conduct their physical, psychological, and spiritual lives independently, without the constraints of restricting routines, dull conventions, and stifling traditions.

Angel Mi-Yi-Ca-El elevates those under her/his protection to the very source of all individualities, which is the origin of creation, the infinite generator of all things, great and small. Under Mi-Yi-Ca-El's friendly guidance, their minds can conceive the Shape of all shapes and make contact with the prepersonal model for all personalities. Then, with their celestial guardian's help, they can bring the uniqueness of each universal molecule into their lives, where it can enhance their personal being, liberate their souls, and free them from the enslavement of expectations and traditions.

Of course, individuality is a wonderful thing—as long as individuals are willing to own all the effects of their uniqueness. Strong and wise, secure and self-aware, those under the protection of Angel Mi-Yi-Ca-El are able to take full responsibility for their thoughts and actions. They are powerful leaders, discrete in their individualism, and yet they are sincere in their respect of others' unique identities. They value the freedom of others just as they value their own. For this reason, those who achieve resonance with this liberating Angel can often become the catalyst for social revolutions. Creative and intellectually free, they are capable of creating new models in such areas as science, technology, finance, applied arts, or mathematical or philosophical research. It is interesting to note that history books rarely record their contributions, however. These powerful innovators often abhor public notoriety, preferring to work behind the scenes, in groups, or even under the cover of pseudonyms!

The harmonic vibrations of Angel Mi-Yi-Ca-El endow those in this guide's care with the ability to handle numbers, make complex calculations, and precisely evaluate quantities. By quantifying numbers, they strengthen their appreciation of the particular identity of a person or a thing. And because their particular gifts encourage

HARMONIC MATCHES FOR MI-YI-CA-EL'S PROTÉGÉS

- *The best matches for success in economic and practical achievements will be among men and women born April 19–23, under the care of Acha-A-Yah.*
- *The best matches for recognition, fame, personal charisma, and social fulfillment will be among men and women born August 17–21, under the care of Le-Caba-El.*
- *The best matches for romance, love, and artistic and intellectual achievements will be among men and women born August 12–16, under the care of Ova-Ma-El.*

the building and distribution of wealth on a large scale, those who invoke Mi-Yi-Ca-El are often given the impetus to work in the economic sector, particularly in mass production and distribution. In fact, if circumstances allow, these men and women are able to create and put into place operational structures through which their successes can be reproduced, thus providing to the greatest number of people the capacity to generate wealth on their own.

If you are in perfect accord with the harmonic vibrations of Angel Mi-Yi-Ca-El, you are a peacemaker who seeks to create and reinforce the cohesion among all things and all beings. By becoming a propagator of communal wealth or bringing your message of unity to others, you ensure your own spiritual and material prosperity. If, on the other hand, you reject Mi-Yi-Ca-El's soft guidance out of pride, you could sink into the abyss of materialism.

Depending on the path you choose, you and all those under the protection of Angel Mi-Yi-Ca-El could become long-appreciated teachers, instructors who transform lives and inspire a following among your pupils. Angel Mi-Yi-Ca-El generously provides the ability to share, and often, those under his/her guidance make it their mission to bring knowledge to their brothers and sisters, thus freeing minds and quenching spiritual thirst.

Angel VAVALI-YAH

OCTOBER 16–20

Enriches sentimental and emotional life. Enhances fecundity and fertility. Increases physical strength. Stimulates intellectual vitality. Provides qualities allowing for regeneration and rebirth. Encourages spiritual growth.

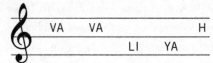

PHONETIC PRONUNCIATION

Va as in Varsity
Va as in Varsity
Li as in Ligament
Ya as in Yard
H Vocalize the final H as a soft exhalation

UNIVERSAL RESONANCE OF THE ANGEL'S NAME

Va Vitalizing factor. Fruitfulness and productivity. Catalyst of variety, vitality, verity, will, and vigor.

Va Vitalizing factor. Fruitfulness and productivity. Catalyst of variety, vitality, verity, will, and vigor.

Li Dynamic learning. The ability to make mental links. Intellectual elevation. An evolving, ascending movement of the mind. Lucidity and enlightenment.

Yah Final vibration of the Angel's name. Receptivity and reflectivity. The presence of the deity; the abundance of the being.

NOTABLE PEOPLE BORN UNDER THE INFLUENCE OF VAVALI-YAH

Angela Lansbury, actress

Arthur Miller, playwright

David Ben-Gurion, first prime minister of Israel

Eugene O'Neill, Nobel Prize winner in literature

Evander Holyfield, boxer

Günter Grass, Nobel Prize winner in literature

John Le Carré, writer

Margot Kidder, actress

Melina Mercouri, actress

Montgomery Clift, actor

Noah Webster, creator of Webster's Dictionary

Oscar Wilde, writer

Rita Hayworth, actress

Tim Robbins, actor

William O. Douglas, former U.S. Supreme Court justice

COLOR HARMONIZATION

White / Black / Red / Violet / Dark gray / Creamy yellow

Guardian Angel Vavali-Yah

In Akkadian, the name Vavali-Yah means, literally, "Love's union elevates itself into vivid, intense emotional energy, thus sublimating into waves of mental intellectual consciousness."

Angel Vavali-Yah encourages men and women to draw from the deepest emotional sources, to channel the vibrant energy they get there, and to elevate themselves to higher levels of thoughts and intellectual activities. Like a tree whose roots draw from the dark underground all of the vital elements that nourish its leafy branches and healthy buds, these grounded individuals maintain their connection to the fertilizing forces while they reach for the sky. When they are in harmony with their sustaining Angel, the friends of Vavali-Yah live life with passion, revel in their senses, and express, without reservation, the sheer joy of being alive.

Having a wedding or baby shower? Looking for someone to adopt your cat's unexpected offspring? Put the friends of Angel Vavali-Yah at the top of the list! To them, fertility is nothing short of a miracle. They marvel at it in all of its aspects—births, rebirths, replanting, seeding, coupling, meetings, love—and long to participate in any ritual that celebrates growth and expansion.

That being said, it will probably not surprise you to learn that these men and women enjoy a profound connection to nature. Sensitive, deep, and acutely appreciative of all life, these caring souls feel the subtle energy that bonds all living things, from the ants in the anthill to the potted plant on the windowsill. Through this intimate contact, they increase in their heart the flow of love that energizes the sap—the very lifeblood—connecting all children of the universe. Most of all, those in kinship with Vavali-Yah have a unique fondness for animals and other living things—and their pets, the pets of others, and even wild animals go out of their way to reciprocate. They are the Dr. Doolittles of their time.

Social environments and their restrictive rules rarely allow for direct expression of feelings that deeply stir the personalities of the men and women who are in harmony with Angel Vavali-Yah. Only during certain phases of their lives, or in specific circumstances, do these people feel they can open the floodgates and allow the huge waves of their love to flow freely. In fact, the sheer force of their feeling can be a bit daunting to less exuberant lovers. Timid types who ask them how they feel had better do so with their running shoes on. They'll make a beeline for the door as soon as they get their answer.

When people call on Angel Vavali-Yah, their physical, sensual, and sexual experiences are refined, without losing any of their original vigor, density, and energy. The harmonic vibrations of Angel

HARMONIC MATCHES FOR VAVALI-YAH'S PROTÉGÉS

- *The best matches for success in economic and practical achievements will be among men and women born April 14–18, under the care of Lela-Ha-El.*
- *The best matches for recognition, fame, personal charisma, and social fulfillment will be among men and women born August 12–16, under the care of Ova-Ma-El.*
- *The best matches for romance, love, and artistic and intellectual achievements will be among men and women born August 17–21, under the care of Le-Caba-El.*

Vavali-Yah open the energy channels through which passions flow. When these passions move through the mind, stimulating the clarity of consciousness and uncovering the secret dimensions of the world, those close to Vavali-Yah experience profound spiritual growth.

If you seek a relationship with your passionate guardian, you will discover many diverse opportunities to express your irrepressible love for life. Those close to Vavali-Yah always realize their most profound desires and transit with increasing joy from the periphery toward the center of the circle of life. If you wish to channel and use the regenerative powers that are your birthright, you need only to invoke your powerful guardian. A sincere request to Vavali-Yah will bring healing to your body, light to your obscure feelings, facility to your thoughts, and clarity to your vision.

With the help of Angel Vavali-Yah, men and women follow their passions, wherever they lead. Zealous and caring, they may become religious missionaries who bring together different religions or ambassadors for peace who facilitate agreements between warring factions. Whatever they choose to do, they know how to live in harmony with their emotions, immerse themselves in the collective reality, and, from a sense of love that encompasses all living things, bring unity, enlightenment, and truth to the world.

Because he/she provides access to the eternal source of love, Angel Vavali-Yah gives those in her/his care the ability to inspire growth in everyone and everything around them. When sincerely in tune with this Angel's vibrations, those in kinship with Vavali-Yah can become agents of change, nurturers of growth, and sowers of the seed of infinite tomorrows.

Angel YELA-HI-YAH

OCTOBER 21–25

Increases enthusiasm in thought and action. Develops initiative. Brightens the intellect. Helps overcome obstacles and difficulties. Increases the desire to express oneself, communicate, and teach.

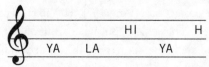

PHONETIC PRONUNCIATION

Ye as in Yes
La as in Large
Hi as in He
Ya as in Yard
H Vocalize the final H as a soft exhalation

UNIVERSAL RESONANCE OF THE ANGEL'S NAME

Ye Mastery. Dexterity, expertise; human action aligned with divine universal principles.

La Dynamic learning. The ability to make mental links. Intellectual elevation. An evolving, ascending movement of the mind. Lucidity and enlightenment.

Hi Spiritual life force. Presence of universal love and the all-permeating spirit. Divine call, divine connection.

Yah Final vibration of the Angel's name. Receptivity and reflectivity. The presence of the deity; the abundance of the being.

Guardian Angel Yela-Hi-Yah

In Akkadian, the name Yela-Hi-Yah means, literally, "The supreme act whose fluid vibrations spiral, rise, and mate with love's energy and the universal spirit."

Those in harmony with Angel Yela-Hi-Yah aren't simply born: they burst into the world with strength and enthusiasm. Angel

COLOR HARMONIZATION

Indigo blue / Cobalt blue / Sky blue / Turquoise blue / Bluish white all in successive stripes, crossed by radiating rays of ocher and sunny yellow

HARMONIC MATCHES FOR YELA-HI-YAH'S PROTÉGÉS

- *The best matches for success in economic and practical achievements will be among men and women born April 9–13, under the care of Ma-Hashi-Yah.*

- *The best matches for recognition, fame, personal charisma, and social fulfillment will be among men and women born August 7–11, under the care of Re-Yi-Ya-El.*

- *The best matches for romance, love, and artistic and intellectual achievements will be among men and women born August 22–26, under the care of Va-Sari-Yah.*

Yela-Hi-Yah encourages leadership and provides those under her/his protection with a strong capacity to unravel situations with simple and enlightening solutions. With the help of this energizing Angel, those born between October 21 and 25 can easily bypass the obstacles that stop others, vaulting over them with an exaltation of the mind, then sprinting toward their goals through the open gates of intellectual and spiritual elevation.

Quick thinking, high spirited, and lively, the men and women born under the protection of Angel Yela-Hi-Yah can appear to others to be impulsive, even reckless. But what seem on the surface to be thoughtless and spontaneous acts are in fact driven by the light of the intellect. Angel Yela-Hi-Yah acts as a true guardian, guiding the actions of those in his/her care, refining their perceptions and widening their objectives. At times, this hovering force is like a master guiding the hand of his young pupil, lightening the weight of the pencil on the paper, patiently demonstrating how to work toward an objective while enjoying the pleasures of success along the way.

In truth, those in kinship with Angel Yela-Hi-Yah have little difficulty enjoying pleasures. Cheerful and buoyant, they are often accused of having too much fun, particularly by those who have forgotten to have any. The friends of Yela-Hi-Yah approach each new day as an adventure and every experience as a launching pad to unexplored happy horizons. Filled with the immediacy and innocence of childhood, indeed, these people can appear to lead their lives as if they were playing. Depending on their personal circumstances, they have the potential for great success in any area that provides them with a favorable atmosphere for their enlightened and enlightening mental insights. Endowed by Yela-Hi-Yah with the ability to cope with—and even enjoy!—sudden challenges, they could achieve important breakthroughs in such areas as physics, chemistry, biology, medicine, language, communication, and transportation. With the help of their adaptable guardian, they are also capable of great physical achievements, drawing upon their mental agility to rally their willpower and win competitions or break records.

If you are born into the care of Yela-Hi-Yah, others may look up to you. Because you have learned the secret of acting with power but without violence, and because you teach without imposing restrictive models upon your students, you are a wonderful example of neither selling out nor selling yourself short. Of course, you can't expect everyone to applaud your success. The ease and lightness with which you overcome what are for others grueling, arduous tasks can make you subject to the sudden hostility and unexplained animosity of some colleagues or even employers. And because you chart your own course, paying no attention to commonly accepted rules or even the standards of your workplace, you can come to believe yourself to be above the law—or the ultimate arbiter of the way things *should* be done. In situations like these, it is important that you keep close to your guardian. Angel Yela-Hi-Yah will make you understand that the qualities that provoke jealousy and hatred in a few—the qualities of leadership and freedom—generate immense joy in others. He/she will also reconnect you to the sources of cosmic love that feed your emotions, feelings, and thoughts. Reestablishing your alliance with the unifying energy of the universe will reinforce your positive and constructive urges and endow you with a strong power of rejuvenation you can use to revive your own spirits as well as those of others.

Yela-Hi-Yah is a spirit of action. Consequently, it is best to invoke this Angel through direct action rather than words. Nothing impresses this Angel more than effectiveness in the face of crisis, unity in response to anger, and the light of intellect dissolving darkness and ignorance. Act in alignment with the celestial energies, and Angel Yela-Hi-Yah will generously share the pure joys of discovery, the eternal light of truth, and the inexhaustible wealth of heavenly love.

Angel SE-ALI-YAH

OCTOBER 26–30

Enlightens the mind and opens access to knowledge.
Stimulates the intellectual search and spiritual quest.
Unfolds the talent for discovery by questioning.
Illuminates the paths leading to the truth.

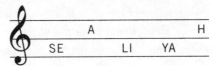

PHONETIC PRONUNCIATION

Se as in Settler
A as in Arrow
Li as in Liberty
Ya as in Yard
H Vocalize the final H as a soft exhalation

UNIVERSAL RESONANCE OF THE ANGEL'S NAME

Se Knowledge brought to consciousness. Deep understanding through clarification of creative forces.

A The original ultimate energy, before form, universal, infinite, unifying.

Li Dynamic learning. The ability to make mental links. Intellectual elevation. An evolving, ascending movement of the mind. Lucidity and enlightenment.

Yah Final vibration of the Angel's name. Receptivity and reflectivity. The presence of the deity; the abundance of the being.

Guardian Angel Se-Ali-Yah

In the Akkadian language, the name Se-Ali-Yah means, literally, "My question surges, bearer of sincere mental intelligence, and the Supreme Being answers by illuminating enlightenment."

There are no pointless questions, especially when those questions are being asked by the savvy men and women born under the

NOTABLE PEOPLE BORN UNDER THE INFLUENCE OF SE-ALI-YAH

Alfred Sisley, painter

Amanda Beard, Olympic swimmer

Annie Potts, actress

Bill Gates, founder of Microsoft

Captain James Cook, explorer

Dylan McDermott, actor

Ezra Pound, poet

François Mitterrand, former president of France

Hillary Clinton, former U.S. first lady

John Adams, U.S. president

Jonas Salk, scientist and inventor of polio vaccine

Julia Roberts, actress

Mahalia Jackson, singer

Richard Dreyfus, actor

Theodore Roosevelt, former U.S. president

Winona Ryder, actress

COLOR HARMONIZATION

Navy blue / Burgundy red / Beige / Spirals of strong green

care of Angel Se-Ali-Yah. Curious and intelligent, probing and irrepressible, these inquisitive people explore the world and the dimensions of the universe by putting every reality to the test. Question authority? They question everything, all in the hopes of reaching a clear understanding of the world around them—and a perfect knowledge of the realms that lie beyond that.

Those who feel as though they have been interrogated by these assertive souls might wonder whether they are sincerely seeking information or just yanking others' chains. The truth is Angel Se-Ali-Yah encourages and nourishes an inexhaustible thirst for knowledge. During the course of their lives, those under the protection of Angel Se-Ali-Yah make a point of uncovering any element that could contribute to the growth of knowledge, the unveiling of truth, the accomplishment of wisdom. In other words, if there's something they want to know, it may be wise to come clean as quickly as possible. Angel Se-Ali-Yah endows men and women with an unshakable belief that truth is not beyond their reach though it may be temporarily covered, buried, hidden, or encoded. With the help of Angel Se-Ali-Yah, they leave no stone unturned and no map, sign, symbol, or image uninterpreted as they collect the fragments, connect the truths, and form the conclusions that lead them to consciousness.

Of course, as any seeker knows, the path to knowledge is not without obstacles. Often, because they want to convince others of the value of their quest and their total objectivity, these men and women become overly analytical. When that happens, their reasoning becomes so complex that they actually become bewildered by their own questions—or lost in a forest of doubts. If, at times like these, they invoke their wise guardian, Se-Ali-Yah will rescue them from despair, lead them safely back into their inner world, and rekindle the flame of truth that is always present in their hearts.

If your birthday falls between October 26 and 30, you think and act cautiously, always questioning what lies before you and probing for any invisible "hazards" before taking a step. Depending on your personal circumstances or preferences, you could be successful in such areas as historical and archaeological research, police investigation, and theoretical scientific research. In more general terms, you live each day of your life as if it were a treasure

HARMONIC MATCHES FOR SE-ALI-YAH'S PROTÉGÉS

- *The best matches for success in economic and practical achievements will be among men and women born April 4–8, under the care of Âlami-Yah.*
- *The best matches for recognition, fame, personal charisma, and social fulfillment will be among men and women born September 11–15, under the care of Mena-Da-El.*
- *The best matches for romance, love, and artistic and intellectual achievements will be among men and women born July 18–22, under the care of Nith-Ha-Yah.*

hunt, searching for buried or hidden material wealth and gathering up scattered or encoded intellectual or spiritual secrets.

Literally hunting for information is not the only route to success for you, however. Angel Se-Ali-Yah generously bestows upon those in her/his care the ability to unravel complex situations through quick and comprehensive analysis, to make well-founded choices, and arrive at enlightening, intelligible decisions. These qualities could make you an excellent catalyst for family and social changes, for progress in industry or business, or exciting breakthroughs in what we consider to be staid institutions such as the judicial system or educational organizations. If, presented with the opportunity, you might even use your talent and inspiration to draw up laws for social reform, anticipating the consequences of the changes you propose, and paving the way for a smooth transition to a more innovative, enlightened time. You could also share the wealth of your probing intellect by offering to participate in research and problem-solving groups, think tanks, or crisis committees in all areas of family, social, and professional life.

Others are bright, but those protected by Angel Se-Ali-Yah are authentic explorers of the intellect, for whom each answered question is another step forward in the journey to the truth. When those in this inquiring Angel's care apply their characteristic questioning to a spiritual quest, their illuminating guardian fills their heart with the universal divine life force, broadens and lightens their pace, and shows them new and simpler ways to attain enlightenment. Then they can compare the fragments of truth they have gathered with the source of all truth and, with the guidance of Se-Ali-Yah, immerse themselves joyfully in the light of total knowledge.

Angel ÂRI-YA-EL

OCTOBER 31–NOVEMBER 4

Opens the doors to joy and happiness. Stimulates free expression of desires, passions, and emotions. Encourages simple and innocent feelings of love. Intensifies relationships by endowing them with the forces of nature.

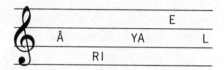

PHONETIC PRONUNCIATION

Â as in Arrow, ending with a soft breath out
Ri as in Reading
Ya as in Yard
El as in Elevation

UNIVERSAL RESONANCE OF THE ANGEL'S NAME

Â The origin of the sensory world; the foundation of human emotions and passions. Enhancement of visual senses and hearing acuity. Supersensitivity.

Ri Rotation, return, renewal; the natural cycles of existence. Radiance. Charisma. Inner vision and foresight on a universal scale. Princely leadership.

Ya Mastery. Dexterity, expertise; human action aligned with divine universal principles.

El Ending vibration of the Angel's name. Principle of excellence; chosen; elite. Elevating force. Source of perpetual transformation and evolution.

Guardian Angel Âri-Ya-El

In Akkadian, the name Âri-Ya-El literally means, "The presence of living beings on this earth, simple and naked," or "Earthly physical sensibility radiates outward, toward the Divine Presence."

COLOR HARMONIZATION

Many shades of gold / Carnal reds / All the greens of nature / Colors of flowers and butterflies

Have you ever wished people could return to a simpler time, when men were men and women were women, and instinct took care of the details? You can. Just stay close to those in harmony with Angel Âri-Ya-El. Earthy and secure, natural and nature loving, these enviable women and men are able to experience freely the simple joys of life on earth, to allow themselves to experience physical pleasure without guilt, and to enjoy the bliss of an endless innocent, happy childhood.

The guardian of every natural instinct and spirit, Angel Âri-Ya-El awakens and enhances the happy vibrations of nature, makes birds sing and leaves rustle, lights up the colors of flowers, enhances the taste of fruit, softens the strokes of lovers. Needless to say, for those in this guardian's protection, life is a bountiful garden where everything in it lies waiting to be discovered, tasted, touched, breathed, admired, loved. The cupids that fly through the air, unabashed by their innocent nudity, or that wait in the branches to stimulate romantic passion with the point of their arrows are a testimony to the springlike freshness and purity of emotions awakened by Angel Âri-Ya-El.

Of course, there are limits to natural living in the contemporary world. Angel Âri-Ya-El doesn't intend for you to march naked into the office or proposition an attractive co-worker, claiming that Cupid made you do it. In fact, those born between October 31 and November 4 will feel this powerful Angel's influence in many different ways. They will see, for instance, that their life on this earth is not a punishment but a happy sojourn. They will welcome their earthly companions—including animals, plants, single-celled organisms, and even minerals—as the sublime and loving gifts of a bountiful Creator. And most of all, with Âri-Ya-El's encouragement, they will truly live in the moment, enjoy the present, and live each second of their lives as it unfolds, without clouding it with comparison to the past or aspirations for the future. For those people, the garden of Eden blooms at their doorstep, each morning the sun brightens the sky with a new light; each day is a rebirth.

If you are one of the lucky few born under the protection of Angel Âri-Ya-El, you may appear to others as if you lack ambition. In this world, where so many are striving for some ineffable joy that will, they hope, materialize someday in the future, your innocence and joie de vivre can look like a waste of time. By invoking Angel Âri-Ya-El, you will receive a remedy for the undeserved judgment of others, particularly those who don't understand the value of stopping to smell the flowers.

Depending on time and circumstances, you and all of those close to Âri-Ya-El will find peace in a rural setting, by joining a community that is close to nature, or by participating in clubs that allow you to explore and observe the natural world. The harmonic vibrations of Angel Âri-Ya-El encourage men and women to seek out, everywhere and in all circumstances, the source and origin of things. Therefore, you will never be contented living a life of pure contemplation. Instead, you will find a way you can live in empathy with life on earth but explore it like an eagle, rising up on the currents of your interest, locating the answers to life's mysteries from above. If circumstances permit, you may literally take to the air and survey your surroundings by plane, hot air balloon, or glider. You may even get your pilot's license. Whether you choose to take your search off the ground or not, Angel Âri-Ya-El bestows upon you and all of those in her/his kinship the ability to elevate themselves, to keep a lofty perspective on things, and to seek out the natural influences on every aspect of life, from the way the moon governs the tides to the effects of DNA on your daily behavior.

Sometimes, those under the protection of Angel Âri-Ya-El, when they are well integrated in contemporary society, may choose an inner path to express their vision. This enables them to draw strength and knowledge from the natural model while living a modern, perhaps urban, life. Wherever you make your home, Angel Âri-Ya-El encourages an empathy toward a natural environment, one in which the things you uncover outdoors are brought in to become functional objects or beautiful design elements.

With the help of Angel Âri-Ya-El, men and women express their love of life by improving life on earth, creating objects that emulate plants, animals, or other natural things, or preserving the natural resources of their planet.

The harmonic vibrations of Angel Âri-Ya-El, amplified by invocation, exalt all sensations, give all emotions a radiating power, and refine thoughts. Those under the protection of Angel Âri-Ya-El

HARMONIC MATCHES FOR ÂRI-YA-EL'S PROTÉGÉS

- The best matches for success in economic and practical achievements will be among men and women born March 30–April 3, under the care of Si-Yata-El.
- The best matches for recognition, fame, personal charisma, and social fulfillment will be among men and women born September 6–10, under the care of Chava-Qui-Yah.
- The best matches for romance, love, and artistic and intellectual achievements will be among men and women born July 23–27, under the care of He-A-A-Yah.

intuitively and subtly perceive that everything that is born and grows on earth has its source in the heavens.

In supreme harmony with Angel Âri-Ya-El, men and women reinforce their loving ties with all of nature, extend their symbiotic union to the whole planet, and embrace all of the suns and planets of the cosmos in the warmth of their passion. Then, when their hearts are filled with wonder, stars flower in the fields of night, suns propel rays of life, and constellations unroll spirals of love.

Angel Â-SALI-YAH

NOVEMBER 5–9

Increases visual and hearing abilities. Develops intuitive intelligence. Bestows unique, distinctive, and unexpected visions. Stimulates analytical abilities. Encourages the search for progress and its transmission to the world.

		H	
Â	LI	YA	
	SA		

PHONETIC PRONUNCIATION

Â as in Arrow, ending with a soft breath out
Sa as in Saffron
Li as in Liberty
Ya as in Yard
H Vocalize the final H as a soft exhalation

UNIVERSAL RESONANCE OF THE ANGEL'S NAME

Â The origin of the sensory world; the foundation of human emotions and passions. Enhancement of visual senses and hearing acuity. Supersensitivity.

Sa Diffusion, radiation. The ability to comprehend and use the forces enclosed in the nucleus. Birth of science, sentience, and sapience. Radiating knowledge. Cosmic fire; archetype of every sun in the universe.

Li Dynamic learning. The ability to make mental links. Intellectual elevation. An evolving, ascending movement of the mind. Lucidity and enlightenment.

Yah Final vibration of the Angel's name. Receptivity and reflectivity. The presence of the deity; the abundance of the being.

NOTABLE PEOPLE BORN UNDER THE INFLUENCE OF Â-SALI-YAH

Alain Delon, actor
Albert Camus, writer
Billy Graham, religious leader
Carl Sagan, astronomer
Christiaan Barnard, medical pioneer
Edmond Halley, astronomer
Ethan Hawke, actor
Ivan Turgenev, writer
Joan Sutherland, opera singer
John Philip Sousa, composer
Margaret Mitchell, writer
Marie Curie, Nobel Prize winner in physics
Milton Bradley, businessman
Raymond Loewy, industrial designer
Sally Field, actress
Sam Shepard, playwright and actor
Walter Perry Johnson, baseball hall of famer
Will Durant, historian
William D. Phillips, Nobel Prize winner in physics

COLOR HARMONIZATION

Many nuances of green / Various blues / Ocher-yellow / Warm rusty browns

Guardian Angel Â-Sali-Yah

In Akkadian, the name Â-Sali-Yah means, "The sensory and sensual world spreads consciousness and knowledge that join in harmony with the Divine Verb."

Who says you can't be in two places at one time? Sensitive and analytical, poetic and practical, the fascinating men and women in harmony with Angel Â-Sali-Yah immerse themselves with equal pleasure in the world's sensory and intellectual dimensions.

An intriguing blend of EQ—emotional quotient—and IQ, those special people born under the care of Angel Â-Sali-Yah are endowed with keen senses—and the startling ability to take in information, either visually or auditorially, and immediately comprehend it. Depending on their personal potential, they can then transform this information into unique and unexpected perceptions, one-of-a-kind mental links, or endless fascinating conversations with friends and colleagues.

With a gift for organizing their thoughts in the form of enlightened, transmittable knowledge, those in kinship with this clever Angel may become known as great observers of their time. Careful chroniclers who always give their reports, letters, or conversations an erudite turn, who never present a fact outside of its context or a conclusion without the reasoning behind it, those born between November 5 and 9 are precise and detailed analysts who shuffle the evidence and deal out something unexpected. In the professional arena, those under the protection of Angel Â-Sali-Yah find many opportunities to develop their talents for analysis and syntheses, particularly in the technology of communication and mass media.

If you were born under the influence of the harmonic vibrations of Angel Â-Sali-Yah, you are endowed with a sharp vision and a deep understanding of the real "facts of life." It is important to you, therefore, that others understand them, too. In order to help other human beings gain access to the information they need to evolve and progress, you and all those under the protection of Angel Â-Sali-Yah may put your commendable energies into helping to build community buildings, theaters, libraries, or schools. You may also inspire technological breakthroughs that promote physical

HARMONIC MATCHES FOR Â-SALI-YAH'S PROTÉGÉS

- *The best matches for success in economic and practical achievements will be among men and women born March 25–29, under the care of Yeli-Ya-El.*
- *The best matches for recognition, fame, personal charisma, and social fulfillment will be among men and women born September 1–5, under the care of Le-Ha-Hi-Yah.*
- *The best matches for romance, love, and artistic and intellectual achievements will be among men and women born July 28–August 1, under the care of Yeratha-El.*

comfort or intellectual progress in the areas of farm engineering, computer science, or the spread of knowledge.

It is important to note, however, that the friends of Â-Sali-Yah can only produce such positive results when their desire to spread knowledge remains totally unencumbered. In other words, you will lose your perceptive and visionary capacities if you are hindered in following your own path or burdened by a job whose sole purpose is the protection of the privileged. When you are constrained in such a way, you lose your freedom of expression. This leads to a form of intellectual blindness and a darkening of your inner vision. Your intriguing perceptions will dry up as surely as a river that has been cut off from its source.

At times like these, it is important that you invoke Angel Â-Sali-Yah. Your perceptive guardian will reveal to you the true cause of your loss of interest in the sensory life, for plants and perfumes, for minerals and color nuances, for the diversity of animal life, the warmth of human feelings, the wealth of ideas. With the help of Â-Sali-Yah, you will remove yourself from the situations that deprive you of the freedom you need to grow and flower.

When in harmony with Angel Â-Sali-Yah, men and women look for the inspiring origin of their beautiful perceptions and their vast knowledge, and Angel Â-Sali-Yah lets them know, hear, and taste the true source of Beauty and Truth. Those under the protection of Angel Â-Sali-Yah may then throw themselves, with total confidence, into daring plans for building complex and sumptuous buildings, such as cathedrals or amphitheaters, or designing futuristic and generous plans for the dissemination of information through education, book publication, or the creation of innovative computer programs.

Given the opportunity, they may even devise peace plans on a national or global scale, clearing an emotional, intellectual, and spiritual path that brings all humans together, regardless of differences.

Filled with the virtues that beckon their perceptions back to their remote, celestial sources, these men and women, during certain phases of their lives, will want to give back to Angel Â-Sali-Yah. Thus, through the mirror of their minds, they project toward the invisible inhabitants of the heavens the colorful beauties and the echoing harmonies that fill their life on earth.

Angel MI-YA-HA-EL

NOVEMBER 10–14

Encourages the sense of responsibility. Reinforces personal and individual values. Facilitates union with celestial forces. Encourages the distribution of profits, benefits, and kind deeds. Helps with success of projects and missions.

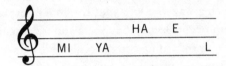

NOTABLE PEOPLE BORN UNDER THE INFLUENCE OF MI-YA-HA-EL

Aleksandr Borodin, *composer*

Auguste Rodin, *sculptor*

Calista Flockhart, *actress*

Claude Monet, *painter*

David Schwimmer, *actor*

Demi Moore, *actress*

Fyodor Dostoyevsky, *writer*

George S. Patton, *U.S. Army general*

Grace Kelly, *actress*

Kurt Vonnegut, *writer*

Leonardo DiCaprio, *actor*

Martin Luther, *Protestant reformer*

Nadia Comaneci, *Olympic gymnast*

Richard Burton, *actor*

Sonia Delaunay, *painter*

Whoopi Goldberg, *actress and comedian*

COLOR HARMONIZATION

Rose / Peach / Apple green / Royal blue / Turquoise / Pastel yellow

PHONETIC PRONUNCIATION

Mi as in Mirror

Ya as in Yard

Ha as in Habit

El as in Elevation

UNIVERSAL RESONANCE OF THE ANGEL'S NAME

Mi The matrix; the model upon which creation is based. Manifestation in the material world. Loving maternal protection.

Ya Mastery. Dexterity, expertise; human action aligned with divine universal principles.

Ha Spiritual life force. Presence of the universal love and all-permeating spirit. Divine call, divine connection.

El Ending vibration of the Angel's name. Principle of excellence; chosen; elite. Elevating force. Source of perpetual transformation and evolution.

Guardian Angel Mi-Ya-Ha-El

In Akkadian, the name Mi-Ya-Ha-El means, literally, "The Divine Verb and celestial love form the protective matrix of my being in its physical manifestation," or "My physical being comes from the celestial matrix that is both action and love."

Who doesn't put off until tomorrow what he or she could do today? The time-conscious men and women born under the influence of Angel Mi-Ya-Ha-El, that's who! The harmonic vibrations of Angel Mi-Ya-Ha-El provide men and women with a sense of immediacy and urgency about many of the things the rest of us put off until . . . well, forever. Those under the protection of this busy guardian minimize the time span between decisions and actions, between getting an idea and making it real, between their thoughts and their words, between the experience of an emotion and the expression of it. They may appear overly impulsive and impatient or maybe even egocentric (these go-getters take on initiative and leadership very quickly!), but they are also extremely active, productive, and generous beings. In fact, they are more interested in the results and success of their achievements than they are by any social status their work brings them. As quickly as they take charge, they will totally change their role, accepting a new position in another town, country, or on another professional, social, or personal level, should the move facilitate their goals.

Considering their quick moves and sudden maneuvering, it can be difficult to trust the interesting souls born in mid-November. People tend to equate moving from interest to interest or job to job with a lack of responsibility. In fact, nothing could be further from the truth. Those under the protection of Angel Mi-Ya-Ha-El develop a strong sense of individuality that inspires them to take charge—and to accept full responsibility for their words and actions. If, by taking a chance, they happen onto thin ice, they will blame no one but themselves. They will simply learn from the experience and head for shore.

If you are in deep harmony with Angel Mi-Ya-Ha-El, you are generous, sincere, and loving toward others. Indeed, in this world of givers and takers, you are a natural-born giver, sharing all you have with others without ulterior motives, strings attached, or a need for control. Neither do you skimp when divvying up your emotions. Friends, colleagues, family, even casual acquaintances all benefit from the magnificent passions of your heart. You offer yourself—and your brilliant ideas—unstintingly to the world. Although, on occasion, envious people will take advantage, you know these covetous souls can do you no real harm. Your guardian, Mi-Ya-Ha-El, connects you to the very source of love. You will always receive more than you give.

HARMONIC MATCHES FOR MI-YA-HA-EL'S PROTÉGÉS

- *The best matches for success in economic and practical achievements will be among men and women born March 20–24, under the care of Ve-Hovi-Yah.*

- *The best matches for recognition, fame, personal charisma, and social fulfillment will be among men and women born August 27–31, under the care of Ye-Hovi-Yah.*

- *The best matches for romance, love, and artistic and intellectual achievements will be among men and women born August 2–6, under the care of Se-A-He-Yah.*

Those in harmony with Angel Mi-Ya-Ha-El create wealth through their diversified achievements and their unquenchable desire to explore and try new ways of generating income. Those who are in particularly close kinship with this celestial guide are often known as people who have the golden touch. That's because they succeed not only in the missions they have chosen but also those that are thrust at them. They simply don't stop until their results surpass everyone's expectations.

Depending on circumstances, and with the help of Angel Mi-Ya-Ha-El, these men and women may become famous inventors. As opposed to researchers and theoreticians, who solve problems in the abstract, those born between November 10 and 14 present their inventions in the form of usable prototypes, ready to go. Prospective financial backers will find this hard to resist.

Whatever career those close to Mi-Ya-Ha-El choose, they will distinguish themselves as people who can materialize things from ideas and breathe new life into languishing projects. When in deep harmony with Angel Mi-Ya-Ha-El, they may become authentic leaders—gurus who open new pathways to achievement and create models that inspire other discoveries and inventions that benefit the world. They can be like the fruit that grows, in its center, the seed of a new tree—and the infinite promise of future harvests.

Angel VE-HOVA-EL

NOVEMBER 15–19

*Reinforces an intimate connection with the forces of life
and love. Encourages alliances and associations. Promotes
fecundity by creative fusion. Stimulates reveries
and imagination.*

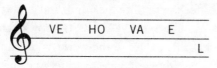

VE	HO	VA	E
			L

PHONETIC PRONUNCIATION

Ve as is Vector

Ho as in Hope

Va as in Vast

El as in Elevation

UNIVERSAL RESONANCE OF THE ANGEL'S NAME

Ve Vitalizing factor. Fruitfulness and productivity.
Catalyst of variety, vitality, verity, will, and vigor.

Ho Spiritual life force. Presence of the universal love and
all-permeating spirit. Divine call, divine connection.

Va Vitalizing factor. Fruitfulness and productivity. Catalyst of variety, vitality, verity, will, and vigor.

El Ending vibration of the Angel's name. Principle of
excellence; chosen; elite. Elevating force. Source of
perpetual transformation and evolution.

Guardian Angel Ve-Hova-El

In Akkadian language, the name Ve-Hova-El means, literally,
"Human fecundity, penetrated by and burning with divine love,
mutates and transforms into fecundity opened to the universe."

When touched by the harmonic vibrations of Angel Ve-Hova-
El, men and women ecstatically immerse themselves into the flow
of life. They are aware of the wonderful fecundity of the world, and
they experience within themselves the cycles of regeneration that

COLOR HARMONIZATION

*Yellow and white (like an egg) /
Cream and amber (milk and honey) /
Blue, turquoise, and tender green
(sky-sea-grass)*

constantly renew every animal, plant, and cell on earth. For them, the countless generations of plants and animals around them are an infinite source of happiness and discovery—in other words, a feast for the senses as well as the intellect. Because Angel Ve-Hova-El puts those he/she loves in touch with the unifying energy of the universe, this energizing Angel endows them with a strong capacity for association, merging, togetherness, coupling, friendly alliances, and enduring love relationships.

Feelings of affection fertilize the minds and guide the actions of those in harmony with Angel Ve-Hova-El. Warm, open, and gregarious, they present themselves to the world as human beings who are deeply in love with every aspect of life. And they pull others into their compassionate world, cultivating deep friendships and love relationships everywhere they go. At certain times in their lives, they may give free reign to their romantic yearnings and deeply felt emotions. This can lead to misunderstanding or can even result in sudden conflicts with those close to them. Consequently, those under the protection of Angel Ve-Hova-El are sometimes thought to be too caring, too intimate, or too affectionate by people who believe it is best to keep unbridled fondness bottled up, repressed, or at least carefully controlled, like something dangerous and explosive.

When faced with such unfair hostilities, those who call on Angel Ve-Hova-El will find the spiritual paths that can save them from the petty meanness and jealousy of their more restrained friends, neighbors, or colleagues. If they invoke their guardian, they will move even closer to the endless source of benevolence and love that fills their hearts.

Angel Ve-Hova-El provides men and women with a deep perception of the intimate and fertile unions at work at all levels of physical and spiritual life. He/she also endows them with the power to consciously and voluntarily participate in the mutual attraction that spawns this fertility. This can make those under Ve-Hova-El successful flirts—and irresistible romantics. Depending on their circumstances and talents, they may express their appreciation for the essential forces of life in the form of poetry or literary prose, artistic expression, scientific discovery, or even mystical revelation. In fact, their art can be quite vivid—like the paintings of

Georgia O'Keeffe. This is because, to those under the influence of this visionary Angel, the images received in dreams and imagination are every bit as real as the impressions picked up in daily life. In other words, for them, psychic and spiritual realities have as much substance as physical ones.

If you are born into the care of Angel Ve-Hova-El, you can develop skill as a writer of fiction, science fiction, fantasy, fairy tales, or any other stories that draw upon your acute perception of the underlying relationships motivating individuals and the fantastic images that color your imagination. Because you are so strongly connected, by your love for life, to all the creatures who share your world, you could become a storyteller with a very direct style, one who enthusiastically reveals details that might be invisible to others.

Whatever career you choose, Angel Ve-Hova-El will see to it that you become an active participant in the cultural enhancement of everyone around you. As long as limits are not imposed upon you, you love to share your discoveries and the beauty of your experiences with others, perhaps through involvement in a cultural group, community theater, or creative writing workshop.

Depending on circumstances in your life, you may reproduce the art, beauty, and refinement you have found at the heart of the living world through artistic expression. You may also be drawn to those careers that build upon your natural inclination to foster productivity and bring about harmony. You may become a mediator of difficult diplomatic, legal, domestic, or relational situations or a matchmaker, bringing people together from all walks of life to form successful alliances, federations, associations, and, yes, love matches.

By deepening their relationship with Angel Ve-Hova-El, men and women can refine their connections with the subtle energies of attraction that travel through the grand universe. By responding to the celestial call, as reflected by Angel Ve-Hova-El, men and women turn their spirits toward the source of all loving words and warm their hearts with the sublime rays that surge from the primal fountainhead: the true origin of earthly love.

INVOCATION

O Angel Ve-Hova-El,
Your eyes filled with light
Cast on my dark path
Stars and galaxies,
Beacons guarding my journey.
O Ve-Hova-El,
Close to you my soul is serene.
I hear the words of Angels
Leading my return to the heavens.
Angel Ve-Hova-El,
Help me, lend me courage,
My dreams in the night caress
The portals of eternity.

HARMONIC MATCHES FOR VE-HOVA-EL'S PROTÉGÉS

- *The best matches for success in economic and practical achievements will be among men and women born July 13–17, under the care of He-Havi-Yah.*

- *The best matches for recognition, fame, personal charisma, and social fulfillment will be among men and women born January 29–February 2, under the care of Me-He-Ya-El.*

- *The best matches for romance, love, and artistic and intellectual achievements will be among men and women born February 23–27, under the care of Ro-A-Ha-El.*

Angel DANI-YA-EL

NOVEMBER 20–24

Encourages achievements that are guided by the principles of social justice. Stimulates activities that call for understanding and compassion. Raises capacity and potential for innovation and transition. Bestows a deep sense of ethics.

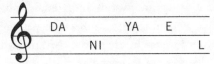

DA		YA	E
	NI		L

PHONETIC PRONUNCIATION

Da as in Dam
Ni as in Need
Ya as in Yard
El as in Elevation

UNIVERSAL RESONANCE OF THE ANGEL'S NAME

Da Discovery. Unveiling the unknown. Drama of all changes. Transference, translocation, translation. Mobility and transfer from one world to another. Appreciative perception of contrasts, differences, and variances.

Ni Nucleus, center, the essential; identity, individuality. Penetration to the center of every reality. Negation and rejection of superficial and perverse realities.

Ya Mastery. Dexterity, expertise; human action aligned with divine universal principles.

El Ending vibration of the Angel's name. Principle of excellence; chosen; elite. Elevating force. Source of perpetual transformation and evolution.

NOTABLE PEOPLE BORN UNDER THE INFLUENCE OF DANI-YA-EL

Benedictus de Spinoza, philosopher and theologian

Billie Jean King, tennis champion

Charles de Gaulle, former president of France

Dale Carnegie, writer and public speaker

Emilio Pucci, fashion designer

George Eliot, writer

Goldie Hawn, actress

Harpo Marx, comedian

Henri Toulouse-Lautrec, painter

Jamie Lee Curtis, actress

Nadine Gordimer, Nobel Prize winner in literature

Nataliya Makarova, ballerina

René Magritte, painter

Robert F. Kennedy, former U.S. senator and attorney general

Scott Joplin, composer and pianist

Voltaire, writer

COLOR HARMONIZATION

Many nuances of blue and white / Colors of skies, vast oceans, mountain peaks / Luminous colors contrasting with dark blue of the night, like shooting stars in deep space

Guardian Angel Dani-Ya-El

In Akkadian language, the name Dani-Ya-El means, literally, "Passage, transition, and innovation arise from the central, unique, immutable law with which the true Verb creates evolving movement."

Would the moral and scrupulous men and women in deep harmony with Angel Dani-Ya-El rather be right or happy? The answer is both. For unless these honest, honorable souls are working on the side of righteousness, unless their personal behavior and social activities draw upon the highest ethical principles, they simply cannot be truly happy.

There is, of course, a difference between being righteous and self-righteous—and we are happy to say that those under the protection of Angel Dani-Ya-El manage to be upright yet flexible. They lead a life of rectitude yet avoid rigidity and always try to exercise compassion, behave with fairness, and show respect for others' feelings. In fact, they are truly and deeply good people, men and women who are motivated by the desire to spread love and justice, not disseminate a particular dogma.

Generous, thoughtful, willing, and able to walk a mile or more in someone else's shoes, the special people who are close to Angel Dani-Ya-El can, with their guardian's help, open their minds to the immutable and universal divine laws and make them a part of our lives right here on earth. Angel Dani-Ya-El encourages practical actions based on theoretical knowledge. He/she also eases the transition from ideas to action, making it simple for those in her/his care to know—then *do*—the right thing. Depending on the circumstances of their lives, they may put their gift for fair and generous judgment at the service of their friends, families, and professional colleagues, resolving conflicts in a way that is acceptable by all and even convincing longtime adversaries to give up their petty differences and act on higher principles.

For those in harmony with Angel Dani-Ya-El, it is as easy to transit between the celestial and terrestrial worlds as it is to take the crosstown bus. This spiritual VIP pass allows these special people to glimpse the reality of immutable eternity, to understand the evolving movement of life, and to know the comparisons and contrasts between the divine ethic and the human justice. By the grace of this virtuous Angel, those in his/her care acquire the ability to cross thresholds of all sorts, including those that separate people, to penetrate to the center of divisive issues and bring a touch of divine justice to earth, thus elevating and enriching their environment. Because they are able to penetrate to the heart of any

HARMONIC MATCHES FOR DANI-YA-EL'S PROTÉGÉS

- *The best matches for success in economic and practical achievements will be among men and women born July 8–12, under the care of Mela-Ha-El.*

- *The best matches for recognition, fame, personal charisma, and social fulfillment will be among men and women born January 24–28, under the care of Ânava-El.*

- *The best matches for romance, love, and artistic and intellectual achievements will be among men and women born February 28– March 4, under the care of Yaba-Mi-Yah.*

issue, those under the protection of Dani-Ya-El can accomplish things that, on the surface, seem paradoxical. Their suggestions are, for example, simple yet profound; their ideas are pure common sense yet breathtakingly innovative. Given the right circumstances, these men and women can solve the problems of the world.

If you were born between November 20 and 24, you may be self-effacing to the extreme—but for good reason. Having an intimate knowledge of such gloriously transformative subjects like universal law and divine ethics, you have little interest in personal prominence. You and all those in kinship with Angel Dani-Ya-El may prefer to put your creative power at the service of teams organized around a cause or project. Depending on your personal circumstances and potential, you may also become a successful manager or excel in any job where you can draw upon your talent as a mediator and your capacity to always do the right thing, even when the most ethical choice is also the most difficult.

If you establish a deep harmony with your pure Angel, you will lead an intense and sincere spiritual life. Indeed, like Robert Kennedy, you will be inspired by the celestial dimensions, then put those higher principles to work to bring about justice here on earth. Angel Dani-Ya-El provides those close to her/him with the immense privilege of traveling from one dimension to another, from latitude to longitude, spiritual dimension to material world. By invoking your guardian, you will put your quest for the truth in motion, moving from periphery to centers and back again, in a lifelong pursuit of knowledge.

Although your path is always illuminated by your own bright principles, you and all of those close to Dani-Ya-El may, at certain times, encounter discouragement and despair, especially if you compare your material well-being to that of those who scorn ethics and reap huge windfalls. By invoking Angel Dani-Ya-El, you will intensify the light of the spiritual beacons that, here and yonder, illuminate the vast universe and strengthen the courage of those who ascend toward justice, beauty, and truth.

Angel HA-HASI-YAH

NOVEMBER 25–29

Encourages access to logical and spiritual knowledge.
Stimulates a talent for communication and teaching. Opens
the door to scientific thought permeated with humanism.

HA	HA		H
		YA	
SI			

PHONETIC PRONUNCIATION

Ha as in Habit

Ha as in Habit

Si as in Signal

Ya as in Yard

H Vocalize the final H as a soft exhalation

UNIVERSAL RESONANCE OF THE ANGEL'S NAME

Ha Spiritual life force. Presence of the universal love and all-permeating spirit. Divine call, divine connection.

Ha Spiritual life force. Presence of the universal love and all-permeating spirit. Divine call, divine connection.

Shi or Si Diffusion, radiation. The ability to comprehend and use the forces enclosed in the nucleus. Birth of science, sentience, and sapience. Radiating knowledge. Cosmic fire; archetype of every sun in the universe.

Yah Final vibration of the Angel's name. Receptivity and reflectivity. The presence of the deity; the abundance of the being.

Guardian Angel Ha-Hasi-Yah

In Akkadian language, the name Ha-Hasi-Yah means, literally, "Human love permeates itself with the wholeness of the divine Being and becomes revealing, radiating, and edifying awareness."

COLOR HARMONIZATION

Blues of the sky /
Earthy greens and ochers /
Colors reconciling sky and earth /
Creamy blues and rusty maroons

HARMONIC MATCHES FOR HA-HASI-YAH'S PROTÉGÉS

- *The best matches for success in economic and practical achievements will be among men and women born July 3–7, under the care of Ye-Yi-Ya-El.*
- *The best matches for recognition, fame, personal charisma, and social fulfillment will be among men and women born January 19–23, under the care of Ye-He-Ha-El.*
- *The best matches for romance, love, and artistic and intellectual achievements will be among men and women born March 5–9, under the care of Ha-Ye-Ya-El.*

Invoking Angel Ha-Hasi-Yah enlightens the mind and spirit and endows those in this guardian's care with a strong capacity for intellectual and spiritual depth. In addition, the harmonic vibrations of Angel Ha-Hasi-Yah actively encourage those close to this Angel to generously share their knowledge and spread the truth. With the help of Ha-Hasi-Yah, men and women transform their brilliant insights into transmissible knowledge and spread what they have learned throughout the world.

Plainspoken, clear, and intelligent, those under the guidance of Angel Ha-Hasi-Yah may become scientific discoverers or enlightened explicators of such abstract subjects as theoretical mathematics, physics, astronomy, and philosophy. They may also excel as teachers in such areas as chemistry, biology, ecology, technology, and human and animal psychology. Professionally, these men and women are particularly comfortable in the business of publishing books or magazines or producing scientific films, all of which allow them to apply their prodigious talents for mental penetration, deep understanding, and clear, powerful communication.

If you are in kinship with Angel Ha-Hasi-Yah, you are blessed with the ability to connect with the highest spiritual vibrations. You are also able to perceive the enlightened messages carried by these celestial frequencies. Strongly immersed in the flow of universal love, you and all those under the protection of Angel Ha-Hasi-Yah navigate gracefully on the ocean of mysticism, avoiding any whirlpools of fanaticism or dogma along the way. When communicating your experiences, either inwardly to yourself or to others, you are careful to always choose exactly the right words. Wise, thoughtful, and deeply spiritual, you are a natural mystic who knows that everything one thinks and says casts a light on the world. You want to be a constant, illuminating beacon, not a flash in the pan.

In your personal, professional, and social life, you are a patient teacher, devoting countless hours and unlimited affection to the development of others. If you attain deep harmony with your patient guardian, you will align your emotional, intellectual, and spiritual sensitivities with the vibrations of the divine harmonies and expand your awareness all the way to the edges of space and time.

Those under the protection of Angel Ha-Hasi-Yah are optimists who always look to the future, think beyond the present time, explore territories beyond their borders, and enlighten their minds with the principles that underlie the cosmos. By invoking Angel Ha-Hasi-Yah, these spiritual travelers acquire the grace to explore, without restrictions, the many dimensions of the universe. Guided by the stars of truth, knowledge, and awareness, those close to this inspiring Angel ascend the crystal staircase that unites them with their Creator, pausing at each step to share their progress with their sisters and brothers on earth.

Angel ÂMAMI-YAH

NOVEMBER 30 – DECEMBER 4

Reinforces the power of the senses and of intuitive perception. Harmonizes the relationship with the physical world. Inspires creative visions. Opens the doors to social success, fame, and material wealth.

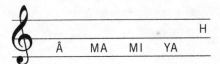

PHONETIC PRONUNCIATION

Â as in Arrow, ending with a soft breath out

Ma as in Matter

Mi as in Middle

Ya as in Yard

H Vocalize the final H as a soft exhalation

UNIVERSAL RESONANCE OF THE ANGEL'S NAME

Â The origin of the sensory world; the foundation of human emotions and passions. Enhancement of visual senses and hearing acuity. Supersensitivity.

Ma The matrix; the model upon which creation is based. Manifestation in the material world. Loving maternal protection.

Mi The matrix; the model upon which creation is based. Manifestation in the material world. Loving maternal protection.

Yah Final vibration of the Angel's name. Receptivity and reflectivity. The presence of the deity; the abundance of the being.

NOTABLE PEOPLE BORN UNDER THE INFLUENCE OF ÂMAMI-YAH

Alfred B. Nobel, *chemist*

Bette Midler, *actress and singer*

Brendan Fraser, *actor*

Britney Spears, *pop singer*

Georges Seurat, *painter*

Gianni Versace, *fashion designer*

Jeff Bridges, *actor*

Jonathan Swift, *writer*

Joseph Conrad, *writer*

Katerina Witt, *Olympic figure skater*

Maria Callas, *opera singer*

Mark Twain, *writer*

Martin Rodbell, *Nobel Prize winner in medicine*

Monica Seles, *tennis champion*

Nikos Kazantzakis, *writer*

Richard Pryor, *comedian and actor*

Wassily Kandinsky, *painter*

Winston Churchill, *former prime minister of Great Britain*

Woody Allen, *actor, writer, and director*

COLOR HARMONIZATION

Peach / Turquoise / Pastel green / Rusty brown / Light gray with specks of flame red and yellow gold

Guardian Angel Âmami-Yah

In Akkadian language, the name Âmami-Yah means, literally, "The matrix source of material worlds is the Verb of Creation itself," or "My people are my primary matrix, source of my models for action and control."

The harmonic vibrations of Angel Âmami-Yah provide those close to this inspiring guardian a strong capacity for adjusting to the physical world of sensations and the ability to act with strength, grace, competence, and success. They live and act in this world with self-assurance and intensity and take to the subtle changes in life's currents like fish swimming in water.

With the help of their celestial guide, these men and women grasp the unseen structures that form the foundation of the world. When in harmony with Âmami-Yah, they can hone this skill, becoming ultrasensitive receptors of ideas and then bringing these innovative visions to life. Depending on the circumstances in their lives and their personal potential, those under the protection of Angel Âmami-Yah demonstrate their gifts as inspired manual artists, creating remarkable or even grandiose works that bring them great admiration—or even fame. They may be sculptors, for example, carving their visions in stone, forging them in metal, or capturing them in molten glass. In whatever medium best expresses their creativity, their works could become public monuments, artfully symbolizing the shared values of a community. They could also become inspirations and guides for painters and sculptors now or in the future.

Those under the protection of Angel Âmami-Yah are guided by the spirit of their times; in turn, they become compassionate, intelligent guides for others. In the personal and professional realm, these men and women can reach the heights of fame, leadership, and material wealth. Their startlingly ingenious ideas and artistic and scientific brilliance move them to the forefront of notoriety. Whether they choose to make their statement as creators of high fashion, painters or sculptors, architects, dancers or singers, politicians, business people, mathematicians, physicians or chemists, financiers or economists, educators, or philosophers, those under the protection of Angel Âmami-Yah always seem to find

HARMONIC MATCHES FOR ÂMAMI-YAH'S PROTÉGÉS

- *The best matches for success in economic and practical achievements will be among men and women born June 28–July 2, under the care of Nel-Cha-El.*

- *The best matches for recognition, fame, personal charisma, and social fulfillment will be among men and women born January 14–18, under the care of Vama-Ba-El.*

- *The best matches for romance, love, and artistic and intellectual achievements will be among men and women born March 10–14, under the care of Mova-Mi-Yah.*

a form of expression that allows them artistic freedom and appeals to the public. Indeed, their creations can provoke such overwhelming demand that they become the subject of mass marketing on an international scale, as Âmami-Yah protégé Britney Spears can attest.

By the grace of this transforming Angel, those in her/his care acquire the power to draw what they need—energy, direction, funding—from the most productive sources. Reciprocally, they then nourish others with the milk and honey they create. Those under the protection of Angel Âmami-Yah are true philanthropists who generously distribute their surplus to those in need. In fact, when the right charity can't be found, those in kinship to this generous Angel will create their own, founding organizations to promote progress in the arts, social advancements, or achievement in areas of interest to them.

If you are in harmony with Angel Âmami-Yah, you are a benevolent, well-adjusted, and happily integrated member of your social group or community. Depending on your background, you might even be a respected elder, spokesperson, or public voice in your social or professional circle—one who can be counted on to express key ideas, defend shared values, and promote those causes in which you believe. You and all of those under Âmami-Yah's guidance express ideas that would remain dormant in other persons. This capacity to create and communicate draws admirers to you who follow your example or use you as a model.

Enlightened by the spiritual examples and inspiring celestial models Angel Âmami-Yah kindly provides, you and everyone in this guardian's care can refine your ability to sense connections between people, things, and ideas. Then, filled with confidence, you can create on earth amazing new models for living drawn from the brightest heavenly realities.

Angel NANA-A-EL

DECEMBER 5–9

Provides a disposition for inner spiritual examination. Develops an understanding of singularities and encourages an individualistic way of living and thinking. Promotes knowledge through the discovery of underlying hidden structures.

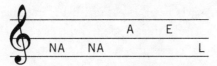

PHONETIC PRONUNCIATION

Na as in Navigate

Na as in Navigate

A as in Arrow

El as in Elevation

UNIVERSAL RESONANCE OF THE ANGEL'S NAME

Na Nucleus, center, the essential; identity, individuality. Penetration to the center of every reality. Negation and rejection of superficial and perverse realities.

Na Nucleus, center, the essential; identity, individuality. Penetration to the center of every reality. Negation and rejection of superficial and perverse realities.

A The original ultimate energy, before form, universal, infinite, unifying.

El Ending vibration of the Angel's name. Principle of excellence; chosen; elite. Elevating force. Source of perpetual transformation and evolution.

Guardian Angel Nana-A-El

In Akkadian language, the name Nana-A-El means, literally, "In the center of the center and deepest core of each individualized being lies the minute presence of the universal creator's gigantic life force."

NOTABLE PEOPLE BORN UNDER THE INFLUENCE OF NANA-A-EL

Alfred Eisenstaedt, *photojournalist*

Aristide Maillol, *sculptor*

David Carradine, *actor*

Dick Butkus, *football great*

Elián González, *famous Cuban émigré*

George A. Custer, *U.S. general*

Gian Lorenzo Bernini, *sculptor*

Jim Morrison, *musician*

John Milton, *writer*

Khalil Gibran, *poet and writer*

Kim Basinger, *actress*

Kirk Douglas, *actor*

Larry Bird, *basketball hall of famer*

Martin Van Buren, *former U.S. president*

Sammy Davis Jr., *singer*

Walt Disney, *animator and entertainment industry mogul*

COLOR HARMONIZATION

Jade green / Ruby red / Topaz-amber / Sapphire-blue cobalt

Men and women in harmony with Angel Nana-A-El are able to penetrate directly into the center of things and, without hesitation, infiltrate the successive layers that cover the seeds of truth. Those under the protection of Angel Nana-A-El know how to connect their minds with what is essential and to make that link in the shortest, most direct way, without wandering off toward materialistic goals or being distracted by shimmering, empty appearances.

The grace of Angel Nana-A-El is the ultimate VIP pass, granting those in this Angel's favor access to what is invisible and hidden. From this privileged vantage point, those close to Nana-A-El can see the inner structures that underlie reality and quench their thirst for truth at the very source of all knowledge.

Clearly, these curious, interesting people have a great deal to offer those near them. However, that offer may not come. These men and women do not enjoy social relationships. In fact, they consider casual friendships to be futile, even a waste of time compared to their quest for the truth. They also avoid everything in the world that would give more importance to appearances rather than to the inner exploration of the self and to profound discoveries. Consequently, depending on circumstances of their lives, they are drawn to those areas of interest where their deep desire for exploration can be exercised, such as chemistry (particularly as applied to extracts or to submolecular analysis), microcosmic physics, genetic biology and the study of chromosomes, nutrition with extracts and nectars, linguistics (particularly linguistic decoding), and the refinement of metals and extraction of essences. In all of their activities, men and women can call upon Angel Nana-A-El to enhance their abilities to uncover the invisible connections and unifying synchronicities that exist in all people and things.

Quiet and introverted, pensive and shy, those under the protection of Angel Nana-A-El are the party guests you can count on *not* to mingle. No matter how lively the company, they always prefer authentic love on a one-on-one basis and intimate friendships to group interactions. What they seek in their relationships is the simple joy of being together based on common aspirations, mutual curiosities, deep examinations, and sincere questioning. In other words: the quest for all facets of the truth.

Angel Nana-A-El provides men and women with minds that cultivate individuality and unveil the uniqueness and specificity of each thing, like the singular qualities and even occlusions that make each gem distinct. With so much focus on distinctiveness and individuality, those under the protection of Angel Nana-A-El are often not able to cope or react adequately when faced with mass phenomena, crowds, and undifferentiated quantities, such as faceless mobs. In other words, they lack the natural ability to work a room or schmooze. Consequently, they are often not exposed to opportunities that can bring them large incomes and great material wealth.

When circumstances demand, the friends of Nana-A-El can fight their reclusive tendencies and make the great effort to be sociable, gregarious, part of a group. And they should be encouraged to do so. Socializing is a human behavior that provides people with a great deal, including financial and emotional security. If these men and women do not control their tendency toward isolation, or if they do not get involved in a relationship with a partner who encourages them to be social, they may lead the life of a hermit, filled with solitude and meditation but emotionally flat. With so much invested in their personal studies, those under the protection of Angel Nana-A-El may also become weak, vulnerable, or even maladjusted in life if their superior ability to penetrate and understand beings and things goes unrecognized by their peers or professional colleagues. They will find security in those pursuits where science and uncompromising knowledge are sought, admired, and rewarded.

The harmonies of Angel Nana-A-El bless men and women with the joys of discovery in a constantly evolving universe. Indeed, this erudite Angel allows those close to him/her to delight in an endless journey through the spiritual depths to the heart of knowledge.

By praying and invoking their powerful guardian, these men and women can reinforce their intimacy with Angel Nana-A-El, who will then lead them on their quest to the very edges of the finite universe and personally connect them with the eternal life force that precedes the emergence of the most subtle forms. There, they can contemplate the Origin of origins and the unique Source of all diversities.

HARMONIC MATCHES FOR NANA-A-EL'S PROTÉGÉS

- *The best matches for success in economic and practical achievements will be among men and women born June 23–27, under the care of Pe-Hali-Yah.*

- *The best matches for recognition, fame, personal charisma, and social fulfillment will be among men and women born February 18–22, under the care of Ha-Bovi-Yah.*

- *The best matches for romance, love, and artistic and intellectual achievements will be among men and women born February 3–7, under the care of Damabi-Yah.*

When they are able to penetrate to the epicenter of everything and link their energies with the forces that underlie all living things, those under the protection of Angel Nana-A-El may become majestic explorers of the immense universe. By integrating microcosms and macrocosms, they can rise up without fear to the celestial dimensions where Angels live.

Angel NIYA-THA-EL

DECEMBER 10–14

Encourages idealism. Gives access to a knowledge of essential structures. Widens the awareness of time and of cyclical returns. Helps in making decisions. Nourishes the ability to innovate.

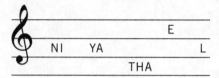

PHONETIC PRONUNCIATION

Ni as in Niche
Ya as in Yard
Tha as in Taxi
El as in Elevation

UNIVERSAL RESONANCE OF THE ANGEL'S NAME

Ni Nucleus, center, the essential; identity, individuality. Penetration to the center of every reality. Negation and rejection of superficial and perverse realities.

Ya Mastery. Dexterity, expertise; human action aligned with divine universal principles.

Tha Experience of time. Evolving temporal cycles eternally recurring. Mutation coupling mortality with immortality.

El Ending vibration of the Angel's name. Principle of excellence; chosen; elite. Elevating force. Source of perpetual transformation and evolution.

Guardian Angel Niya-Tha-El

In Akkadian language, the name Niya-Tha-El means, literally, "Knowledge inspired by the Divine Creator develops into action and mastery, acting within time with the aim to travel beyond time."

HARMONIC MATCHES FOR NIYA-THA-EL'S PROTÉGÉS

- *The best matches for success in economic and practical achievements will be among men and women born June 18–22, under the care of Levavi-Yah.*
- *The best matches for recognition, fame, personal charisma, and social fulfillment will be among men and women born February 13–17, under the care of A-Ya-Â-El.*
- *The best matches for romance, love, and artistic and intellectual achievements will be among men and women born February 8–12, under the care of Mana-Qua-El.*

Nobody's perfect, but those exacting men and women in harmony with Angel Niya-Tha-El come close! Deliberate and careful, they have the ability to act with precision and nearly always without error. That's because their actions are guided by the deep currents that underlie all of existence. Bold, even dashing, a force to be reckoned with in the world, those under the protection of Angel Niya-Tha-El get involved in life's experiences without hesitation or fear, even in complex situations where others might express reluctance about the consequences or turn away in fear.

In their private and professional lives, those under the protection of Angel Niya-Tha-El are excellent advisers, able to open new routes to a goal. Of course, some of the routes they suggest may appear perilous to less stouthearted types. Nevertheless, their sense of direction is unerring, and, while the paths they travel may seem to risk life and limb—or at least sanity—they will almost certainly get where they are going, and with aplomb.

With the help of Angel Niya-Tha-El, women and men are able to sense what lies beneath the polished surface of any situation or person. While others are captivated by appearances or bewitched by beauty, they see down to the hidden and lasting nucleus of all reality. As a result, those under the guidance of Angel Niya-Tha-El produce unique and clear syntheses based on solid knowledge and precise solutions that are relevant to their time.

If you are attuned to the harmonic vibrations of Angel Niya-Tha-El, you have a great ability to concentrate and focus, a strong capacity for uncovering the essential elements or the nitty-gritty of any situation, and a powerful intuitive knowledge of the cycles that govern the development of events in time. Whether it's feast or famine, up or down, or time to reap or sow, you understand that "this, too, shall pass." Besides, whatever the cycle, you might even make the best of it! An intimate connection with Angel Niya-Tha-El allows men and women to ride the waves of time with a clear awareness and a powerful intuition about how trends arise, disappear, and then return. You and all those under the protection of Angel Niya-Tha-El can succeed in occupations that develop over time: for example, financial investments that rise and fall or cyclical or seasonal artistic creation such as fashion and interior design, design and marketing of gift products, or the publication of popular books. And if you don't make it on the first try, you aren't likely to get discouraged. You know that your potential for success is recurrent and constantly renewed. You merely need to gather your formidable forces and try again.

By invoking Angel Niya-Tha-El, you and everyone born between December 10 and 14 are led to guide your actions by the pure ideas you draw from the deep and spiritual sources of life. Consequently, the material wealth that results from your hard work can come to feel like more of a burden to you than a reward. For this reason, you will be inspired to share what you have generously with others rather than using or accumulating it for your own benefit. You and everyone who is touched by Niya-Tha-El recognize that your treasure lies in your capacity to draw from the universal storehouse of dynamic ideas and in your ability to work within the flow of time. You have no need to hoard.

Depending on the depth of your spiritual connection with the harmonies of Angel Niya-Tha-El, you may be an idealist whose actions are based on authentic moral standards and pure truth. Where others struggle with moral dilemmas, you reject purely selfish decisions without quibbling. If your circumstances lead you to choose an intellectual occupation, you may become an excellent historian, archaeologist, archivist, art restorer, museum curator, or patron of art works related to the knowledge of past civilizations and history.

Those under the protection of Angel Niya-Tha-El may sometimes appear to be naive and utopian. Indeed, they are people who will voluntarily rid themselves of all possessions, whether intellectual or material, if such measures will promote their spiritual well-being. However, with the help of Angel Niya-Tha-El, such simple goodness is not the cause of their generous actions but their ultimate reward, the result of their deep closeness with the real nature of life and the cycles of time.

Angel Niya-Tha-El teaches men and women under her/his protection and all those who invoke him/her sincerely the secrets of eternal renewal. Then, by showing them the paths of Light, this Angel guides their souls to the celestial bridge that leads to immortality.

Angel MEBA-HI-YAH

DECEMBER 15–19

NOTABLE PEOPLE BORN UNDER THE INFLUENCE OF MEBA-HI-YAH

Arthur C. Clark, writer

Bill Pullman, actor

Brad Pitt, actor

Don Johnson, actor

Edward E. Barnard, astronomer

Erskine Caldwell, writer

Gustave Eiffel, civil engineer

J. Paul Getty, oil baron

Leonid Brezhnev, former premier of the
   Soviet Union

Ludwig van Beethoven, composer

Margaret Mead, anthropologist

Maurice Wilkins, Nobel Prize winner
   in medicine

Philip K. Dick, writer

Ray Liotta, actor

Steven Spielberg, film director and
   producer

COLOR HARMONIZATION

Ebony black / Glittering black /
The reflective transparency of fine
diamonds / Scintillating gold /
Glitter of stars / The light of dawn

Encourages patience. Promotes knowledge through experience. Bestows the energy and courage needed to begin again or start over. Rewards material and physical perseverance by spiritual elevation.

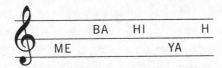

PHONETIC PRONUNCIATION

Me as in Meter

Ba as in Battle

Hi as in He

Ya as in Yard

H Vocalize the final H as a soft exhalation

UNIVERSAL RESONANCE OF THE ANGEL'S NAME

Me The matrix; the model upon which creation is based. Manifestation in the material world. Loving maternal protection.

Ba The universal paternal force; that which contains the code of all codes. The formative energy generating all data and shapes. The energy that begins all lives, all manifestations, all experiences.

Hi Spiritual life force. Presence of the universal love and all-permeating spirit. Divine call, divine connection.

Yah Final vibration of the Angel's name. Receptivity and reflectivity. The presence of the deity; the abundance of the being.

Guardian Angel Meba-Hi-Yah

In Akkadian language, the name Meba-Hi-Yah means, literally, "The matrix of all forms of life is inhabited by the divine love."

Mountain climbers tell of the vastly changeable, intriguingly perilous events that characterize each climb. One minute they are ascending, quite literally, to the top of the world; the next they are visiting some obscure cave, known only to a handful of hardy spelunkers who came before them. Women and men who live in harmony with Angel Meba-Hi-Yah report similar experiences as they navigate the unpredictable terrain of their emotional worlds.

In the eyes of those close to them or their colleagues, the personalities of those under the influence of Angel Meba-Hi-Yah are, in turn, obscure and superficial, shut tight against intruders and totally accessible, ponderously heavy and light and breezy. And just when friends have gotten a grip on the range of emotion they can expect from Meba-Hi-Yah's protégés, these men and women surprise everyone around them by totally changing their ways of living and thinking, as if a new light had suddenly revealed some essential realities that were unknown to them before. It goes without saying that relationships with these people are never dull. In fact, the lives of those who are close to Angel Meba-Hi-Yah can unfold like a Steven Spielberg film, complete with unexpected twists, visits from alien personalities, and, at the end, glorious redemption.

Just as a sudden calm follows every storm, life is not always tumultuous for those close to Meba-Hi-Yah. At certain times in their lives, they solidly anchor their existence in the real world. Then, when their apprehension is limited to visible and tangible concerns, when they are led by the desire to improve their social position or their personal enjoyment, they can function day to day, content in their comfortable routines. In such circumstances, Angel Meba-Hi-Yah provides them with perseverance and tenacity, a resistance to adversity, and the patience to learn from those times when things are slow, heavy, and difficult.

Indeed, slower times can be educational times. Because they see themselves as the inheritors of ideas, thought structures, methods, and techniques developed through the ages, those

HARMONIC MATCHES FOR MEBA-HI-YAH'S PROTÉGÉS

- The best matches for success in economic and practical achievements will be among men and women born June 13–17, under the care of Cali-Ya-El.
- The best matches for recognition, fame, personal charisma, and social fulfillment will be among men and women born February 8–12, under the care of Mana-Qua-El.
- The best matches for romance, love, and artistic and intellectual achievements will be among men and women born February 13–17, under the care of A-Ya-Â-El.

under the protection of Angel Meba-Hi-Yah can learn customs and traditions, programs and formulas, then implement them themselves. When they continue to draw from the vibrations of Meba-Hi-Yah, they can apply what they have learned to professions related to arts and crafts, mechanical, electronic, or technical repairs, experimentation in scientific or medical laboratories, restoration of ancient works of art, or of anything requiring them to follow an accepted procedure, whether simple or complex. Over time, those born between December 15 and 19 can develop great dexterity and, therefore, tremendous expertise at their craft. They could receive great recognition and honors from their contemporaries. They could also apply their considerable powers of perseverance to the perfection of a specific method or skill, the refining of a formula, or becoming good, patient, and persistent teachers of their craft.

If you live in deep harmony with your creative guardian, you may experience a complete turnaround, a life-changing experience, a complete and sudden metamorphosis that brings about a total reversal of the values that guide your life. When sincerely invoked, Angel Meba-Hi-Yah draws men and women out of the darkness of caves into the serenity of the heavens, transmutes their troubled emotions into mystical love, frees their thoughts from the heavy realities of life, and leads their spirit to the heavenly realm. After such an encounter, you will be guided, not by any earthly desires, but by continuous feelings of wonder and perpetual surprise.

If you feel weighed down by everyday life and materialism, the influence of Angel Meba-Hi-Yah will beckon to you, like a spiritual call. When you are ready, your guardian will connect you with the spiritual dimensions of the world and touch off a transformative process of personal growth. Although your friends and family may wonder about your motives, your suddenly changed life, and perhaps even your sanity, you will be too busy exploring your inner life, participating in educational seminars, or delving into the mystical, philosophical, or religious realms to concern yourself with their opinions. You will have gone beyond the here and now to a world where everything is possible and the only thing worth searching for is the truth.

Meeting on the path of life with the inspiring, life-changing Angel Meba-Hi-Yah is one of the happiest and most intense experiences a human can have. Bathe in the harmonies of this consciousness-heightening Angel and he/she will reconnect you with your origin and light your way to your divine destiny.

Angel POVI-YA-EL

DECEMBER 20—24

Develops a talent for oration and speech. Reinforces vitality. Stimulates and refines manual dexterity. Enriches personal and social relationships.

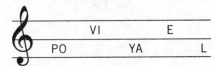

PHONETIC PRONUNCIATION

Po as in Poetry

Vi as in Victory

Ya as in Yard

El as in Elevation

UNIVERSAL RESONANCE OF THE ANGEL'S NAME

Po Inspiration-expiration. A facility for speech, prose, poetry, expression, and proclamation. Power, possibility, passion. Pronunciation, vocalization of the universal language.

Vi Vitalizing factor. Fruitfulness and productivity. Catalyst of variety, vitality, verity, will, and vigor.

Ya Mastery. Dexterity, expertise; human action aligned with divine universal principles.

El Ending vibration of the Angel's name. Principle of excellence; chosen; elite. Elevating force. Source of perpetual transformation and evolution.

NOTABLE PEOPLE BORN UNDER THE INFLUENCE OF POVI-YA-EL

Bob Hayes, *Olympic sprinter*

Chris Evert, *tennis champion*

Diane Sawyer, *television journalist*

Emperor Akihito of Japan

Frank Zappa, *musician*

Giacomo Puccini, *composer*

Howard Hughes, *millionaire businessman*

James Hadley Chase, *writer*

Jane Fonda, *actress*

Joseph Smith, *Mormon religious leader*

Kieffer Sutherland, *actor*

Kit Carson, *pioneer*

Phil Donahue, *talk-show host*

Steve Garvey, *baseball hall of famer*

COLOR HARMONIZATION

Yellow / Lavender / Indigo blue / The deep green of foliage / Pastel rose with notes of mauve lilac

Guardian Angel Povi-Ya-El

In Akkadian language, the name Povi-Ya-El means, literally, "Passionate human speech reflects the active power of the Divine Verb."

Who coined the last really memorable line you heard? You know, the one that stands out in your memory long after the party is over, the last song is sung, and the dinner conversation is just a fuzzy memory? If the remark was pithy, the speech eloquent, or the song unforgettable, it may have originated with one of the garrulous, inventive men and women born under the protection of Angel Povi-Ya-El. When in harmony with this tongue-loosening spirit, people communicate their vitality, passion, and joie de vivre, and they do so through their words and actions, enthusiastically and flamboyantly. Angel Povi-Ya-El endows men and women with cheerful and communicative personalities that they manifest in spite of any adversities they encounter throughout their lives.

Their explosive, warm, and vibrant personalities attract many friends to these gregarious souls, who accumulate interesting and diverse acquaintances the way others collect rocks or stamps or parking tickets. Genuine people who inspire the sincere admiration of everyone within earshot, the protégés of Povi-Ya-El are often at the center of a fluid and diverse social network that forms around them.

Because those under the protection of Angel Povi-Ya-El are so extroverted, others (specifically, envious others!) may deem them superficial people who lead chaotic lives. They may even shrug off their spontaneous eloquence as impulsive or even irrational. In those cases, naysayers will almost certainly learn not to repeat such errors. The harmonies of Angel Povi-Ya-El provide those under her/his protection with deep spiritual understanding, which guides these men and women inexorably toward the truth. Once there, they quickly separate the productive, transforming, and beneficial facts of the matter from the superfluous matter, like an ardent flame burning away the impurities to produce fine gold.

Angel Povi-Ya-El encourages men and women to develop a personal style based on honesty. At this Angel's knee, they learn to be civil without hypocrisy and courteous without pretension. If you are under this Angel's protection, you attain your goals with talent, discretion, and humility. Despite your intense, occasionally noisy ways of relating to the world, you are a selfless achiever, working toward your goals with little thought of prestige, power, or material gain. Nevertheless, the recognition of others and an income sufficient for a comfortable life will almost certainly be provided to you. When in harmony with Angel Povi-Ya-El, people are inspired to speak and work out of a love for beauty and goodness. This is an attribute those who issue checks can appreciate.

HARMONIC MATCHES FOR POVI-YA-EL'S PROTÉGÉS

- *The best matches for success in economic and practical achievements will be among men and women born June 8–12, under the care of Le-A-Vi-Yah.*
- *The best matches for recognition, fame, personal charisma, and social fulfillment will be among men and women born February 3–7, under the care of Damabi-Yah.*
- *The best matches for romance, love, and artistic and intellectual achievements will be among men and women born February 18–22, under the care of Ha-Bovi-Yah.*

With the help of this straightforward guardian, you and everyone in the friendship of this eloquent Angel can develop careers in those fields requiring dexterity, tact, precision, and attention to detail. You may succeed, for example, as a fashion designer, goldsmith, perfumer, carpenter, interior designer, stockbroker, surgeon, poet, or in any area where actions or words must immediately follow ideas and thoughts. Depending on your personal circumstances, you may also succeed in occupations such as speakers, teachers, or television or radio journalists, like Diane Sawyer and Phil Donahue.

Without appearing to specifically seek out material goods, those under the protection of Angel Povi-Ya-El providentially receive, at the right time and in sufficient amounts, enough income to fulfill their desires. In turn, they always find the right way to express their sincere thanks to those who are at the source of their good fortune. The right words to express their deep gratitude are consistently on the tips of their tongues. With those words, they charm their benefactors and render their enemies powerless.

When in deep harmony with Angel Povi-Ya-El, men and women reach to the ultimate source of the generative energy to ensure the quality of their actions and the loving warmth of their words. Through Angel Povi-Ya-El, the power of the Verb of Creation penetrates their minds, invests them with spiritual control, and clearly presents them with the divine ideals they will use as models in the final stage of their ascension to the eternal worlds.

Angel NEMA-MI-YAH

DECEMBER 25–29

Encourages exploration by imagination. Develops intuitive and futuristic visions. Stimulates an understanding of the inner, deep, and invisible levels of beings and things. Paves the way for discoveries and innovation.

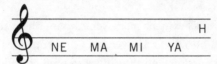

PHONETIC PRONUNCIATION

Ne as in Nepal

Ma as in Matter

Mi as in Mirror

Ya as in Yard

H Vocalize the final H as a soft exhalation

UNIVERSAL RESONANCE OF THE ANGEL'S NAME

Ne Nucleus, center, the essential; identity, individuality. Penetration to the center of every reality. Negation and rejection of superficial and perverse realities.

Ma The matrix; the model upon which creation is based. Manifestation in the material world. Loving maternal protection.

Mi The matrix; the model upon which creation is based. Manifestation in the material world. Loving maternal protection.

Yah Final vibration of the Angel's name. Receptivity and reflectivity. The presence of the deity; the abundance of the being.

Guardian Angel Nema-Mi-Yah

In Akkadian language, the name Nema-Mi-Yah means, literally, "Thinking penetrates the essence of all things, names them, and leads them to new forms of expression."

NOTABLE PEOPLE BORN UNDER THE INFLUENCE OF NEMA-MI-YAH

Annie Lennox, *singer*

Anwar el-Sadat, *former president of Egypt*

Carlos Castaneda, *writer*

Conrad Hilton, *hotel executive*

Denzel Washington, *actor*

Gerard Depardieu, *actor*

Helena Rubinstein, *cosmetics entrepreneur*

Henry Miller, *writer*

Humphrey Bogart, *actor*

Johannes Kepler, *astronomer*

Johnny Otis, *musician*

Kary B. Mullis, *Nobel Prize winner in chemistry*

Louis Pasteur, *chemist and biologist*

Marlene Dietrich, *actress*

Woodrow Wilson, *former U.S. president*

COLOR HARMONIZATION

White / Mauve / Dark violet / Sparkles of rose

HARMONIC MATCHES FOR NEMA-MI-YAH'S PROTÉGÉS

- *The best matches for success in economic and practical achievements will be among men and women born June 3–7, under the care of He-Qua-Mi-Yah.*
- *The best matches for recognition, fame, personal charisma, and social fulfillment will be among men and women born March 10–14, under the care of Mova-Mi-Yah.*
- *The best matches for romance, love, and artistic and intellectual achievements will be among men and women born January 14–18, under the care of Vama-Ba-El.*

The harmonic vibrations of Angel Nema-Mi-Yah enliven the mind with strong and unexpected images, sudden inspirations, free associations of seemingly illogical ideas, and imaginary visions that transcend the ordinary thinking of everyday life. When in harmony with Angel Nema-Mi-Yah, women and men learn not to reject such intrusions even if others think them eccentric; rather, they come to appreciate their ability to see into the future and their capacity to understanding the dazzling intuitions that are bestowed upon them by Angel Nema-Mi-Yah.

Inventive, quick-witted, and psychic, those under the protection of Angel Nema-Mi-Yah can be successful in occupations that demand intuition, imagination, and the ability to predict, and especially in those fields where prophecy merges with innovation, such as fashion, advanced technology, and theoretical or experimental science. Their actions always create surprise and wonder, and their ideas often produce breakthrough results that define the cutting edge. Depending on their personal circumstances, those under the protection of Angel Nema-Mi-Yah are often recognized for their novel perspectives on everything from their work to the latest news headlines.

Prophecy can be a daunting power. Those who have it either embrace it or push it away. With the help of Angel Nema-Mi-Yah, those in her/his kinship learn to follow their intuitions, dig deep into people's minds, and uncover life's secrets. They also learn to bring back from their psychic journeys images that give life and color to their ideas and shape to their dreams.

If you are in harmony with Angel Nema-Mi-Yah, you see the invisible center at the heart of every reality as clearly as you see any tangible thing. Inspired by such intuitions, you can be counted on to offer an interpretation—of work situations or of relationships—that is so new and unique that it actually redefines people's everyday experience. In particular, you and all those who are guided by this innovative Angel are capable of a deep and fascinating analysis of the world, one that breaks the limits of current understanding. Your innovative thoughts, although disruptive to the status quo and sometimes extreme, often contribute to the advancement of a particular knowledge, science, or technique. Such ideas may quickly become enlightening models for others, the jumping-off points for other forward thinkers.

Men and women who live in kinship with Angel Nema-Mi-Yah are able to uncover precisely and to express accurately, in one word or expression, the absolute essence of an object, a situation, a person, or group. For example, they can recognize each plant in a field by its characteristics while also appreciating the aesthetic quality of the scenery. Or they can identify each person in a group by the subtleties of his or her personality while also understanding the feelings that bring them together or set them apart. For this reason, they are known to have a gift for naming and renaming beings and things. Depending on their personal circumstances, these men and women may use this talent to make breakthroughs in the field of classification (perhaps in the areas of botany or chemistry), perfumery (who do you think comes up with those compelling names?), or advertising, communications, or public relations.

By providing those in her/his care with rich intuitions and a fertile imagination, this exciting guide encourages those he/she loves to explore the many dimensions that form the universe, to know the many frontiers that separate them, and to move beyond them.

Under the protection of Nema-Mi-Yah, women and men can easily find their way when they travel from matter to the spirit of matter, from the depth of matter to the enlightenment of the mind, and can, when the time has come, rise up from the surface of the earth to the heights of the heavens.

Angel YE-YA-LA-EL

DECEMBER 30–JANUARY 3

Encourages an active way of life. Develops charisma. Helps in intelligently implementing high impact projects. Brings success by harmonizing purposes, thoughts, and actions.

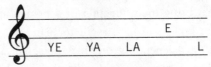

PHONETIC PRONUNCIATION

Ye as in Yes

Ya as in Yard

La as in Lama

El as in Elevation

UNIVERSAL RESONANCE OF THE ANGEL'S NAME

Ye Mastery. Dexterity, expertise; human action aligned with divine universal principles.

Ya Mastery. Dexterity, expertise; human action aligned with divine universal principles.

La Dynamic learning. The ability to make mental links. Intellectual elevation. An evolving, ascending movement of the mind. Lucidity and enlightenment.

El Ending vibration of the Angel's name. Principle of excellence; chosen; elite. Elevating force. Source of perpetual transformation and evolution. .

Guardian Angel Ye-Ya-La-El

In Akkadian language, the name Ye-Ya-La-El means, literally, "The Verb of Creation vibrates and generates the fluid of intellect that spirals and crystallizes in mental molecules."

There are people in the world around whom parties seem to spontaneously form, just the way electrons gather around the nucleus of an atom. Often, these are the people who are in harmony with guardian Angel Ye-Ya-La-El. Pragmatic, precise, and accurate,

---

NOTABLE PEOPLE BORN UNDER THE INFLUENCE OF YE-YA-LA-EL

Anthony Hopkins, *actor*

Elizabeth Arden, *cosmetics entrepreneur*

Famke Janssen, *actress*

Henri Matisse, *painter*

Isaac Asimov, *writer*

J. D. Salinger, *writer*

J. R. R. Tolkien, *writer*

John von Neumann, *mathematician*

Mel Gibson, *actor*

Paul Revere, *patriot*

Rudyard Kipling, *writer*

Sergio Leone, *film director*

Tia Carrere, *actress*

Tiger Woods, *golf champion*

Val Kilmer, *actor*

COLOR HARMONIZATION

*Iridescent colors of crystal /
Bluish white / Salmon rose /
Warm gold*

without a hint of self-doubt or uncertainty, these social movers and shakers use their natural leadership ability, ingenuity, and love of action to create memorable—even unforgettable—events and situations. In fact, the friends of Ye-Ya-La-El often acquire a reputation for bringing people together, creating relationships between unlikely partners, and generally excelling at the people mix, either in the social or professional realm. Just what, you may ask, do these people collectors gain by all this social juggling? Diverse people bring with them diverse possibilities. Those under the protection of Angel Ye-Ya-La-El take advantage of the many opportunities their friends bring their way. They integrate any new ideas that arise into their current projects with the agility of a potter adding clay to the growing form. And in the end they bring forth a more beautiful finished piece.

Angel Ye-Ya-La-El bestows upon those close to him/her the ability to understand, at a glance, the nuances of emotion that exist between people and the undertone of any social gathering. Thus, those under this social Angel's protection take to any roomful of people like fish to water, ably reading the nonverbal messages of those around them and communicating their own thoughts in actions, gestures, and eloquent words.

If you are in harmony with Angel Ye-Ya-La-El, you may be drawn to professions that require a strong personal presence or occupations that allow you to operate autonomously, without distractions, hesitations, waiting periods, or excessive planning. Depending on your personal circumstances, you may become involved in scientific or archaeological explorations, cover-story reporting, political activism, police investigations, litigation, public relations, fundraising, lobbying, stage direction, or film production.

In your private and professional life, you and all those born under the influence of Ye-Ya-La-El stay busy. You are constantly working with your hands, exercising your mind, working on artistic activities, putting together collections of objects, or gathering friends so they can share your interests and passions.

If you are in deep harmony with this Angel, you are known to be a charismatic, attractive, and fascinating personality. Thanks to your nearly magical power to act and through the grace of Angel Ye-Ya-La-El, every step on the path to success lies illuminated

HARMONIC MATCHES FOR YE-YA-LA-EL'S PROTÉGÉS

- *The best matches for success in economic and practical achievements will be among men and women born May 29–June 2, under the care of Hare-Ya-El.*
- *The best matches for recognition, fame, personal charisma, and social fulfillment will be among men and women born March 5–9, under the care of Ha-Ye-Ya-El.*
- *The best matches for romance, love, and artistic and intellectual achievements will be among men and women born January 19–23, under the care of Ye-He-Ha-El.*

before you. Thus, what is unseen by others is clear to you; celestial intelligence abides in your words; and human beings unite in your behalf to harvest the fruit of your ideas and actions.

Angel Ye-Ya-La-El gives to those in her/his protection a capacity for simultaneous action and thought. This means that you can act immediately—even impulsively—but with amazing appropriateness. Ye-Ya-La-El also bestows on those in his/her kinship the ability to overcome obstacles, leaping over pitfalls and difficulties like a character in a video game. By exercising the gifts of this guardian and refining desires and goals, you and everyone close to Ye-Ya-La-El can attain unity between your thoughts and actions and experience deep within yourself the transforming power of ideas.

With the help of Angel Ye-Ya-La-El, women and men happily elevate their minds to the very Source of all actions, of all thoughts, of all preeminence, and of all simultaneity. Then, bathed in eternal light, those under the protection of Ye-Ya-La-El can help the Angels reproduce their thoughts on earth, and they read in the spirit of Angels the words that reveal immortality.

Angel HA-RA-HA-EL

Generates visions and intuitions concerning the future. Encourages the exploration of elevated ways to resolve problems. Helps to lead a lifestyle guided by celestial ethics and enlightened by the laws of love and compassion.

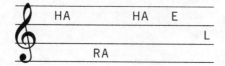

PHONETIC PRONUNCIATION

Ha as in Habit
Ra as in Rational
Ha as in Habit
El as in Elevation

UNIVERSAL RESONANCE OF THE ANGEL'S NAME

Ha Spiritual life force. Presence of the universal love and all-permeating spirit. Divine call, divine connection.

Ra Rotation, return, renewal; the natural cycles of existence. Radiance. Charisma. Inner vision and foresight on a universal scale. Princely leadership.

Ha Spiritual life force. Presence of the universal love and all-permeating spirit. Divine call, divine connection.

El Ending vibration of the Angel's name. Principle of excellence; chosen; elite. Elevating force. Source of perpetual transformation and evolution.

NOTABLE PEOPLE BORN UNDER THE INFLUENCE OF HA-RA-HA-EL

Clarence King, geologist
Diane Keaton, actress
E. L. Doctorow, writer
Elvis Presley, singer
Emily Green Balch, Nobel Peace Prize winner
Isaac Newton, physicist and founder of Newtonian physics
Joan of Arc, warrior and saint
Juan Carlos, king of Spain
Julia Ormond, actress
Katie Couric, television journalist
Nicolas Cage, actor
Robert Duvall, actor
Simone de Beauvoir, writer
Stephen Hawking, theoretical physicist
Umberto Eco, writer
Werner Heisenberg, theoretical physicist

COLOR HARMONIZATION

Sunny pale yellow / Orange stripes on large areas of dense cobalt blue

Guardian Angel Ha-Ra-Ha-El

In Akkadian language, the name Ha-Ra-Ha-El means, literally, "Penetrated by universal Love, human beings are enlightened by the divine spirit that brings them to the Creator."

Men and women who are in harmony with Angel Ha-Ra-Ha-El lift their minds to the heights of intelligent thought, constantly widen the field of their understanding, and look for the highest point of view: the vantage point that allows them to see the bigger picture.

If you were born under the protection of Angel Ha-Ra-Ha-El, your desire to glimpse the world from above and free yourself from realities that narrow or constrain your perception may manifest itself in the place you choose to make your home. Because you are drawn to vast horizons and a wide perspective, you may find comfort in a loft apartment or stilt house or on a balcony or elevated porch. Indeed, the right perch may even make you more receptive to spiritual messages. You may experience powerful dreams when camping at the top of a mountain or sleeping on a high floor of a building or under the limitless immensity of a wide-open, starlit sky.

If your birthday falls between January 4 and 8, you may feel that things are quite literally "looking up." That's because Angel Ha-Ra-Ha-El encourages her/his protégés to follow the ascendant path, opens up the way to the top, and stimulates a permanent upward momentum. It is important to note that constant climbing can be a challenge. But the Angel Ha-Ra-Ha-El always illuminates the path with the warm and bright rays of celestial love and provides his/her favored travelers with the energy they'll need to fuel the journey to emotional, intellectual, and spiritual growth. And at each step of the ascension, Ha-Ra-Ha-El bestows generous gifts upon those in her/his care, including new and bright visions that allow them to enlighten their current understanding of the world and to direct their search toward dimensions of the universe that are still mysterious to them.

Make no mistake: Angel Ha-Ra-Ha-El is one spiritual Sherpa who will lead you far from the beaten path. Men and women who choose to follow his/her breathtaking trails can find themselves strongly isolated from ordinary social life. They can even experience the kind of profound loneliness that both geniuses and psychopaths experience. If, by luck or design, they find their place in an artistically or intellectually open milieu, such as an astronomy lab, a large university, an association of writers, or a center for spiritual research, their unique visions are bound to draw attention and generate true respect. If not, those under the protection of Angel

Ha-Ra-Ha-El might have to protect themselves from the hostile, jealous, or simply inept people who are quick to categorize or misinterpret their visionary perceptions.

It may be helpful to note that one person's aerie may be another's lonely pinnacle. From the outside, those under the protection of Angel Ha-Ra-Ha-El can appear to be dreamers who have taken up permanent residence in the cloudier realms. In fact, because of the vastness of the perspective they embrace, friends of Ha-Ra-Ha-El see what is down below and what is up above with the same clarity and can discern what is coming for the future just as well as they can brilliantly analyze the present. Needless to say, with the loving and shining help of Angel Ha-Ra-Ha-El, it is possible to call the usual assumptions into question, refine your intellectual capacities, build your knowledge from primal truths, and live—in the light of the highest ethical ideals—a deep spiritual life.

Because the men and women who connect their minds to the harmonic vibrations of Angel Ha-Ra-Ha-El show a strong capacity for predicting the future, for prophecy and divination, "seeing" is a tangible part of their reality. Indeed, they are valued for their prophetic gifts, particularly if they become involved in fields where experts anticipate future ways of life, uncover long-term trends, or "foresee" cultural needs. These fields include many realms of research, ncluding sociological or technological research and development, marketing, or publishing. However, those under the protection of Ha-Ra-Ha-El must show great caution when distributing their considerable gifts among their contemporaries. Prophecy is among the most beautiful fruits of the celestial harvest when it is gathered from the highest branches of the tree of universal law. In other words, precognition is a gift best used with responsibility. Men and women who sincerely respond to the call of Angel Ha-Ra-Ha-El should also remember that messengers—no matter how well intentioned—can meet with disapproval, condemnation, and, depending on the social climate of the times, excommunication from a religious institution. Share your wisdom cautiously—and be glad you aren't living in an earlier time when no list of possible punishments was considered complete unless it included banishment or execution.

HARMONIC MATCHES FOR HA-RA-HA-EL'S PROTÉGÉS

- *The best matches for success in economic and practical achievements will be among men and women born May 24–28, under the care of Meba-Ha-El.*

- *The best matches for recognition, fame, personal charisma, and social fulfillment will be among men and women born February 28–March 4, under the care of Yaba-Mi-Yah.*

- *The best matches for romance, love, and artistic and intellectual achievements will be among men and women born January 24–28, under the care of Ânava-El.*

In spite of the risks, those of you who count the grace of Angel Ha-Ra-Ha-El among your many blessings have much to celebrate. You always choose the high roads and celestial apexes. And you travel them courageously, knowing they will ultimately lead you to the loving source, eternal Creator of our planet, of all the stars, of all living things, in all spaces and in all times.

Angel MITSA-RA-EL

JANUARY 9–13

Provides a gift for accuracy, precision, and adequacy.
Stimulates the energy to free oneself from conventions.
Helps in resolving delicate and inextricable situations.

		E	
MI			L
	TSA	RA	

PHONETIC PRONUNCIATION

Mi as in Miracle
Tsa as in Tsar
Ra as in Rama
El as in Elevation

UNIVERSAL RESONANCE OF THE ANGEL'S NAME

Mi The matrix; the model upon which creation is based. Manifestation in the material world. Loving maternal protection.

Tsa Exit; liberation. Movement toward the exterior, directional explosion. Righteousness, holiness. Perfect orientation of moral intentions.

Ra Rotation, return, renewal; the natural cycles of existence. Radiance. Charisma. Inner vision and foresight on a universal scale. Princely leadership.

El Ending vibration of the Angel's name. Principle of excellence; chosen; elite. Elevating force. Source of perpetual transformation and evolution.

Guardian Angel Mitsa-Ra-El

In Akkadian language, the name Mitsa-Ra-El means, literally, "Suddenly coming out of the matrix, one is able to see and reflect the future of the universe in its totality, its diversity, and its wholeness."

COLOR HARMONIZATION

Many greens, from the tender yellow-green of spring to deep forest green /
Sunny rays of summer

HARMONIC MATCHES FOR MITSA-RA-EL'S PROTÉGÉS

- *The best matches for success in economic and practical achievements will be among men and women born May 19–23, under the care of Yezala-El.*

- *The best matches for recognition, fame, personal charisma, and social fulfillment will be among men and women born February 23–27, under the care of Ro-A-Ha-El.*

- *The best matches for romance, love, and artistic and intellectual achievements will be among men and women born January 29– February 2, under the care of Me-He-Ya-El.*

Still waters run deep—and the quietly visceral men and women under the protection of Angel Mitsa-Ra-El are a great example. Thoughtful and discreet, these people are blessed with a temperament that allows them to go through long periods of maturation and patient preparation in the secret realms of their hearts. There, they refine their intentions and align them with their powerful minds.

Not just thinkers but doers, the friends of Mitsa-Ra-El conceive their ideas and act on them much the same way an embryo transforms itself in the darkness of the egg. Their ideas are conceived in solitude, grow in silence, then suddenly break through their protective shell into the clarity of daylight. At that point, the protégés of Mitsa-Ra-El come out of their "shells," too—to take on their goals and impress the world with massive achievements that are remarkable in scale and transformative power.

Angel Mitsa-Ra-El encourages deep introspection, including an ongoing inner examination of the underlying structures that make up reality, an awareness of the inner currents that feed the lives of beings and things, and an exploration of the paths that deliver them to the radiant light of truth. Deserving members of the spiritual heavyweight class, the friends of Mitsa-Ra-El often receive brilliant intuitions—even prophetic visions—which fire their aspirations and guide their future plans.

If you are close to this visionary guardian, you may be successful in an occupation or activity involving military or social strategy, theoretical experimentation, film or stage direction, ethnological or ethological exploration, religious missionary undertaking, architecture, encyclopedic writing, or innovative industrial entrepreneurship. Whatever career you choose, you can be sure you will attract notice. The scale of your achievements and the speed, innovation, and style with which you complete each assignment dazzle those around you. In fact, the quality of your work even makes up for your periods of incubation—and the resulting delays—that precede your impressive creative spurts.

Angel Mitsa-Ra-El predisposes those under her/his protection to an explosive intellectual mobility that gives them an exceptional aptitude for conceiving and inventing new modes of physical or virtual transmission, such as rapid air and ground travel or futuristic systems of communication. These, however, are certainly not the only options available to a deep thinker and spiritual visionary like you. Those who are in kinship with Angel Mitsa-Ra-El are often extremely sensitive to the rules, customs, laws, or practices that limit the horizons of those less fortunate. When your heart is filled with compassion, you may take on the role of a redresser of wrongs, a defender of social justice, and a veritable superhero to those in need. Indeed, your magnificent talents can turn a local cause into a national or international mission! In fact, you are so willing to put your money where your mouth—or sympathy—is, you might even leave a lucrative or comfortable position and devote yourself entirely to speaking, writing, educating, or directing films or publishing books that will enlighten others about the worthy cause you espouse.

In your private, social, and professional life, you and all those under the protection of Angel Mitsa-Ra-El always know to avoid closed-in places, no-win situations, and relationships that limit individual freedom. You are particularly careful to leave the door open when your enter business relationships, sign contracts, or select a club or a church. Should you find yourself mired in a difficult relationship or business liaison, you need only invoke your guardian. Angel Mitsa-Ra-El will extricate you faster than a good attorney.

Too many constraints imposed upon those under the protection of Angel Mitsa-Ra-El always result in their running off in directions that others consider unpredictable yet are, in reality, characteristically well planned. Trust your trailblazing guardian to point you always toward the freedom road. The harmonic vibrations of Angel Mitsa-Ra-El connect men and women with the most radiant energies of the universe. Allow these energies to awaken your freedom of choice, and you will be guided inevitably to the ultimate source of truth.

INVOCATION

O Angel Mitsa-Ra-El,
Your eyes illuminate the heavens,
Your chant awakens the planets
And praises the eternal dawn.
O Mitsa-Ra-El,
Help,
Guide,
And reveal to me
The hopes of my soul.
O Angel Mitsa-Ra-El,
I am coming back,
A vibrant spark
Freed from the mortal fears,
To the source of celestial fires.

Angel VAMA-BA-EL

JANUARY 14–18

Stimulates productive vitality. Provides the power for expansion. Frees up creative abilities. Paves the way for an easy and happy way of life. Give access to abundance and wealth.

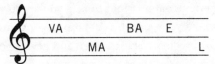

PHONETIC PRONUNCIATION

Va as in Valor
Ma as in Master
Ba as in Battle
El as in Elevation

UNIVERSAL RESONANCE OF THE ANGEL'S NAME

Va Vitalizing factor. Fruitfulness and productivity. Catalyst of variety, vitality, verity, will, and vigor.

Ma The matrix; the model upon which creation is based. Manifestation in the material world. Loving maternal protection.

Ba The universal paternal force; that which contains the code of all codes. The formative energy generating all data and shapes. The generic code that begins all lives, all manifestations, all experiences.

El Ending vibration of the Angel's name. Principle of excellence; chosen; elite. Elevating force. Source of perpetual transformation and evolution.

Guardian Angel Vama-Ba-El

In Akkadian language, the name Vama-Ba-El means, literally, "The life force penetrates the matrix, which encodes, molds, and manifests all forms of being, in their future and their evolution."

NOTABLE PEOPLE BORN UNDER THE INFLUENCE OF VAMA-BA-EL

Albert Schweitzer, Nobel Peace Prize winner

André Michelin, founder of Michelin Tires

Aristotle Onassis, businessman

Benjamin Franklin, writer, scientist, and statesman

Cary Grant, actor

Danny Kaye, actor

Faye Dunaway, actress

Gene Krupa, musician

James Earl Jones, actor

Jim Carrey, comedian and actor

Kate Moss, fashion model

Kevin Costner, actor

Lloyd Bridges, actor

Martin Luther King Jr., Nobel Peace Prize winner

Muhammad Ali, boxing champion

Sade, singer

COLOR HARMONIZATION

Apple red and green / Yellow peach / Grape purple

Too much of a good thing is . . . even better! Just ask the innovative men and women born under the protection of Angel Vama-Ba-El. Through the grace of their celestial guardian, they receive the gifts of fecundity, creation, and expansiveness, all of which they manifest in the joy and enthusiasm that colors everything they do. Playful, adventurous, and ingenious, these irresistible raconteurs—like Jim Carrey, Aristotle Onassis, and Danny Kaye—seem to draw material, emotional, intellectual, and spiritual wealth without much effort on their behalf. In truth, they earn their rich rewards with their productive ideas and the original ways with which they bring their dreams to life.

Those under the protection of Angel Vama-Ba-El enjoy abundance in all areas, and their wealth usually increases over time thanks to the formidable vitality of the thoughts, emotions, and goals that created it in the first place. For example, with the help of Angel Vama-Ba-El, those under this generous Angel's care not only create new financial formulas that generate strong returns, they also concoct new systems for revitalizing the businesses in which they have invested. Their financial security is thus ensured, and their active minds get a revitalizing workout in the bargain.

But just because these constructive, much-blessed men and women bring in the bucks, that doesn't mean they have a "what's mine is mine" attitude. The harmonies of Angel Vama-Ba-El activate energies that inspire women and men to be generous, nearly without limits. During the course of their lives, they seem to draw their wealth from an immense lake that is permanently fed by invisible underground springs. The more they distribute the resources that come their way, the more there seems to be to go around.

If you were born between January 14 and 18, your interests are as diverse as your talents. At work, you may be a jack-of-all-trades, familiar with all kinds of skills, from computer programming to whipping up gourmet lunches for your group to landing that big account to fixing that infernal copy machine. To your colleagues, there seems to be no limit to the things you can do. You accomplish whatever you put your mind to with power, innate know-how, and usually massive success. In the social arena, those under the protection of Angel Vama-Ba-El are often less famous than are their ideas and productions. But don't despair! If you were to seek popularity

HARMONIC MATCHES FOR VAMA-BA-EL'S PROTÉGÉS

- *The best matches for success in economic and practical achievements will be among men and women born September 11–15, under the care of Mena-Da-El.*

- *The best matches for recognition, fame, personal charisma, and social fulfillment will be among men and women born November 30–December 4, under the care of Âmami-Yah.*

- *The best matches for romance, love, and artistic and intellectual achievements will be among men and women born December 25–29, under the care of Nema-Mi-Yah.*

or personal glory in the creative things you do, your storehouse of ideas and inspirations would surely dry up, along with the source of your wealth. Rather than concerning yourself with notoriety, focus on the ways you can share your celestial gifts with others. Then you will be free to live the comfortable, happy, life of a bon vivant, filled with happy moments and stimulating relationships. All you need to do is follow the rich example provided by your industrious guardian, and you will be blessed with charm, generosity, an attractive personality, and the enduring love of others.

And while you're meditating on your divine Angel, you might consider your own spiritual nature as well. The busy men and women endowed by Vama-Ba-El are often so busy producing tangible results that they do not apply themselves to inner exploration. By invoking your guide sincerely and often, you will learn to seek the spiritual lesson in everything you do. You may even discover how to find in your work opportunities for reflection and meditation. If you work in an office, for example, you might invite some co-workers to join you in an early morning yoga class. If you spend considerable time on the road, you might make a point of building at least one cultural, artistic, historical, or religious destination into your weekly itinerary. Such soul breaks will nourish your spirit and may even increase your productive brainstorms.

When invoked, the Angel Vama-Ba-El heightens the intellectual powers of those in his/her care, awakens their ability to produce, and connects their ideas to the organizing laws of the universe. Touched by this Angel's intellectual lightning, those under the protection of Angel Vama-Ba-El illuminate the world and penetrate the depths of never-ending creation. Then, filled with wonder at their active participation in sublime, infinite invention, these men and women generously spread on earth the flowers, fruits, and sprouts they abundantly harvest in the celestial gardens.

Angel YE-HE-HA-EL

JANUARY 19–23

Stimulates a desire for appropriate action. Energizes the will and encourages initiative. Connects with the cohesive forces of universal love. Helps in the development of a charismatic personality. Promotes synchronicity.

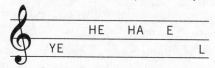

PHONETIC PRONUNCIATION

Ye as in Yes

He as in Hero

Ha as in Habit

El as in Elevation

UNIVERSAL RESONANCE OF THE ANGEL'S NAME

Ye Mastery. Dexterity, expertise; human action aligned with divine universal principles.

He Spiritual life force. Presence of the universal love and all-permeating spirit. Divine call, divine connection.

Ha Spiritual life force. Presence of the universal love and all-permeating spirit. Divine call, divine connection.

El Ending vibration of the Angel's name. Principle of excellence; chosen; elite. Elevating force. Source of perpetual transformation and evolution.

Guardian Angel Ye-He-Ha-El

In Akkadian language, the name Ye-He-Ha-El means, literally, "The supreme, imperative Verb of the Creator says, 'Let love be the unifying substance of all beings and evolution.'"

The world is putty in the hands of those strong-willed, creative men and women under the protection of Angel Ye-He-Ha-El. Or at least it seems that way! Determined and lively, endowed with a distinct vision of the way they believe things ought to be, those whose

Buzz Aldrin, pioneer astronaut

Christian Dior, fashion designer

David M. Lee, physicist

Dolly Parton, singer and actress

Edgar Allan Poe, writer

Federico Fellini, film director

Geena Davis, actress

Gertrude B. Elion, Nobel Prize winner in medicine

Jack W. Nicklaus, golf champion

Paul Cezanne, painter

Plácido Domingo, opera tenor

Princess Caroline of Monaco

Sir Francis Bacon, writer

Skeet Ulrich, actor

Telly Savalas, actor

COLOR HARMONIZATION

Lots of white / Lots of black / Red, to spice and warm / Violet-purple

HARMONIC MATCHES FOR YE-HE-HA-EL'S PROTÉGÉS

- *The best matches for success in economic and practical achievements will be among men and women born September 6–10, under the care of Chava-Qui-Yah.*
- *The best matches for recognition, fame, personal charisma, and social fulfillment will be among men and women born November 25–29, under the care of Ha-Hasi-Yah.*
- *The best matches for romance, love, and artistic and intellectual achievements will be among men and women born December 30–January 3, under the care of Ye-Ya-La-El.*

birthdays fall between January 19 and 23 are furnished with a strong ability to guide events in their own and other people's lives. Indeed, when in tune with the harmonic vibrations of Angel Ye-He-Ha-El, these revolutionaries can mold the world around them, dramatically transforming their environment and the people in it by the sheer strength of their thoughts. In their private relationships and professional friendships, such persons stimulate others with their contagious enthusiasm and easily convince them to share their feelings, join them in deep alliances, and in the end work toward creating their vision of the world.

The guardian of visionaries of all kinds, Ye-He-Ha-El supports the fanciful dreams of all her/his protégés, whether they are weavers of poetry, like Edgar Allen Poe, or creators of cinematic spectacle like Federico Fellini. No matter how outrageous their aesthetic, those in deep harmony with Angel Ye-He-Ha-El know they will succeed in everything they undertake—and that they are limited in their accomplishments only by the number of their desires and goals. Their countless degrees from the school of experience and their ability to change professions as casually as others change hats ensure that they will rarely fail—and only in undertakings that require more consistency and stability than they can muster.

Independent souls, the protégés of Ye-He-Ha-El prefer to act on their own whether in private or professional occupations. To put it mildly, they are not fans of groupthink and participate in collective projects only if they can take a leadership position. Being at the head of the pack enables them to give priority to their own goals—and their goals are always worthy of consideration. Their competence, initiative, and self-determination guides those under the protection of Angel Ye-He-Ha-El toward positions of leadership in artistic, social, business, industrial, or scientific research projects.

Considering their need for autonomy, drive to excel, and stubborn insistence on self-determination, those close to Ye-He-Ha-El may not long survive in a group setting. Or the group may not survive them. At any rate, their involvement in any organization is often short-lived, but their presence is always the source of remarkable events, unexpected discoveries, and providential—even miraculous—success. If they do carve out a niche in a corporate or group setting, an exciting time is guaranteed for all. Angel Ye-He-Ha-El opens the doors to action, encourages physical and intellectual motion, and, by stimulating individual free will, provides those under his/her protection with the necessary energy to face constant and ongoing challenge.

If you achieve deep harmony with Ye-He-Ha-El, you can connect spiritually with the forces that govern the universe. Through such contact, you will find the intellectual strength and moral righteousness that will guide you in your lifelong search for pure truth.

By invoking your independent Angel, you will activate the power of your will, which is the source of your individual freedom, and immerse yourself in the spiritual life force that unifies all beings and things. Then, with the help of your celestial guide, you can merge with the universal Creation and find exquisite joy in even the most minute creative act.

The friends of Ye-He-Ha-El are not just enlightened folk; they draw their inner illumination from the very source of the light. Consequently, those under the protection of this guardian can generally be expected to exemplify generous natures, high purposes, and the purest ethical principles. They are as powerful as locomotives—and usually run on the right track. But if you or other friends of Ye-He-Ha-El become overly influenced by your own success or too immersed in your own individuality, you may find your values turned upside down. Then, when your personal desires drive your goals, you will spiritually derail. You may even cross the line between personal power and tyranny, arrogance, deceit, manipulation, or demonic corruption. Blinded by the radiance of their gifts, the wise ones lose their way and see themselves as the unique source of their magical powers. However, by invoking Angel Ye-He-Ha-El, you and everyone close to this loving Angel will clearly identify the divine source of your talents and constantly search the paths of progress and spiritual elevation.

When in harmony with Angel Ye-He-Ha-El, men and women purify their desires and purposes in the pure celestial fountains, and their hearts beat in rhythm with the love of the universe's Creator.

Angel ÂNAVA-EL

JANUARY 24–28

Encourages humility. Stimulates comprehensive knowledge.
Gives priority to simplicity and authenticity in all things.
Supports a sincere search for spiritual and intellectual truth.

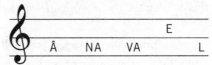

PHONETIC PRONUNCIATION

Â as in Arrow, ending with a soft breath out
Na as in Nativity
Va as in Value
El as in Elevation

UNIVERSAL RESONANCE OF THE ANGEL'S NAME

Â The origin of the sensory world; the foundation of human emotions and passions. Enhancement of visual senses and hearing acuity. Supersensitivity.

Na Nucleus, center, the essential; identity, individuality. Penetration to the center of every reality. Negation and rejection of superficial and perverse realities.

Va Vitalizing factor. Fruitfulness and productivity. Catalyst of variety, vitality, verity, will, and vigor.

El Ending vibration of the Angel's name. Principle of excellence; chosen; elite. Elevating force. Source of perpetual transformation and evolution.

Guardian Angel Ânava-El

In Akkadian language, the name Ânava-El means, literally, "Out of a being's humility comes the ultimate wealth that nourishes the soul."

There are those who think highly of themselves and those of whom others think highly. The harmonic vibrations of Angel Ânava-El encourage men and women to go beyond the superficial,

NOTABLE PEOPLE BORN UNDER THE INFLUENCE OF ÂNAVA-EL

Artur Rubinstein, *pianist*

Ava Gardner, *actress*

Bridget Fonda, *actress*

Douglas MacArthur, *U.S. Army general*

Jackson Pollock, *painter*

Lewis Caroll, *writer*

Linda Blair, *actress*

Mairead Corrigan-Maguire, *Nobel Peace Prize winner*

Mary Lou Retton, *Olympic gymnast*

Mikhail Baryshnikov, *dancer and choreographer*

Neil Diamond, *singer*

Robert Burns, *poet*

Virginia Woolf, *writer*

Wayne Gretsky, *hockey hall of famer*

Wolfgang Amadeus Mozart, *composer*

COLOR HARMONIZATION

Gray / White / Cream /
Spots of orange /
Large strikes of sunny yellow

to understand the true essence of everyone and everything around them, and to be so profoundly aligned with the germinal powers of fundamental truth that they stand as an example of quiet charisma and deep wisdom .

Angel Ânava-El provides those close to her/him with the privilege of not being dazzled by the shimmer of superficiality. Instead, these special people delve deep to find the unmatched light that shines at the heart of all reality. Unimpressed by the airs of others, those close to this forthright Angel are unlikely to put on the dog themselves. They would rather spend their time uncovering deception, penetrating veils and masks, and, stimulated by a love for truth, searching out the deep or remote sources and motivations of those nearby. And what they seek, these celestially inspired detectives will almost certainly find. As those under the protection of Angel Ânava-El put together each successive piece of the puzzle, their determination and fervor grows. Until the entire picture is revealed, they are simply unstoppable.

When in harmony with Angel Ânava-El, men and women overcome—without fanfare or other attention-getting tactics—the antiquated rules imposed by tradition. As if working in an underground revolution, they think beyond the beliefs that stifle, reject ideas that tranquilize the masses, and question, within themselves, the common sense of conventional wisdom. When circumstances allow, these freethinkers can produce brilliant accomplishments in nearly every field of endeavor, including science or philosophy, art or literature. Whatever area attracts them, they produce works that are remarkable in the depth of the intuition, understanding, and skill necessary for their completion.

If you are in harmony with Angel Ânava-El, you are a quiet, unpretentious achiever who avoids, as much as possible, what you see as the chaos, the carnival, and the complexity of social life. Because you are attracted to the depths, not the shallows, of life, you can be something of a problem at a party. Small talk wastes your time, and you have no interest in social games and exchanges. Still, you are a popular and loyal friend, one who prefers an inner search or a quiet tête-à-tête to a boisterous mob scene.

Thoughtful and probing, wise and fair, the friends of Ânava-El are deeply appreciated as advisers, particularly in the professional

HARMONIC MATCHES FOR ÂNAVA-EL'S PROTÉGÉS

- *The best matches for success in economic and practical achievements will be among men and women born September 1–5, under the care of Le-Ha-Hi-Yah.*
- *The best matches for recognition, fame, personal charisma, and social fulfillment will be among men and women born November 20–24, under the care of Dani-Ya-El.*
- *The best matches for romance, love, and artistic and intellectual achievements will be among men and women born January 4–8, under the care of Ha-Ra-Ha-El.*

arena. No matter what your current job, you will certainly be called upon to guide your colleagues and share your unique ideas with them. You may sidestep or turn down the promotion that comes with such responsibility, though. Because you are, above all else, a humble seeker of deep truths, you may have little desire to court notoriety, receive honors or titles, self-promote, or appear to outshine others, even if you deserve to do so. In truth, the situation is out of your hands. Your light is simply too big to hide. Powerful people see in you authenticity, honesty, truth, and ability. They will see to it that you receive all of the protection, recognition, and material support due you.

Those under the protection of Angel Ânava-El are often the originators of foundations or organizations in which they can work behind the scenes, in anonymity. Whether they apply their talents in an organization of their own creation or workplace of someone else's invention, these women and men find their rewards in the accomplishments of the organizations, not in their own aggrandizement. They are happiest in professional situations that match their integrity and their lofty goals.

Kinship with Angel Ânava-El guarantees that the intellect will always pierce ignorance, that it will separate what is worth knowing from what is not, and that it will reunite the soul with the origin of all life. By the grace of this perceptive Angel, men and women immerse their minds in the eternally fertile light of the universal Creator and illuminate the path to their goals. Then, having attained glory, those under the protection of Angel Ânava-El return to earth to show others the right path, the one that can be described in only one word: *humility.*

Angel ME-HE-YA-EL

JANUARY 29–FEBRUARY 2

Encourages a loving, maternal role. Develops a placid, calm, and patient temperament. Provides flexibility and adaptability. Supplies the necessary gifts for encouraging birth, growth, and maturity.

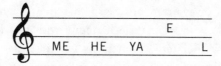

PHONETIC PRONUNCIATION

Me as in Mesopotamia

He as in Hero

Ya as in Yard

El as in Elevation

UNIVERSAL RESONANCE OF THE ANGEL'S NAME

Me The matrix; the model upon which creation is based. Manifestation in the material world. Loving maternal protection.

He Spiritual life force. Presence of the universal love and all-permeating spirit. Divine call, divine connection.

Ya Mastery. Dexterity, expertise; human action aligned with divine universal principles.

El Ending vibration of the Angel's name. Principle of excellence; chosen; elite. Elevating force. Source of perpetual transformation and evolution.

Guardian Angel Me-He-Ya-El

In Akkadian language, the name Me-He-Ya-El means, literally, "The matrix and the model of the Love-Being encourage evolution and growth."

What do talk-show host Oprah Winfrey and humanitarian actor Paul Newman have in common? They are both embraced by the harmonic vibrations of Angel Me-He-Ya-El, a uniquely enlightening

NOTABLE PEOPLE BORN UNDER THE INFLUENCE OF ME-HE-YA-EL

Alva Myrdal, *Nobel Peace Prize winner*

Anton Chekhov, *writer*

Boris Spassky, *chess champion*

Christie Brinkley, *actress and model*

Clark Gable, *actor*

Emanuel Swedenborg, *mystic and scientist*

Farrah Fawcett, *actress*

Franklin D. Roosevelt, *former U.S. president*

Franz Schubert, *composer*

Gene Hackman, *actor*

Heather Graham, *actress*

James Joyce, *writer*

Norman Mailer, *writer*

Oprah Winfrey, *talk-show host, actress, and producer*

Paul Newman, *actor*

Tom Selleck, *actor*

COLOR HARMONIZATION

Peach iridescence / Rose-mauve / Green / Blue / All on a white, semitransparent veil

HARMONIC MATCHES FOR ME-HE-YA-EL'S PROTÉGÉS

- *The best matches for success in economic and practical achievements will be among men and women born August 27–31, under the care of Ye-Hovi-Yah.*
- *The best matches for recognition, fame, personal charisma, and social fulfillment will be among men and women born November 15–19, under the care of Ve-Hova-El.*
- *The best matches for romance, love, and artistic and intellectual achievements will be among men and women born January 9–13, under the care of Mitsa-Ra-El.*

guardian who inspires gentle actions, protective gestures, comforting and encouraging words, feelings of love and compassion, constructive goals, and unifying thoughts.

In fact, the spiritual focus of the *Oprah Winfrey Show* and Newman's philanthropic efforts are characteristic of the concerned, compassionate men and women born into this Angel's care. In all circumstances, whether professional or private, those under the protection of Me-He-Ya-El seek to nourish, care for, and keep dangers away from others so that they might grow and evolve. People who attain true harmony with this loving guide come to view their environment as part of a natural system. Throughout their lives, they do everything they can, with love, to protect, improve, and beautify their world—and enlarge the prospects of the beings in it.

There are, of course, those naysayers who believe that the efforts of individuals cannot change the world. Nevertheless, those born into the care of this bountiful guardian are well equipped to give it a shot. Judicious, reflective, and free from prejudice, these people are able to find the win-win option in every situation. They excel at any job that requires a fair distribution, whether that means divvying up the world's resources or calming a group of covetous kids. They also have the patience to encourage growth, respect for the traditions, methods, and systems that have stood the test of time, and an indefatigable desire to help, in any capacity, at any moment. With Me-He-Ya-El's help, these special men and women can succeed in occupations such as portfolio management, child education, helping the needy, medical care, psychological counseling, social and legal work, and the protection of nature.

But while the rest of us are still arguing about the questions, what makes the protégés of Me-He-Ya-El so sure they have the answers? With the help of this discerning Angel, those in her/his care immerse themselves, body and soul, in discovering the mystery of the origin of life. When they have learned enough, they confidently reproduce on earth the fairness, love, and wisdom our guardian Angels inspire. Consequently, when what goes around comes around, the friends of Me-He-Ya-El will no doubt bring it!

If you are in kinship with Angel Me-He-Ya-El, you are in intimate contact with the subtle energies and vital substances that nourish life. Because these forces purify and protect you from useless uncertainties and harmful doubts, you develop a trusting and generous personality that works as a catalyst for calm and harmony in the world. If your destiny places you in the midst of social unrest, or if you are confronted with people in crisis, you and all those under the protection of Angel Me-He-Ya-El need only draw from that peaceful center within you to give help, assistance, care, and consolation. Depending on circumstances, you can be an effective organizer for charitable causes or devote your time to the growth and education of your own children. Both options take full advantage of your celestially inspired talents.

You and all of the friends of Angel Me-He-Ya-El are most fulfilled when you act out of your feelings of love for your fellow living creatures. Conversely, you may lose your courage and efficiency if you allow yourself to be influenced by hostile, vengeful, or destructive intentions. When you are faced with difficult situations, opposition, or provocation, it is important that you return to your calm, still center. This deep, placid core is like a lake that is fed by a rapidly moving river. Although the water that rages into it sends ripples across the lake's surface, the white water is absorbed and calmed. Your guardian will see to it that the quiet and fluid strength of your character will envelop your churning emotions as well.

With the help of Angel Me-He-Ya-El, you and everyone born between January 29 and February 2 are endowed with effortless patience and a keen intellect. These qualities allow you to acquire a deep knowledge of the rhythms, seasons, and cycles that guide the birth and growth of all living things. They also enable you to find an interesting and secure future as, for example, a trustworthy financial adviser, able to face market fluctuation without panicking, or an agent who must help those he or she guides to wait for better days. You may "mother" a business, legal, or intellectual project by nourishing and protecting it, or you may guide a beloved child's growth to maturity.

By the grace of Angel Me-He-Ya-El, the minds of men and women are warmed by the fire of the supreme Creator's love, and their souls receive the imprint of life's eternity. Thus enlightened by such imperishable truth, the protégés of this Angel do everything they can to implement on earth the celestial models that exalt the heavens.

Angel DAMABI-YAH

FEBRUARY 3–7

Stimulates intellectual curiosity. Sharpens the gift for exploring, uncovering, and discovering. Encourages the return to sources, origins, and principles. Opens the way to change and innovation.

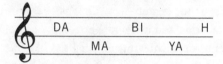

PHONETIC PRONUNCIATION

Da as in Darling
Ma as in Matter
Bi as in Bee
Ya as in Yard
H Vocalize the final H as a soft exhalation

UNIVERSAL RESONANCE OF THE ANGEL'S NAME

Da Discovery. Unveiling the unknown. Drama of all changes. Transference, translocation, translation. Mobility and transfer from one world to another. Appreciative perception of contrasts, differences, and variances.

Ma The matrix; the model upon which creation is based. Manifestation in the material world. Loving maternal protection.

Bi The universal paternal force; that which contains the code of all codes. The formative energy generating all data and shapes. The generic code that begins all lives, all manifestations, all experiences.

Yah Final vibration of the Angel's name. Receptivity and reflectivity. The presence of the deity; the abundance of the being.

COLOR HARMONIZATION

*White / Cream /
Black and white checks /
White, black, and yellow threads
elaborately interwoven and knotted
on warm sienna /
Specks of bright red and royal blue*

Guardian Angel Damabi-Yah

In Akkadian language, the name Damabi-Yah means, literally, "Unveiling universal archetypes, models, and forms, while penetrating the mysteries of the Creator Verb."

It is no surprise that Charles Lindbergh, William Burroughs, and Betty Friedan number among the protégés of this guardian Angel. The harmonies of Angel Damabi-Yah fuel the desire for journeying to unknown territories and new dimensions, encourage exploration of new worlds, and invigorate hopes of discoveries and innovations. Adventurous, achieving personalities like those mentioned above—all of whom have revolutionized a field of endeavor, pushed the envelope of an art form, or created a movement—are typical of the men and women who have been touched by Damabi-Yah.

It is said that a great journey begins with a single step. In the case of those born between February 3 and 7, adventure begins with thought. With the help of Angel Damabi-Yah, explorers reflect at length before they embark, taking time to refine their objectives and increase their odds of success before they act. Then, those under the protection of Angel Damabi-Yah enthusiastically and courageously pull up anchor and set off for faraway, mysterious, sometimes dangerous lands.

It should be noted that there are two types of challenging trips: adventures that require inoculations and possibly a good flotation device, and those that are less geographical than they are journeys of the mind. Depending on their personal circumstances, those in harmony with Angel Damabi-Yah can initiate or join exciting explorations at sea or on land, open new ways of reaching the earth's summits, penetrate dense forests to look for unique medicinal plants, or trek through an arid desert to mine a deposit of precious stones. There is no doubt that those under the protection of Angel Damabi-Yah are already anticipating their explorations into space and are preparing their departure toward extraterrestrial worlds, but they are also launching themselves into intellectual and artistic voyages they can make without ever leaving terra firma! Angel Damabi-Yah encourages women and men to scale the heights of understanding. Endowed by their brilliant Angel with the capacity to connect mentally with invisible spiritual forms that are the models for life on earth, these people are also able to decode, interpret, and translate celestial messages into day-to-day language. No wonder so many of these people are writers and performing artists known to have much to say!

If you open your heart to Angel Damabi-Yah, you can mobilize people and social institutions on behalf of your highest desires. For example, you might inspire others to disseminate information about innovative ideas, to pave the way for surprising innovations, or to reveal the profound truths you have learned as the result of your daring explorations. You will almost certainly find an audience. The discoveries made by the friends of Angel Damabi-Yah are remarkable in the strength of their impact and in their ability to revolutionize thought.

In the course of your fascinating life, one thing is certain: your day-to-day existence will not be ordinary. Whether at home or en route to some exotic locale, whether at work or in the social milieu, you move beyond the limits of timid habits and safe traditions. And wherever your lively intellect leads you, you always come back more knowledgeable, with more to offer those near you, and with new ideas for adventures to come. You may even lead your contemporaries on a more progressive path, one that charts a course to innovation in the fields of science, technology, medicine, geography, astronomy, psychology, theology, education, social organization, industry, or commerce.

Because you draw your inspiration and rewards mostly from celestial principles and because you tend to roam those spiritual territories where generosity, beauty, and truth reign, you and all those under the protection of Angel Damabi-Yah can sometimes find it difficult to earn the necessary income for your material security and comfort. By consciously invoking Angel Damabi-Yah, you will learn how you can best bring your brilliant discoveries to the world, thus encouraging those with means to provide you with the salary or reward you deserve.

When in deep harmony with Angel Damabi-Yah, the minds of men and women go beyond appearances, overcome obstacles of space and time, and speed up their incessant ascending motion to reach the source of all beginnings, the origin of all lives, and the light that uncovers all mysteries.

HARMONIC INVOCATION

O Angel Damabi-Yah,
Help me.
Help my hopes
To cross bridges
Over somber abysses.
O Damabi-Yah,
Your love scorches the tenebrous
darkness
And your song in the Angels' choir
Resonates beyond all times.
O Angel Damabi-Yah,
I chant your name,
My soul refines prayers,
Preparing its next journey
Toward the fountains of light.

MATCHES FOR
DAMABI-YAH'S PROTÉGÉS

- *The best matches for success in economic and practical achievements will be among men and women born August 22–26, under the care of Va-Sari-Yah.*
- *The best matches for recognition, fame, personal charisma, and social fulfillment will be among men and women born December 20–24, under the care of Povi-Ya-El.*
- *The best matches for romance, love, and artistic and intellectual achievements will be among men and women born December 5–9, under the care of Nana-A-El.*

Angel MANA-QUA-EL

FEBRUARY 8–12

Encourages the completion of all projects that are undertaken. Provides wealth and abundance. Stimulates the sense of balance and sharing. Promotes practical modes of action that have fruitful and permanent results. Reinforces confidence in the future.

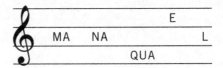

PHONETIC PRONUNCIATION

Ma as in Matter
Na as in Narrow
Qua as in Karma
El as in Elevation

UNIVERSAL RESONANCE OF THE ANGEL'S NAME

Ma The matrix; the model upon which creation is based. Manifestation in the material world. Loving maternal protection.

Na Nucleus, center, the essential; identity, individuality. Penetration to the center of every reality. Negation and rejection of superficial and perverse realities.

Qua Intelligence; knowledge of the principles of calculation, evaluation, quantification. Equilibrium and balance. Multiplication of natural riches and material abundance. Cosmic consciousness.

El Ending vibration of the Angel's name. Principle of excellence; chosen; elite. Elevating force. Source of perpetual transformation and evolution.

NOTABLE PEOPLE BORN UNDER THE INFLUENCE OF MANA-QUA-EL

Abraham Lincoln, *former U.S. president*

Boris Pasternak, *Nobel Prize winner in literature*

Burt Reynolds, *actor*

Charles Darwin, *naturalist*

Christina Ricci, *actress*

Dmitri Mendelyev, *chemist*

Franco Zeffirelli, *film director*

James Dean, *actor*

Joe Pesci, *actor*

Jules Vernes, *writer*

Laura Dern, *actress*

Mark Spitz, *Olympic swimmer*

Seth Green, *actor*

Thomas Edison, *inventor*

COLOR HARMONIZATION

Intense green / Peachy rose / Lilac / Creamy beige / Silvery gray / Dark brown

Guardian Angel Mana-Qua-El

In Akkadian language, the name Mana-Qua-El means, literally, "All integral and complete forms multiply, grow, and reproduce themselves in ascending evolution." Or, "My share is equal with that of the cosmos and grows eternally."

Whose bookshelves aren't overflowing with partially read books and unfinished novels, whose closets not packed with half-finished projects? Those close to Angel Mana-Qua-El! The harmonic rhythms of this powerful guardian provide women and men with the power to accomplish all their goals, complete their thoughts, and fully realize their desires. In fact, with the help of Angel Mana-Qua-El, these people browse freely through the inexhaustible wealth of the universe, using what they find there as the inspiration for even more goals and dreams! Never overwhelmed or perplexed by which of their favorite projects to get to first, these can-do men and women take on each new enterprise with measure, balance, and harmony.

In fact, though the rest of us may rack our brains, ideas rain upon the friends of Angel Mana-Qua-El like celestial manna. And they can handle it! Curious, intelligent, and interested, these men and women thrive on detecting what makes life on earth work and understanding how, with just a little effort, they might make it work even better. For example, these resourceful people don't just plant the crops, they find a bountiful source of pure water to irrigate them. In the professional sphere, they might acquire the copyright for successful books or films, create a new formulation for a particularly helpful pharmaceutical or cosmetic product, or invest in a new company with strong and innovative ideas. They generate wealth through the wide distribution of their products and the dissemination of their ideas. And they aren't flash-in-the-pan types, either. On the contrary, the intellectual, artistic, industrial, or commercial successes created by those close to Angel Mana-Qua-El show consistent growth and remarkable longevity.

If you are in harmony with Angel Mana-Qua-El, you can create an incredibly rich emotional life. You can, in fact, go through existence with your hands full, your arms laden with the flowers of friendship, your houses alive with children and the people you love. By the grace of your guardian, you generously communicate

HARMONIC MATCHES FOR MANA-QUA-EL'S PROTÉGÉS

- The best matches for success in economic and practical achievements will be among men and women born August 17–21, under the care of Le-Caba-El.
- The best matches for recognition, fame, personal charisma, and social fulfillment will be among men and women born December 15–19, under the care of Meba-Hi-Yah.
- The best matches for romance, love, and artistic and intellectual achievements will be among men and women born December 10–14, under the care of Niya-Tha-El.

the inner joy that inhabits your heart to others. People may even comment that you light up when you smile. Indeed, the light that shines in your eyes reflects the radiance of celestial beauty.

Those under the protection of Angel Mana-Qua-El develop stable and balanced personalities, rarely fearful of the future. And what is there to fear? You know that the beneficial power of Providence will compensate for any small failures on your part; therefore, you exude confidence. In fact, it is this deep trust that everything will turn out well in the end that inspires your characteristic stick-to-it-iveness. So what if others call it stubbornness? Your insistence on following through on every project, always building on solid foundations, and only considering your work finished when it becomes public is what will make you a success!

And speaking of your work, it is important to note that those under the protection of Angel Mana-Qua-El are happy when they work with their hands or when engaged in occupations that have practical (rather than purely intellectual, philosophical, or theoretical) applications. Depending on your personal circumstances, you may feel fulfilled in fields like architecture, sculpture, pottery, landscaping, interior design, high-quality arts and crafts, mechanics, or clock making.

Guardian Angel Mana-Qua-El introduces those in her/his care to the mysterious dynamics of abundance and to the flexible laws of unconditional generosity that ensure the reproduction and distribution of wealth. These people learn from their celestial master that material wealth will disappear if it is not redistributed, that beauty withers away if not admired, and that all thoughts are incomplete if not shared.

When in deep harmony with this profound guide, minds attune to the eternal vibrations that underlie all of the universe's creations, souls receive the celestial light, and hearts welcome the many riches that the Creator's love has given them for eternity. Then, filled with such providential gifts, those in kinship with Mana-Qua-El thank the heavens by recreating celestial beauty, greatness, and goodness on earth.

Angel A-YA-Â-EL

FEBRUARY 13–17

Stimulates empathy with others. Sharpens emotional sensitivity. Allows access to the sources and origins of all things. Provides the gift for interpretation and decoding. Encourages the capacity for judging with certainty and accuracy. Connects with collective memory.

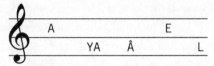

PHONETIC PRONUNCIATION

A as in Arrow

Ya as in Yard

Â as in Arrow, ending with a soft breath out

El as in Elevation

UNIVERSAL RESONANCE OF THE ANGEL'S NAME

A The original ultimate energy, before form, universal, infinite, unifying.

Ya Mastery. Dexterity, expertise; human action aligned with divine universal principles.

Â The origin of the sensory world; the foundation of human emotions and passions. Enhancement of visual senses and hearing acuity. Supersensitivity.

El Ending vibration of the Angel's name. Principle of excellence; chosen; elite. Elevating force. Source of perpetual transformation and evolution.

Guardian Angel A-Ya-Â-El

In Akkadian language the name A-Ya-Â-El means, literally, "The infinite energy of the Verb of Creation transmutes into a source of emotional sensitivity and a supply of universal memory and intelligence."

NOTABLE PEOPLE BORN UNDER THE INFLUENCE OF A-YA-Â-EL

Arcangelo Corelli, composer

Chaim Potok, writer

Chuck Yeager, aviator and test pilot

Galileo Galilei, scientist

George Segal, sculptor

Grant Wood, painter

Henry Brooks Adams, historian

James Ingram, musician

Jane Seymour, actress

Jerry Springer, talk-show host

Jim Brown, football legend

John McEnroe, tennis champion

Matt Groening, cartoonist

Michael Jordan, basketball legend

"Red" Barber, baseball broadcaster

Rene Russo, actress

Susan B. Anthony, women's rights advocate

COLOR HARMONIZATION

Silvery and gold rays, projected on black circles and in perpetual motion / Luminous light on a swirling black background

HARMONIC MATCHES FOR A-YA-Â-EL'S PROTÉGÉS

- *The best matches for success in economic and practical achievements will be among men and women born August 12–16, under the care of Ova-Ma-El.*
- *The best matches for recognition, fame, personal charisma, and social fulfillment will be among men and women born December 10–14, under the care of Niya-Tha-El.*
- *The best matches for romance, love, and artistic and intellectual achievements will be among men and women born December 15–19, under the care of Meba-Hi-Yah.*

When in harmony with Angel A-Ya-Â-El, men and women develop paradoxical personalities, remarkable because of their original, unconventional points of views and the deep, long-lasting consensus that yet forms around their ideas. Angel A-Ya-Â-El encourages men and women to use their highest degree of intellectual power to articulate unconventional arguments—acute logical reasoning that leads to precise, fair, and penetrating conclusions.

At first such analyses may generate embarrassed, resistant, or even hostile reactions, since others fear that the sought-after changes will shake up usual ways of thinking and lifestyles, alter priorities in emotional, intellectual, and spiritual values, change the order of social mores and laws, and alter the interpretation of events, large and small, past and present. However, with the help of Angel A-Ya-Â-El, these people base their reasoning upon intuitions that are so deep and inner visions so accurate that their conclusions end up being adopted by everyone in search of the enlightening and beautiful truth.

Consequently, during the course of their social, professional, or private lives, those under the protection of Angel A-Ya-Â-El are sometimes subject to social isolation during periods of time when most people are opposed to their ideas. Such times are interspersed with periods of notoriety, adulation, and sometimes prestige, when their unusual approach turns out to be the most enlightening and efficient in resolving a serious crisis or promoting understanding of an inexplicable phenomenon.

When in harmony with Angel A-Ya-Â-El, women and men rarely let themselves be distracted by offers of power and leadership that would force them to speak loud and clear in the midst of chaos. They prefer instead to cultivate private relationships that do not confuse their emotional sensitivity and do not alter their acute inner perception. It is through the example of their life, the brilliant intelligence of their message, and the accuracy of their science, rather than through social struggle and victories, that those under the protection of Angel A-Ya-Â-El are given supremacy and power on earth, as a reflection of the spiritual power they constantly draw from the heavens.

The harmonic vibrations of Angel A-Ya-Â-El provide men and women with the capacity to catalyze intellectual growth in their environment by communicating their ideas and their methods, which become, for many, trustful guides and powerful sources of inspiration. These people can become, depending on life's circumstances, mentors and counselors that are very much appreciated and venerated by a small group, a community, a nation, and even a worldwide organization.

Enlightened by the presence of pure universal principles that underlie all realities and stirred by energies that create all life, those under the protection of Angel A-Ya-Â-El like to mirror the truths that organize the universe and the forces of love that unite and vitalize all beings, without altering or tarnishing them with selfishness or vanity.

Such women and men often receive, accept, and succeed in promoting noble and humanitarian causes—working, for example, at improving the schools of an area or a country, improving health care, or providing the principles for the writing of new laws in favor of long-term justice.

When thinking and acting in harmony with Angel A-Ya-Â-El, these people do not pay any attention to sales or public relations that surround their involvement because they consider that real success comes from the participation of everyone contributing as best they can to a common task through intellectual accuracy, honest intentions, celestial inspirations, and universal compassion.

Protégés of Angel A-Ya-Â-El can also apply their hermeneutic talents to interpreting archaeological vestiges, now-silent unspoken languages, and confusing myths and can return such archaisms to their rightful place in the history of the origins of life and the causes of human evolution. Angel A-Ya-Â-El then launches those under his protection toward celestial dimensions where all words, all events, and all meditations vibrate, a place out of space and time that eternally pulses with the complete memory of the origin of the world and the whole history of humanity.

Angel HA-BOVI-YAH

FEBRUARY 18–22

Promotes a way of life based on love and feelings. Connects with the pulsation of life and fertility. Develops charm and joie de vivre. Stimulates the forces of renewal, of regeneration, and of youth.

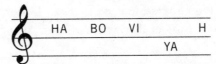

PHONETIC PRONUNCIATION

Ha as in Habit

Bo as in Border

Vi as in Victory

Ya as in Yard

H Vocalize the final H as a soft exhalation

UNIVERSAL RESONANCE OF THE ANGEL'S NAME

Ha   Spiritual life force. Presence of the universal love and all-permeating spirit. Divine call, divine connection.

Bo   The universal paternal force; that which contains the code of all codes. The formative energy generating all data and shapes. The generic code that begins all lives, all manifestations, all experiences.

Vi   Vitalizing factor. Fruitfulness and productivity. Catalyst of variety, vitality, verity, will, and vigor.

Yah Final vibration of the Angel's name. Receptivity and reflectivity. The presence of the deity; the abundance of the being.

Guardian Angel Ha-Bovi-Yah

In Akkadian language, the name Ha-Bovi-Yah means, literally, "Love forms and codifies all of the vital reproductive principles."

How would Sisyphus feel if, while pushing his boulder, he looked up to see someone zipping past, rolling his own stone

NOTABLE PEOPLE BORN UNDER THE INFLUENCE OF HA-BOVI-YAH

Anaïs Nin, writer

Cindy Crawford, model

Drew Barrymore, actress

Frédéric Chopin, composer and pianist

George Washington, first U.S. president

Hubert de Givenchy, fashion designer

Ivana Trump, socialite and entrepreneur

Jeff Daniels, actor

Jennifer Love Hewitt, actress

John Travolta, actor

Kelsey Grammer, actor

Nicolaus Copernicus, astronomer

Sidney Poitier, actor

Toni Morrison, Nobel Prize winner in literature

William Baldwin, actor

COLOR HARMONIZATION

Autumn colors:
yellow-greens, deep flame, rust /
Vibrant red /
All colors of joyous spring: dense greens /
Strawberry / Cherry / Peach

uphill as if it were a ball—and the Sisyphean challenge we call life was just a game? He would feel much the same way the rest of us do when we encounter the agile, able protégés of Angel Ha-Bovi-Yah! Bright and optimistic, these eager women and men charge through life with a nearly total indifference to life's difficulties. And why should they worry? The harmonic vibrations of their guardian enables them to quickly find solutions to sticky situations, to overleap any obstacles they encounter, and to joyfully stay the course that will lead them to emotional and spiritual growth.

And for these enthusiastic students at the school of upbeat experience, lifelong growth is assured. Angel Ha-Bovi-Yah connects the minds of those he/she loves with the vitalizing energy that unifies the universe. Consequently, the men and women in her/his care are endowed with great powers of reproduction and creativity. If they achieve deep harmony with this educating Angel, their lives become a celebration, a constant whirl within the dance that is the spectacle of life, a joyous hymn in the living cathedral of a deep, tree-lined forest.

When in kinship with Angel Ha-Bovi-Yah, those born between February 18 and 22 develop cheerful, lively, and friendly personalities that are full of charm and joie de vivre. Needless to say, they come fully equipped with all the psychological options conducive to sincere friendships, fruitful relationships, and vibrant romantic love. Circumstances permitting, these people reach the pinnacle of the good life when they are in proximity with the living forces of nature, such as alpine rapids and lakes, flowers and orchards, fields and woodland creatures. In this kind of a bucolic setting, they are able to share their feelings of love with all living things—humans, animals, or plants.

If you are fully connected to Angel Ha-Bovi-Yah, you have a deep love of nature and an innate empathy with the reproductive and generative forces that perpetually recreate the world. It is possible that you will express this empathy by bringing forth a large and happy family. You may also tap the power of fertility through gardening (Ha-Bovi-Yah has given you a green thumb), organic farming, silviculture, or the rebuilding of natural environments. You may also hone your regenerative skills by practicing

HARMONIC MATCHES FOR HA-BOVI-YAH'S PROTÉGÉS

- *The best matches for success in economic and practical achievements will be among men and women born August 7–11, under the care of Re-Yi-Ya-El.*
- *The best matches for recognition, fame, personal charisma, and social fulfillment will be among men and women born December 5–9, under the care of Nana-A-El.*
- *The best matches for romance, love, and artistic and intellectual achievements will be among men and women born December 20–24, under the care of Povi-Ya-El.*

alternative medicine or becoming involved in any kind of occupation that cures by regenerating energy or improving health.

If you are a friend of Ha-Bovi-Yah, you are known for your willingness to reach out, in the spirit of love and renewal, to resolve the conflicts, crises, or confusing emotional situations that confound those around you. Indeed, those under the protection of this attractive guardian can become powerful people magnets, attracting a coterie of loyal friends, attentive students, and respectful disciples. Your own powers of attraction may provide you with a mission to educate, teach, distribute goods and wealth, share your knowledge, and give psychological, sociological, economic, and financial support to those who gather at your feet. You may inspire one of your own protégés to develop a design or architectural construction based on your ideas. You may even create models yourself in the areas of science, medicine, and linguistics that will be the basis for many future innovations.

By invoking Angel Ha-Bovi-Yah, men and women can attract, at any age, the energy of prime youth and constantly draw from the pure fountain of eternal renewal. When in deep harmony with Angel Ha-Bovi-Yah, women and men, girls and boys, connect with the invisible presence of love, which encompasses and unifies all beings and things. Then, the sadness of old age and the dark worries of adolescence melt under the sun of the joy of love and forever disappear in the swirling vitality of the mind that touches truth and immerses itself in beauty.

Angel RO-A-HA-EL

FEBRUARY 23–27

Reinforces visionary powers. Generates initiative and stimulates abilities for leadership. Develops the courage to face the intellectual, moral, and spiritual truth and provides the energy necessary to spread its influence.

PHONETIC PRONUNCIATION

Ro as in Rock
A as in Arrow
Ha as in Habit
El as in Elevation

UNIVERSAL RESONANCE OF THE ANGEL'S NAME

Ro Rotation, return, renewal; the natural cycles of existence. Radiance. Charisma. Inner vision and foresight on a universal scale. Princely leadership.

A The original ultimate energy, before form, universal, infinite, unifying.

Ha Spiritual life force. Presence of the universal love and all-permeating spirit. Divine call, divine connection.

El Ending vibration of the Angel's name. Principle of excellence; chosen; elite. Elevating force. Source of perpetual transformation and evolution.

Guardian Angel Ro-A-Ha-El

In the Akkadian language, the name Ro-A-Ha-El means, literally, "The spiraling swirl of circular forces colliding with the protouniversal energy transmutes into a calm ocean of spiritual love." Or, "The original, primordial radiance carries and spreads all existences and all the forces of being and evolution."

COLOR HARMONIZATION

Fresh crisp sky blue / Turquoise / Virginal white with spots of yellow, red, and green

HARMONIC MATCHES FOR RO-A-HA-EL'S PROTÉGÉS

- *The best matches for success in economic and practical achievements will be among men and women born August 2–6, under the care of Se-A-He-Yah.*
- *The best matches for recognition, fame, personal charisma, and social fulfillment will be among men and women born January 9–13, under the care of Mitsa-Ra-El.*
- *The best matches for romance, love, and artistic and intellectual achievements will be among men and women born November 15–19, under the care of Ve-Hova-El.*

Angels are messengers of truth. Angel Ro-A-Ha-El, in particular, helps those in her/his care to "face the truth" without being blinded by its brilliance or frightened by its power. He/she also guides these men and women to share the truth, in all its purity and integrity, with others. When in harmony with this luminous Angel, people project the light of intellect straight to the heart of reality and carry the truth like a banner into their daily lives.

Endowed with the qualities of initiative and decisiveness, those under the protection of Angel Ro-A-Ha-El often develop firm, daring, judicious, penetrating, willful characters that can seem a bit authoritarian and imperious. If it's a jungle out there, then these courageous, self-driven individuals are the kings and queens of that jungle. If they take on that role, it is a sign that their hearts and minds have fallen under the control of their considerable wills. This can lead to becoming authoritarian in their relationships and intellectually tyrannical, emotionally imperialistic, and unreasonably proud. When in harmony with Angel Ro-A-Ha-El, however, those in this guardian's protection tend to their inner lives first. With the grace of their celestial guide, they develop personalities that are daring but judicious, forceful but loving, firm but full of moral resolution. These qualities make them standouts among their peers. Once they attract the notice of others, they are often offered positions of leadership through which they can spread their enlightening knowledge, their futuristic visions, and their progressive plans.

The protégés of Angel Ro-A-Ha-El are people in the know. Self-assured and definite in their opinions, they can worry those who aren't quite so intuitive. They can also be perceived as a threat by colleagues, peers, and insecure bosses who seek to preserve their positions and, therefore, dread dynamic, self-starters who can influence the status quo. However, the innate sense of authority and unerring awareness of the truth of any situation makes those under the guardianship of Ro-A-Ha-El invaluable members of the team in emergencies or when the survival of a cause, group, institution, or nation is at stake. These are the leaders you want on your side when the chips are down.

If you are in harmony with Angel Ro-A-Ha-El, you may find it necessary to distance yourself from situations that demand political concessions, diplomatic circumlocutions, or hidden agendas. These and other circumstances that require you to stretch the truth—sometimes beyond recognition!—put you in direct conflict with your desire to live in truth. To keep your sanity, you should seek out activities in which moral rectitude is rewarded and occupations where your forthright manner might bring you prestige, honor, and success. You might succeed, for example, as a university professor, high-level technician, a research scientist, financial consultant, judge, theologian, or in any other field where truth is brought to light.

By sincerely invoking Angel Ro-A-Ha-El, you can feed your inner life with enlightening inner visions, open direct access to the invisible forces that rule the universe, and share in the powerful energy that unites all creatures to their Creator. In contact with the fiery celestial forces that launch all evolution and protect the consistency of universal laws, that rule over all worlds and encourage all freedoms, you and all those under the protection of Angel Ro-A-Ha-El can test the strength of your stalwart courage and the value of your indomitable will.

With the help of Angel Ro-A-Ha-El, men and women draw on the inexhaustible source of divine love and receive vital messages that foretell the infinite truth. If they also renounce a life of strictly earthly pleasures, they can associate their free wills with the will of the Supreme Master and Creator. Then, guided by Angel Ro-A-Ha-El, those in kinship with this proud Angel will receive the answer to all their questions, penetrate the mysteries of the universe, and, freed from doubt and fear of death, cross the spiritual threshold that leads to the vast territories of the celestial kingdom.

For those who sincerely invoke this Angel, Ro-A-Ha-El illuminates the wonders of creation and reveals the mysteries of the origin of the world. Let him/her lead you to the source of celestial love.

Angel YABA-MI-YAH

FEBRUARY 28–MARCH 4

Encourages a dynamic, active, and productive lifestyle. Opens the way to autonomy and independence. Develops a sense of mission and responsibility. Stimulates vital energy, growth, and development.

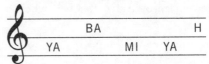

PHONETIC PRONUNCIATION

Ya as in Yard
Ba as in Battle
Mi as in Mission
Ya as in Yard
H Vocalize the final H as a soft exhalation

UNIVERSAL RESONANCE OF THE ANGEL'S NAME

Ya Mastery. Dexterity, expertise; human action aligned with divine universal principles.

Ba The universal paternal force; that which contains the code of all codes. The formative energy generating all data and shapes. The generic code that begins all lives, all manifestations, all experiences.

Mi The matrix; the model upon which creation is based. Manifestation in the material world. Loving maternal protection.

Yah Final vibration of the Angel's name. Receptivity and reflectivity. The presence of the deity; the abundance of the being.

NOTABLE PEOPLE BORN UNDER THE INFLUENCE OF YABA-MI-YAH

Antonio Vivaldi, *composer*

Daniel C. Tsui, *Nobel Prize winner in physics*

Dr. Seuss, *children's author*

Glenn Miller, *bandleader and musician*

Hershel Walker, *professional football player*

Itzhak Rabin, *former prime minister of Israel*

Jackie Joyner-Kersee, *Olympic track and field athlete*

Jennifer Jones, *actress*

Linus Pauling, *Nobel Peace prize winner*

Mikhail Gorbachev, *former Soviet president*

Miriam Makeba, *singer*

Steven Chu, *Nobel Prize winner in physics*

COLOR HARMONIZATION

Steel blue / Forest green / Apple green / Orange / Rust brown / Plum red / Creamy white

Guardian Angel Yaba-Mi-Yah

In the Akkadian language, the name Yaba-Mi-Yah means, literally, "My actions emanate from the matrix of the Supreme Being."

While others wait for someone to take difficult situations off their hands, those born under the protection of Angel Yaba-Mi-Yah can't wait to take matters into theirs. Independent, captains of their own ship, these direct and self-directed individuals are determined to run the show—and often do so, sometimes beginning in early childhood. Neither do they outgrow this tendency. Indeed, the single-minded men and women born between February 28 and March 4, like Dr. Seuss and Jackie Joyner-Kersee, keep a tight hold on the reins until the end of their lives, changing the course of their lives with daring but always well-planned personal initiatives.

Take-charge people are not usually easygoing people, and those in harmony with Angel Yaba-Mi-Yah are no exception. Active and dynamic, prone to stormy phases and impetuous behavior, these autonomous and independent men and women are blessed with an unshakable determination to succeed, sometimes at the expense of those around them. Whether in their private or professional lives, those under the protection of Angel Yaba-Mi-Yah do not hesitate to set themselves up as an example and implement their new ideas or plans without hesitation or discussion. They rarely abandon their projects and always take time to follow through on all the details that will make them succeed. This quality—and their personal dynamism—makes them popular and even inspirational with their co-workers. Circumstances allowing, they may acquire prestige as training coaches, educators for children or adults, or directors of health centers for the physically or mentally disabled.

Yaba-Mi-Yah is an Angel with a mission—and he/she is more than willing to share that sense of destiny with anyone in her/his care. Consequently, the protégés of this celestial guide tend to view any activity that intrigues them as a duty, a responsibility they will fulfill at any cost. Needless to say, these firebrands accomplish just about everything they set their minds to, undertaking works of great scope. Their names are often attached to great accomplishments.

If you are born under the protection of Angel Yaba-Mi-Yah, you can become a real mover and shaker; an active participant in the

HARMONIC MATCHES FOR YABA-MI-YAH'S PROTÉGÉS

- *The best matches for success in economic and practical achievements will be among men and women born July 28–August 1, under the care of Yeratha-El.*
- *The best matches for recognition, fame, personal charisma, and social fulfillment will be among men and women born January 4–8, under the care of Ha-Ra-Ha-El.*
- *The best matches for romance, love, and artistic and intellectual achievements will be among men and women born November 20–24, under the care of Dani-Ya-El.*

development of powerful industrial and commercial firms, the construction of complex buildings, the management of large agricultural farms, the implementation of important social, economic, or financial reforms, or the logistic implementation of rescue plans or humanitarian aid. In fact, you can succeed in all activities that require strong capacities for organization, coordination, anticipation, and innovation, but you are in no danger of getting trapped in an "all work and no play" lifestyle. Men and women who connect with Angel Yaba-Mi-Yah like to promote expansion and growth in their environment and love to share their gifts with others. Consequently, they rarely develop socially isolated personalities. In exchange for their efficient and generous contributions, those under the protection of Angel Yaba-Mi-Yah receive money, credit, contracts, social consideration, and fame.

If you sincerely invoke your luminous guardian, you can be connected with the invisible forces that structure and vitalize beings and things. You will also open the pathway to a veritable treasure trove of inner visions and inspirations that will feed your personal creativity, ensuring that you'll always be ready with a great idea or brilliant and fair solution.

At certain times in your life, in order to benefit fully from your spiritual connection with Angel Yaba-Mi-Yah, you must put your need for action on hold, set aside your search for the next accomplishment, and listen carefully to the harmonic message communicated to you by your guardian Angel. With your body and mind at rest, you can immerse your spirit in the pure water of the universal matrix and let your intelligence draw its models from the unique source of all growth.

Aligning your goals and behavior with Angel Yaba-Mi-Yah, you avoid the dangers of physical and mental agitation, impulsive action, excessive willfulness, and the no-holds-barred quest for independence. You also receive the gift of patience, which motivates you, when necessary, to postpone action so you can widen your perception or take in more information. Allowing yourself time to absorb wisdom will ensure that your plans reach maturity.

You and all those in kinship with this dynamic Angel are blessed with a potent personal will, reinforced by the power to achieve. This can tempt the friends of Yaba-Mi-Yah to accelerate their growth and production and leave their mark on history.

For this reason, Angel Yaba-Mi-Yah encourages those under his/her protection to "turn their tongue in their mouths seven times before speaking," and asks them to abide by the saying that "practice makes perfect." And when they decide to generate followers in the art of action to change the world and want to teach methods that bring them material, intellectual, and spiritual success, Angel Yaba-Mi-Yah invites them to reconsider their real motivations, to elevate their thoughts to the true origins of their gifts, and to become the mindful disciples of a celestial Master.

Angel HA-YE-YA-EL

MARCH 5–9

Provides serenity. Encourages freethinking and liberating actions. Encourages togetherness, solidarity, and brother- and sisterhood. Opens the way to tolerance. Resolves conflicts through mediation, equanimity, and harmony.

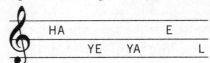

PHONETIC PRONUNCIATION

Ha as in Habit
Ye as in Yes
Ya as in Yard
El as in Elevation

UNIVERSAL RESONANCE OF THE ANGEL'S NAME

Ha Spiritual life force. Presence of the universal love and all-permeating spirit. Divine call, divine connection.

Ye Mastery. Dexterity, expertise; human action aligned with divine universal principles.

Ya Mastery. Dexterity, expertise; human action aligned with divine universal principles.

El Ending vibration of the Angel's name. Principle of excellence; chosen; elite. Elevating force. Source of perpetual transformation and evolution.

Guardian Angel Ha-Ye-Ya-El

In the Akkadian language, the name Ha-Ye-Ya-El means, literally, "The principle of universal unifying attraction turns into ascending, evolving action," or, "God, through love, energizes and inhabits the Verb of Creation."

When in harmony with Angel Ha-Ye-Ya-El, women and men develop personalities that appear paradoxical: deeply contemplative yet able to take action; endowed with a strong inner life but

NOTABLE PEOPLE BORN UNDER THE INFLUENCE OF HA-YE-YA-EL

Alan Greenspan, Federal Reserve Board chair

Bobby Fischer, chess champion

Gabriel García Márquez, writer

Ivan Lendl, tennis champion

Jake Lloyd, actor

Janet Guthrie, race car driver

Linda Fiorentino, actress

Maurice Ravel, composer

Michael Eisner, Disney chief

Michelangelo, painter

Niki Taylor, fashion model

Pier Paolo Pasolini, film director and writer

Piet Mondrian, painter

Sophia Grojsman, master perfumer

Yuri Gagarin, Russian cosmonaut and first man in space

COLOR HARMONIZATION

Red / Black / White / Violet / Yellow

happily engaged in the outside world. Spend a few minutes in conversation with them, and they'll dazzle you with their deep thoughts on the origin of the universe, then they'll lighten things up with a dose of their breezy, at times even childish, humor.

You would think that this sort of duality might be difficult to maintain. Not so for the friends of this complex Angel. Endowed by Ha-Ye-Ya-El with the ability to balance and unify extremes, the men and women born between March 5 and 9 effortlessly combine meditation with movement, firmness with tolerance, and a respect for tradition with the deep drive to evolve. Those under the protection of Angel Ha-Ye-Ya-El also intensify and enrich their lives by drawing their values from both the reservoir of the past and the currents of the future. Thus, they constantly work to deepen their inner lives without ever losing their awareness of the invisible forces that link their progress to the evolution of the world.

We have all heard the saying, "As above, so below." To those men and women who keep close to Angel Ha-Ye-Ya-El, it has a profound meaning. Ha-Ye-Ya-El encourages those he/she loves to incessantly explore every aspect of reality; to discover what's up in the timeless cosmos, then use what they have learned to clarify their understanding of what is in process on this earth. When in harmony with this transformative guide, people can be successful scientists, philosophers, historians, or publishers of exploration and discovery books. In truth, those under the protection of Angel Ha-Ye-Ya-El can also excel in all occupations, whether physical or intellectual, that require the ability to balance opposing forces or unify the energies of seemingly divergent groups. They are naturals in such fields as mediation and in some areas of law, economics, or sports, and they will certainly succeed in education, where they can exercise every day their desire to accelerate evolution.

If you were born under the protection of Angel Ha-Ye-Ya-El, you may have discovered the power of your free will very early in life. You are also likely to have learned, even as a child, that all humans possess the same privilege, though some are more reluctant than you are to use it. If you are like many of the protégés of Ha-Ye-Ya-El, you may find that your life has been a constant effort to increase the bounds of your own freedom, not for any selfish reason, but as an educational tool. If one learns by experience, you might reason,

HARMONIC MATCHES FOR HA-YE-YA-EL'S PROTÉGÉS

- *The best matches for success in economic and practical achievements will be among men and women born July 23–27, under the care of He-A-A-Yah.*
- *The best matches for recognition, fame, personal charisma, and social fulfillment will be among men and women born December 30–January 3, under the care of Ye-Ya-La-El.*
- *The best matches for romance, love, and artistic and intellectual achievements will be among men and women born November 25–29, under the care of Ha-Hasi-Yah.*

then you might as well get your Ph.D. Go for it! What you will learn will enable you to think more deeply, fight ignorance, restore hope, love more fully, and dissolve hatred.

Not that anyone is likely to hate *you*. The men and women guided by Ha-Ye-Ya-El are usually quite charismatic, and, thanks to the serenity they project even when they're under pressure, they are the rocks others cling to for reassurance and a soothing feeling of solidarity. Depending on your personal circumstances, you could become a crack mediator of political or labor crises, a skilled (and unflappable) designer of transportation systems, a memorable communicator, or a learned and amusing friend. Who wouldn't value such a companion? Thanks to your balanced guardian, you are neither overly restrained nor heavy-handed with your advice. A true freethinker, you are also the source of an endless supply of ideas, which you generously share with anyone who asks for help.

The women and men who connect with Angel Ha-Ye-Ya-El draw their intellectual and spiritual energy from the inexhaustible source of universal abundance, enkindle their desires with the fire of divine love, and gather on the earth the spiritual harvest with which Angel Ha-Ye-Ya-El rewards them for their efforts. When they are in deep harmony with this Angel, their thoughts reach all the way to the Angels' domain, where the mind can glimpse the ultimate truth. Here, the friends of Ha-Ye-Ya-El learn the ultimate purpose of their noble actions. Then, ever more serene, they resume their march on this earth and generously share with their journeying companions the enlightening fruits of their radiant knowledge.

Angel MOVA-MI-YAH

Develops patience and ability for waiting. Encourages propagation and reproduction of ideas and goods. Reinforces communion with the rhythms and cycles of nature. Stimulates regeneration, rebirth, and healing.

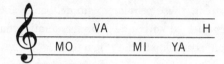

PHONETIC PRONUNCIATION

Mo as in Mobility

Va as in Varsity

Mi as in Mission

Ya as in Yard

H Vocalize the final H as a soft exhalation

UNIVERSAL RESONANCE OF THE ANGEL'S NAME

Mo The matrix; the model upon which creation is based. Manifestation in the material world. Loving maternal protection

Va Vitalizing factor. Fruitfulness and productivity. Catalyst of variety, vitality, verity, will, and vigor.

Mi The matrix; the model upon which creation is based. Manifestation in the material world. Loving maternal protection.

Yah Final vibration of the Angel's name. Receptivity and reflectivity. The presence of the deity; the abundance of the being.

Guardian Angel Mova-Mi-Yah

In the Akkadian language the name Mova-Mi-Yah literally means, "The universe is circular, everything originates from its end, and everything ends at its origin."

NOTABLE PEOPLE BORN UNDER THE INFLUENCE OF MOVA-MI-YAH

Albert Einstein, *Nobel Prize winner in physics*

Andrew Young, *religious leader and civil rights activist*

Antonin Scalia, *U.S. Supreme Court justice*

Billy Crystal, *comedian and actor*

Chuck Norris, *martial artist and actor*

Darryl Strawberry, *baseball player*

Frank Borman, *pioneer astronaut*

L. Ron Hubbard, *writer and founder of Scientology*

Liza Minelli, *singer and actress*

Michael Caine, *actor*

Pope Pius XII

Ralph Abernathy, *Baptist clergyman and civil rights activist*

Rupert Murdoch, *media mogul*

Sharon Stone, *actress*

COLOR HARMONIZATION

Carmine red / Dark, deep sky blue / Sunny egg yellow / White and black

HARMONIC MATCHES FOR MOVA-MI-YAH'S PROTÉGÉS

- *The best matches for success in economic and practical achievements will be among men and women born July 18–22, under the care of Nith-Ha-Yah.*
- *The best matches for recognition, fame, personal charisma, and social fulfillment will be among men and women born December 25–29, under the care of Nema-Mi-Yah.*
- *The best matches for romance, love, and artistic and intellectual achievements will be among men and women born November 30– December 4, under the care of Âmami-Yah.*

Men and women who live in harmony with Angel Mova-Mi-Yah develop active, productive, yet patient personalities. Tolerant souls who are capable of long waits without even drumming their fingers, those close to Mova-Mi-Yah approach life without rushing. They nurture their thoughts before acting or speaking and listen to others before jumping to conclusions. In short, they are the forbearing, accepting parents, teachers, and friends of our dreams.

While most of us adopt the rush to judgment as part of our mental fitness plan, these people remain deliberate and calm, as if they have been blessed with a deep understanding that situations and human beings develop in their own time.

Angel Mova-Mi-Yah ensures that those under her/his protection will evolve and create in the same mysterious way nature does: slowly and through each necessary phase, including fertility and growth, hibernation and rebirth, reproduction and birth.

Consequently, those in harmony with Angel Mova-Mi-Yah acquire a great sensitivity to rhythms, seasons, and cycles, which represent the transforming force of time. Instead of forcing an issue, they faithfully go with the flow, increasing their knowledge of the world, creating their own plans, and undertaking their actions. In their private and professional lives, these individuals display a knack for building anew with old materials, creating new shapes by combining known structures, adapting familiar tools to unusual uses, and awakening in old traditions the seeds of renewal and progress.

All great developments begin with a tiny seed, and the harmonies of Angel Mova-Mi-Yah stimulate the ability to perceive the minute—even invisible—essence of every being and thing. Depending on the circumstances of their lives, these discerning people can be very successful in areas such as technical and biochemical discovery, commerce and mass distribution, the stock market, and all occupations where success, fame, and prestige are based on constant progress and evolution.

If you are inspired by Angel Mova-Mi-Yah, you can call upon your guardian to awaken your memory, reinforce your imagination, combine your rich memories with your innovative goals, and arouse in you new ideas that enhance progress and stimulate growth. Your innate patience and ability to nurture will then enable you to guide your creation to its full maturity.

If you are in harmony with your celestial guide, you carefully study changes that occur in your environment, then, after deliberation, adopt methods, techniques, and programs that improve the situation. The company you work for, any institution you are affiliated with, and, certainly, your grateful friends appreciate this ability in you. Your prudent advice enables them to move forward without destroying the past, to resolve crises without losing money or face.

If, by invocation, you attain a deep connection with Mova-Mi-Yah, your mind will rise to the supreme model of all shapes of the universe and reach to the very source of creation in the universe. Then, with the help of your heavenly guide, you can draw freely from the infinite and eternal invisible universe to transform your world. Endowed with the power to apply their will to recreate the world, the friends of Mova-Mi-Yah often undertake deeply transformative paths, enlightening their inner lives and changing external reality. This tendency may explain the number of religious, spiritual, and political leaders born under this Angel's care.

If learning the truth sets one free, those close to Mova-Mi-Yah are on a journey to liberation—and not just their own. They are innovators who create systems that are infinitely open, prophets who—before uttering the words that free the soul—stop and question the heavens. For Angel Mova-Mi-Yah, who encourages men and women to change the world, knows no good or evil, and never puts celestial authority above people's freedom and responsibility on earth.

INVOCATION

O Angel Mova-Mi-Yah,
Your immense and fertile spirit
Sows the heavens
With eternal seeds.
O Mova-Mi-Yah,
The spirals of your joy
Announce to the universe
The birth of renewal.
O Angel Mova-Mi-Yah,
Help me, inspire my heart.
In your garden
The futures blossom,
And I admire, serene soul,
The pristine petals of origins.

Angel HOVA-VI-YAH

MARCH 15–19

Eases transitions, passages, and discoveries. Encourages changes, mutations, and metamorphoses. Promotes the emergence of renewal and spring. Activates love feelings and friendship.

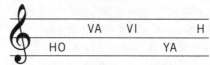

PHONETIC PRONUNCIATION

Ho as in Horizon
Va as in Varsity
Vi as in Victory
Ya as in Yard
H Vocalize the final H as a soft exhalation

UNIVERSAL RESONANCE OF THE ANGEL'S NAME

Ho Spiritual life force. Presence of the universal and all-permeating spirit. Divine call, divine connection.

Va Vitalizing factor. Fruitfulness and productivity. Catalyst of variety, vitality, verity, will, and vigor.

Vi Vitalizing factor. Fruitfulness and productivity. Catalyst of variety, vitality, verity, will, and vigor.

Yah Final vibration of the Angel's name. Receptivity and reflectivity. The presence of the deity; the abundance of the being.

Guardian Angel Hova-Vi-Yah

In Akkadian language, the name Hova-Vi-Yah means, literally, "Love and respect of life and of all living things unifies humans with God."

Change is inevitable—and Angel Hova-Vi-Yah invites everyone born into her/his influence to design, create, and live the change

NOTABLE PEOPLE BORN UNDER THE INFLUENCE OF HOVA-VI-YAH

Andrew Jackson, former U.S. president

Bonnie Blair, Olympic speed skater

Bruce Willis, actor

Edgar Cayce, psychic medium

Glenn Close, actress

Irène Joliot-Curie, Nobel Prize winner in chemistry

James Madison, former U.S. president

Jerry Lewis, comedian and actor

John Updike, writer

Kurt Russell, actor

Nat King Cole, singer

Rob Lowe, actor

Rudolf Nureyev, ballet dancer

Ruth Bader Ginsburg, U.S. Supreme Court justice

Vanessa Williams, actress

COLOR HARMONIZATION

Dark browns of tree bark / Vibrant yellow of the first flowers of spring / Electric violet of heather / Silvery sparkles like raindrops / Dark gray of clouds before a storm

they choose. Indeed, those in this exciting guardian's care may pass through any number of changes. That's because the harmonies of their celestial guide inspire them to close a cycle and open a new one, to throw themselves beyond the present and toward the future, and to escape the world that they know and discover new ones. Hova-Vi-Yah asks all living beings to travel on the spiraling path of his/her spiritual energy, to elevate life's experiences, become brightened by the light of consciousness, and widen the field of knowledge.

Those born between March 15 and 19 and everyone who sincerely calls upon Hova-Vi-Yah may aspire to become powerful and efficient agents of metamorphoses, creators of the cocoons in which they will transform their personalities and their environment in an exceptionally profound way. Just as a vertically rising spiral forms successive circles, all linked together in a perfect, unbroken continuity, Angel Hova-Vi-Yah helps those under his/her protection to innovate without destroying, to bring out the new while respecting the old. Inspired by this revolutionary guardian, women and men throw themselves boldly forward, carried by the rising currents of life. From this high position, they can admire and respect the value of all living creatures' life experiences. They can also glimpse their own dynamic potential.

If you are born under the protection of Angel Hova-Vi-Yah, you view the place you are now—in your spiritual, intellectual, and personal evolution—as a platform from which you can spring into an exciting future. You also see all doors, even those that are seemingly closed to you, as thresholds to new horizons. Consequently, you and all those under the guidance of Angel Hova-Vi-Yah act as relay stations, internally converting present energy into a fantastic future energy without destroying either of them.

Being able to glimpse the future and boldly go where so many others are afraid to go—into the vast unknown—can make a person very smart. It is interesting, then, that those under the protection of Angel Hova-Vi-Yah can be rather paradoxical when it comes to their own expertise. In fact, if you are like many of those born in the care of this Angel, you may even resist being pigeonholed as an expert in any given area. Those influenced by Hova-Vi-Yah often feel that locking oneself into any one field of endeavor limits them and slows down their drive to expand. You may prefer to be an expert at everything, someone who is comfortable in every arena. If you must be considered a specialist, you prefer to specialize in gaps and quantum leaps and any other intellectual variations that liberate thought.

In your personal, family, social, and professional life, you may excel in every situation where a transformer is needed, that is, a relay person who can redirect forces and energies for the common good. Your vision will always expand and remain high, even if you concentrate your talents on small details. Endowed with a passionate heart and blessed with an understanding that encompasses and respects everything, you and all those under the protection of Angel Hova-Vi-Yah are driven by a natural desire to implement change in order to uncover the truth. Consequently, you may accomplish great things in all areas of life. You may distinguish yourself in any occupation that draws upon your innate ability to unite while preserving the diverse values of each individual involved.

A word to the wise, however: in spite of your efforts to respect family, social, or religious traditions while moving toward a more dazzling future, you may be seen as a threat to the established order. You may even be viewed as an iconoclast or irresponsible adventurer, especially by those who consider themselves the preservers of the past. If you look back in history, you will discover that this kind of misunderstanding has led to such punishments as voluntary exile, excommunication, and banishment. When confronted with such old-fogeyism, you and all the friends of Hova-Vi-Yah need only invoke your celestial guardian. He/she will reinforce your transformative power and invite you to refine your inner being. Angel Hova-Vi-Yah will make you a possessor of the truth. In that state of grace, no one can imprison you.

Throughout their lives, those under the protection of Angel Hova-Vi-Yah learn how to open the narrow doors that can unlock systems, offer their thoughts as bridges to unexplored territories,

HARMONIC MATCHES FOR HOVA-VI-YAH'S PROTÉGÉS

- *The best matches for success in economic and practical achievements will be among men and women born November 10–14, under the care of Mi-Ya-Ha-El.*
- *The best matches for recognition, fame, personal charisma, and social fulfillment will be among men and women born June 3–7, under the care of He-Qua-Mi-Yah.*
- *The best matches for romance, love, and artistic and intellectual achievements will be among men and women born June 28–July 2, under the care of Nel-Cha-El.*

and act as relays to hidden dimensions. These men and women cannot fail in their mission because, thanks to Angel Hova-Vi-Yah's harmonic vibrations, the eternal call of divine love echoes in their minds. It connects each minute part to the greater whole, creates myriad differences and separations in order to eternally stir the desire to unite in love, and reinforces the fertilizing power of movements that transform lives.

ACKNOWLEDGMENTS

We wish to express our heartfelt thanks to Martine Fougeron de Monès, our dearest friend and first critic, for her unabated encouragement to pursue our writers' task; to her sons, Nicolas de Monès, age ten, and Adrien de Monès, age nine, for being our youngest readers; to Gerald M. Hertz, Esq., and Gloria Lusinger Hertz, who freely stayed to defend us in the darkest times of our life; to our parents, grandparents, ancestors, and guardian Angels, for holding the thread of our terrestrial existence; to Ellen Silver at City & Company, for creating our first link with the New York publishing world; to Sandra Martin at Paraview, our literary agent, for quietly dispelling our writers' anxieties with her words of truth and love; to Barbara Lagowski for the sincerity of her stimulating questions, her sense of humor, and her mindful editing of the English version of our manuscript; and to Harper San Francisco publishers, and David Hennessy and Renée Sedliar, our editors, for making from our manuscript a book on the edge of the third millennium.